STEPPING OFF THE

RELATIONSHIP ESCALATOR

UNCOMMON LOVE AND LIFE

AMY GAHRAN

Published in the United States by Off the Escalator Enterprises, LLC
PO Box 4385, Boulder, Colorado 80302

First Edition (print)
ISBN: 978-0-9986470-1-2

Cover Design: Gina McLaughlin

This book is based primarily on original research, through an online survey conducted by Amy Gahran in 2013-14 with 1500 participants. All quotes from this survey presented in this and other Off the Escalator books and content are true, and used with permission of survey participants as a condition of participating in the survey. However, names and other identifying information have been changed to protect the identity of participants. Similarities in names or other descriptive characteristics between any subjects of this book and any other person are purely coincidental.

Additional quotes come from interviews or social media posts, in all cases quoted here with explicit permission of the subject.

Other sources (such as scholarly papers or news articles) are quoted or cited briefly in this book, in accordance with the fair use provision of U.S. copyright law (17 U.S. Code § 107). All sources are listed in the endnotes of this book. Links to all online sources cited in this book:

Bit.ly/OffEscNotes1

For Michael,
"You are what you is."

TABLE OF CONTENTS

HOW TO USE THIS BOOK

First of all, this book is the product of participation. Your voice counts! I'd love to hear what you have to say. So, please tell me what you think about this book, or your observations and questions about unconventional relationships in general:

OffEscalator.com/Contact

Also, this book is a launching point for a variety of resources about unconventional intimate relationships. Some of these resources are my own, and some are offered by other authors, thinkers and communities. You can find these resources on the website for the Off the Escalator project: **OffEscalator.com/Resources**

This is only the beginning. This book is the first in a series of books. I collected more than enough valuable information in my initial survey to support at least two other books. As of this writing, Book 2, *10 Common Questions About Unconventional Relationships,* is already written and will be published later in 2017.

Book 3, *Off the Escalator, In the Closet* has largely been assembled. Due out in 2018, it will address how people navigate being public or private about their unconventional relationships. Also, it will explore how anyone can help make the world a friendlier place for unconventional relationships.

To learn more about this project, and to participate, please subscribe to the Off the Escalator email list: **OffEscalator.com/Updates**

Twitter: @OffTheEscalator
Facebook page: Facebook.com/OffEscalator

This book also is designed to support discussion and interaction. At the end of each part there is a list of discussion questions. If you wish, you may answer these questions online: **OffEscalator.com/Resources/Book1Questions**

On the website, you will also be able to take surveys, quizzes, or share your own story. You can answer anonymously if you like. Just be aware that by engaging in this online interaction, you grant the *Off the Escalator* project permission to use your responses in future books and other content.

However, you don't need to go online or share any information in order to take what you learn in this book further. Simply considering the discussion questions offered in this book on your own, or using them to start conversations with others, can prove enlightening — or at least, interesting.

Each quote from my survey that is included in this book represents a snapshot in time, from 2013-14. Life moves on. Undoubtedly, many quotes no longer reflect the current circumstances, relationships or views of participants. I cannot rewrite the history of what participants originally said, but I will post online an updated version of my survey. Anyone will be able to take this, including prior participants who wish to offer an update.

This book includes a glossary, since words used to describe traditional relationships often don't suit unconventional relationships well.

Please support this independent project. See **OffEscalator.com** for ideas. Thanks!

PREFACE:

THE STORY OF THE ESCALATOR

What is a relationship?

In the broadest sense, we have relationships with everyone we know or interact with to any significant extent: neighbors, friends and coworkers; teammates, classmates and fellow volunteers; parents, siblings and children. Any of these relationships might feel quite close and important, or not. It all depends.

However, those types of connections usually are not what most people mean when they say they're "in a relationship." Instead, that loaded little phrase typically implies a very specific type of relationship: one that involves the intimacy of affection, sex and romance. One that looks and works a certain way, and that generally is deemed especially important.

The ubiquitous phrase, "in a relationship," tends to evoke a familiar storyline with well-known characters and symbols: a fairy tale with a happy ending, or at least a romantic comedy.

There's a name for the common set of social norms that shape intimate relationships in most Western societies: the *Relationship Escalator*. I did not coin this term, nor have I been able to track down its precise origins.[1] However, this term has arisen over the last several years, mostly among people who needed to find ways to talk about how intimate relationships, and society, are changing.

In a nutshell, the traditional Relationship Escalator looks like this: two (and only two) people progress from initial attraction and dating, to becoming sexually and romantically involved and exclusive, to adopting a shared identity as a couple, to

3

moving in together and otherwise merging their lives — all the way up to marriage and kids, 'til death do you part.

There is absolutely nothing wrong with this approach. The Relationship Escalator is popular for a reason: it works quite well for many people.

It's just not the only game in town.

There is a broad spectrum of intimate relationships. This book is about the ways that people are stepping off this Escalator to explore unconventional approaches to intimate relationships. If you're curious about what these options are, or whether they might apply to you or to people you know, this book can be your guide. You'll hear what hundreds of people have to say about their unconventional relationships, in their own words.

But first, to understand what can make intimate relationships less conventional, it helps to have a very clear picture of what a very traditional relationship might look like. I've had the opportunity to hear many people describe what they believe makes their own relationships unconventional — that's the process which formed the basis of this book. This insight clarified several common customs that shape how intimate relationships work, and how they tend to fit in with the rest of society and life.

The trouble is, talking about abstract social norms easily gets dry and tedious. People and stories are far more interesting. So, as a backdrop to the real stories of unconventional relationships featured throughout this book, here I offer the fictional tale of a highly traditional relationship — one that rides the Relationship Escalator right from the beginning, and all the way to the top. I will occasionally refer back to this story throughout this book, for contrast.

In the story below, the **bold text** calls attention to the many terms, milestones, value judgments, expectations, obligations, tradeoffs, benefits and privileges commonly associated with Escalator relationships. It can be surprising to realize how thoroughly Relationship Escalator norms are embedded into almost every part of life (in this example, life in the U.S.).

Bundled together and brought into focus, the many indicators of the Relationship Escalator may sound odd since they're often taken for granted. By calling attention to things commonly associated with social norms, I am not trying to denigrate them. "Normal" does not equal "thoughtless" or "boring."

Some of the Escalator indicators noted in this story might sound old-fashioned. However, that is part of what makes them traditional. Society keeps changing, but some norms have surprising staying power.

Real life is always more nuanced than social norms. Thus, few relationships on the more traditional end of the spectrum include all of the indicators noted in this story. Also, many of these indicators (such as falling in love, living together and building a family) also can be found in relationships that are quite unconventional.

Still, it's common for intimate relationships to hit many of these familiar, time-honored marks — or for people to hope that their relationships will look rather like this:

*Chris meets Dana, and they feel a strong spark of mutual attraction. They start talking and hanging out a bit, and then they go out on **dates** — just the two of them, quite **romantic**. They kiss. They feel excited.*

*More dates follow — so now they **are dating**. They start **having sex**. When they are out together, they often hold hands or engage in other socially acceptable **public displays of affection**. They develop regular patterns of daily communication, with lots of phone calls, texting and social media interaction. As they **fall in love**, they obsessively think and fantasize about each other.*

*Their kind of love is **reflected everywhere in the media**. Popular love songs and romantic movies and TV somehow all seem to be about them.*

*Things **get serious** when they begin to **tell each other, "I love you."** That's when they start to feel **committed**. Of course, this commitment involves **monogamy**: they stop dating others, having sex and flirting with others, and frequenting bars alone. Their **online dating profiles vanish**. They become **Facebook official** by tagging each other as being "in a relationship with..."*

*At this point, Chris and Dana start considering themselves **a couple**. They start **saying "we"** quite often. When speaking to others, they usually refer to each other as **"my boyfriend"** or **"my girlfriend."** And between themselves, they start using **terms of endearment**, such as "honey" or "babe," at least as often as they address each other by name.*

*As their emotional bond deepens, they become somewhat **possessive** of each other. So they feel, and sometimes act, jealous whenever somebody else seems interested in, or interesting to, their partner. They're also uncomfortable about each other's prior relationships, so it's helpful that they are **not close to their exes**.*

*Chris and Dana now **spend almost all their free time together**. This means they see their friends far less often, but they assume their friends understand and support this.*

*Other people start **referring to them as a unit**: "Chris & Dana." They are each other's **default companion** for almost any occasion, especially high-profile events like holiday parties, where invitations ask for a +1.*

They **meet each other's family and friends** — although several of their single friends lament how little they see them these days. Now, Chris & Dana **socialize primarily with other committed couples.**

After a few months of serious dating, Chris & Dana do what they've always assumed **must happen next:** they **settle down** and **move in together.** They **share a bed** and start to **merge their finances.**

They **display each other's photo at work,** and they **feel free to note the existence of their relationship** in casual conversations, even with coworkers or strangers. This is **not considered oversharing,** even though everyone assumes that Chris & Dana have sex with each other.

They start **making all major decisions together,** and many minor ones too. They discuss or at least **assume a long-term shared future.** They become **mutually accountable** about their behavior and how they spend their time. They believe they really are **The One** for each other.

When Chris enters a prestigious graduate program in another state, Dana **makes a career sacrifice** so they can move and stay together. They support each other's goals, interests and dreams, which fortunately mostly align well; the ones that **don't align so well mostly fade away.**

One night, Chris **pops the question** to Dana over a candlelit dinner, and Dana enthusiastically accepts. **Flashing their new rings,** they publicly announce their **engagement** with much excitement, and they are **unanimously congratulated.**

They easily acquire a **marriage license.** Their **wedding** is **held in a church** and is **attended by many friends and family,** who all bear **gifts.**

Chris & Dana save their money — helped, in part, by **marital tax breaks.** Eventually, they purchase a home together.

When they **have children,** there is **no question about their right or ability to parent.** They feel immense pride in having created a **real family.** Their **relatives show respect** for, and take pride and interest in, Chris & Dana's marriage and family.

All along, Chris & Dana's relationship has felt completely **natural** and **meant to be,** as if their lives could not have unfolded any other way.

Inevitably, their marriage is occasionally troubled by conflict and resentment. Sometimes they hurt each other's feelings, and they chafe at each other's annoying habits. At times they yearn for something different — usually silently, since they **fear growing apart.** They believe the only way to significantly change their relationship would be to **break up.** That would entail **divorce,** major life disruption, and stigma for them and their kids. That would be a **failure.** The idea of **being alone** (without their **other half)** and having to **start over** fills them with dread.

*Chris & Dana never consider having other sexual partners, even though sometimes their own sexual connection feels rather stale, and they occasionally feel attracted to others. But **fidelity** is crucial to them, so they stay **faithful** to each other, even after many years together. They still share affection and sex. They still love each other — perhaps not with the passion of their initial romance, but their love is still mutual and genuine.*

*Overall, their life together feels fruitful. Its patterns feel familiar and comforting, and not just to them. **Other people easily understand how to interact with Chris & Dana;** they know what to expect from the couple, and what's appropriate.*

They still each maintain connections with friends, but their friendships mostly don't feel as close or important as they once did.

*When Chris has a sudden heart attack, Dana is immediately notified as **next of kin.** At the hospital, Dana need only mention that they are married to **attend Chris' bedside** and **make medical decisions** while Chris is incapacitated. Fortunately, Chris makes a full recovery, with a large part of the costs covered by the **spousal health insurance** that is a benefit of Dana's employment.*

*Their kids grow up and move out, and the **empty nesters** peaceably share middle and old age. They develop some separate hobbies and renew and deepen ties with friends and community.*

*After many years, Dana grows frail and ill. Chris, their children and their grandchildren lovingly **provide care and support** to the very end. At Dana's funeral, everyone offers condolences to Chris and praises their **perfect marriage.** And for Chris, who'd never wanted any other kind of life and love, it was indeed perfect. After all, they'd done everything **right,** achieving the kind of **happily ever after** that **everyone should hope for.***

*Like many people, Dana neglected to create a formal will. So after Dana's death, Chris **automatically inherits, with no legal questions or tax hassles,** most of Dana's estate, and assumes sole ownership of their joint assets. Also, Chris begins to receive **survivor benefits from Social Security,** as well as Dana's **pension income.** Such material things don't make up for missing Dana fiercely every day, but they do help Chris get through the remainder of life.*

...Again, the story of Chris and Dana's relationship probably doesn't completely mirror your own, or those of people you know. Few relationships ride the Escalator in every detail. Usually, it's a matter of degrees: how much a specific relationship resembles the form, trajectory, milestones and goals of the Relationship Escalator.

There is considerable variation on the Escalator. The details of what it looks like, and the amount of pressure to ride it, vary by nation, generation, culture and subculture.

Also, the Escalator is a bit of a moving target, thanks to social evolution. For instance, these days, many couples manage to pretty much ride the Escalator without getting married, having kids, or being socially joined at the hip. And now in many countries (including, as of this writing and for the time being, the U.S.), any two unrelated adults can legally marry, regardless of sexual orientation.

That said, the Relationship Escalator does not exist in a vacuum. Race, class, religion, cultural background, sexual orientation, gender identity, disability and other context can color what it means to ride the Escalator. That's because social norms tend to accommodate social privilege — a thorny topic explored in this book.

Part 1 of this book examines how the Relationship Escalator works, and why some people step off the Escalator.

People ride the Escalator for many reasons. Often, this is a conscious, deliberate choice that honors innate desires, preferences and goals. It can support the kind of life that many people wish to lead and help them be the kind of people they wish to be. This traditional structure fits and serves many people well. Usually, its tradeoffs feel acceptable.

Meanwhile, some people hop on the Escalator without being fully aware that they have other valid options.

While the Escalator comes with steep obligations, it also offers many perks that can be difficult to achieve otherwise. As the amount of bold text in Chris and Dana's story indicates, society has developed myriad ways to accommodate, encourage, recognize, support and favor Escalator relationships. This creates a strong incentive to ride the Escalator, even when it might not be such a great fit. It's also a big reason why it can be so daunting to step off the Relationship Escalator.

Nevertheless, many people do step off the Escalator. Here's why...

INTRODUCTION:

WHAT UNCONVENTIONAL
RELATIONSHIPS CAN LOOK LIKE

Love is not one-size-fits-all. Fortunately, neither are intimate relationships. But that might not seem obvious, based on almost every love song and relationship advice book ever written.

It's quite common to treat loving, intimate relationships as if there is one basic blueprint for how they should look and work. This popular approach does not guarantee that you'll find love, or keep it, or that a relationship will feel wonderful and be trouble-free. However, it may seem like the only viable path to love, happiness and connection.

If you haven't felt quite comfortable in your intimate relationships, if you haven't been finding love that feels right or works well for you — maybe it's not just about you, or the partners you've chosen, or how good your relationship skills are. The problem might be your expectations about how intimate relationships are supposed to work.

In this book, unconventional relationship options are not about the gender or sexual orientation of partners. Rather, this is about the role that intimate relationships can play in life, how they can be shaped to suit the people in them — and even what counts as a real relationship.

Understanding the diversity of intimate relationships can help you have better relationships, no matter what they look like. This awareness also can help you appreciate relationships that might look pretty different from your own.

The *Relationship Escalator* is the set of traditional social norms for intimate relationships. Most of us are raised to believe that the Escalator is the only option for how intimate relationships should work. For some people, the traditional approach feels quite natural and good. For others, not so much.

What might it look like, and feel like, to make relationship choices that depart significantly from the Escalator?

Together, you and the people you love can craft relationships that honor what makes you unique — your emotional needs, preferences for housing or sex, desires for variety and stability, life goals and changes, and capabilities and constraints. You can define what family, home and commitment mean to you, or strike your own balance between independence and interdependence.

The result might not resemble a Disney movie. Still, it can work, It even can work quite well.

The catch is: options for stepping off the Escalator are not always obvious. It can be difficult to consider, let alone explore, paths you don't even know exist — or which you've heard (or assumed) always lead to failure.

Remember Chris and Dana, the fictional couple who rode the Escalator so perfectly in the preface? What if the Escalator had not been such a great fit for them? Their story might have unfolded very differently.

Here are a few alternate storylines for Chris and Dana. Parts 2-6 of this book explore each of these options, and many others, in greater depth.

First, Chris and Dana might adapt their relationship to accommodate profound differences that would be deal breakers on the Escalator, such as:

- *Dana does not wish to be a parent, and Chris strongly wants children. So, with Dana's consent, Chris helps a close friend, Izzy, become a parent. Chris spends time at home with Dana, and also at Izzy's home nearby, where they co-parent their child.*

- *Dana prefers to live a nomadic life. Chris is very much a homebody. They share periods of intense, meaningful intimacy, punctuated by gaps of weeks or months where they focus on the rest of their lives and barely communicate. These pauses feel natural to them and keep their relationship vital. Over the years, they enjoy many blissful reunions.*

Or they might find ways to embrace logistical issues which would bar the path to the Escalator, such as permanent distance or limited time:

- *Although they live two times zones apart, Dana and Chris meet by chance and connect deeply. Neither wishes to relocate. They enjoy their visits every few months, with lots of communication in between.*

- *Chris and Dana fall in love while Chris is on a six-month work assignment. They explore and enjoy their relationship during that time, and let go of it when Chris returns home. They remember each other fondly and remain in occasional contact.*

They might blur traditional lines between friends, lovers and partners; or they might not always give top priority to a lover or spouse:

- *Since high school, Dana and Dakota have had an exceptionally strong, close friendship. Although they are not sexual or romantic partners, they are very affectionate. They often hug, cuddle and express mutual affection and commitment. Dana marries Chris — but for big occasions like weddings or holiday parties, Dana sometimes invites Dakota rather than Chris. When Dakota suffers a serious accident, Dana moves in with Dakota for a year to provide care and household support. Chris appreciates their friendship and supports these choices.*

- *Chris and Dana enjoy each other's company, and their sexual chemistry is smoking hot. However, they do not share romantic feelings for each other, nor do they wish to live together. They develop an enduring friendship where they regularly share sex, as well as considerable mutual respect and appreciation. They also hang out together socially and collaborate on projects.*

Or they might agree that their relationship does not require sexual exclusivity:

- *Chris has never wanted sex, and Dana is a highly sexual person. Their marriage is focused on love, commitment, family and companionship. Dana explores sex with others, with Chris' consent and support.*

- *Dana and Chris value sexual variety, so they have sexual encounters with others at swinger clubs and resorts. This keeps their own sexual connection vital. Several fellow swingers become close friends.*

- *Chris travels frequently for work, and on these trips sometimes enjoys brief sexual liaisons with others. They discuss this. Dana approves but prefers not to hear details. Occasionally Dana also discreetly enjoys other sexual liaisons under the same don't ask don't tell arrangement.*

Perhaps they don't wish to merge their lives, and so maintain more individual autonomy than the Escalator normally allows:

- *Dana and Chris each adore their respective homes and treasure having time alone. They never move in together, but visit each other several times a week and talk daily.*

- *Chris and Dana cringe when people refer to them as a unit, "Chris & Dana." They actively maintain their own friendships, and they often socialize and travel independently. They share a home but keep separate bedrooms, sharing a bed only when they both really want to. They also maintain separate finances. When Chris moves for graduate school, they continue their relationship long distance, while Dana's career advances.*

They might foster deeply emotionally invested or committed relationships with other partners:

- *Over the course of their 10-year Escalator relationship, Chris and Dana realize that monogamy is not a good fit for either of them, sexually or emotionally. They both wish to have other intimate partners, without sacrificing their connection. They discuss this thoroughly and agree to explore consensual nonmonogamy. They attend various local groups and navigate a bumpy learning curve. Eventually, they arrive at an approach that works well for them and their other partners, whom they love dearly.*

- *After falling in love with Tracy and developing a sense of commitment in that relationship, Chris also falls in love with Dana. Tracy knows about this and supports Chris and Dana's relationship. Both relationships involve sexual and romantic intimacy. Both relationships grow to coexist in a peaceful, complementary fashion. Over time, Dana and Tracy develop their own friendship.*

And if their desire or ability to continue their relationship subsides, they can let go and move forward in peaceful ways that don't cast this as a failure:

- *After many years of marriage, Dana's sexual orientation has evolved profoundly, so Dana can no longer be a sexual or romantic partner to Chris. They discuss this, sort through many difficult feelings, and plan to peacefully transition their relationship. They continue to share a home until their children are grown. In the meantime, they also agree*

> *to explore other sexual and romantic relationships. They remain very close friends — even closer in some ways since they no longer need to keep secrets from each other.*

These scenarios are not the product of imagination or speculation. All of them are quite real — as are many, many other options for unconventional relationships.

More than 1500 people in unconventional intimate relationships shared their experiences with me, through an online survey I conducted in 2013-2014. I was stunned by the level of response to this survey. Many of the responses were 1500-2500 words long, or longer — really, personal essays.

These stories described a rich diversity of circumstances and creativity, of joy and heartbreak, of dreams and reality. Many participants expressed enthusiasm and gratitude for the opportunity to let people know they exist. Too often, their kind of love is overlooked or discounted by society.

The vast majority of people who answered my survey have managed to find viable, if unusual, ways to share love and intimacy. And while unconventional relationships also have their ups and downs, they can be fulfilling and rewarding. For instance, three-fourths of the people who responded to my survey reported that overall, they feel very, or mostly, satisfied and happy in unconventional relationships.

In this book, and others in this series, I share their stories with you.

This book features plenty of quotes, shown in italics. These are attributed to real people who took my survey. I've identified participants by name or pseudonym, according to their wishes. Where no preference was expressed, I selected a pseudonym at random. A few quotes come from conversations I've had online and elsewhere — and I've used these only with direct permission. Also, some quotes come from publicly available documents, articles and resources (sources cited).

Altogether, 334 individuals are quoted in this book alone. In the two forthcoming books in this series, even more participants will be quoted.

What can you expect from this book?

If you are contemplating stepping off the Relationship Escalator, then this book offers useful guideposts. You won't be flying totally blind into uncharted territory. Seeing the unconventional relationship choices that others have made can show you what's possible. This book also highlights many issues to consider about venturing off the Escalator.

If you prefer more traditional relationships, this book can help you think more deeply and broadly about this choice, too.

This book is not a how-to guide. It does not list instructions for stepping off the Escalator; there are too many options, and everyone's path is unique. However, reading this book can jump-start your personal process of inquiry and exploration. It can help you think creatively and clearly about any kind of intimate relationship. It can help you ask better questions, clarify what you might want (or not want), and negotiate more compassionately and effectively.

This project is about stories, not statistics. It is a journalistic effort, not a scholarly study. The goal of my survey was to gather personal accounts, identify themes and patterns, and share experiences and insights. While a fairly large number of people responded to my survey, this group was entirely self-selected and definitely does not represent the population at large.

Thus, this book can tell you what is happening in many unconventional relationships. But it does not attempt to answer questions such as "What percentage of all relationships are consensually nonmonogamous?" or "How common is it for unconventional relationships to last longer than five years?" The few statistics I do offer are drawn strictly from my survey and should not be applied more widely.

Where possible, I do cite relevant research done by others. I wish there was more of this. However, surprisingly scant research has done into relationships that don't fit neatly into categories such as monogamy, infidelity, married, single or dating. There are many relationship experts and researchers, but so far, their work has mostly been shaped by Escalator assumptions.

I have attempted to present unconventional relationships fairly. I try to be fair to the Escalator, too. My core assumption is that any intimate relationship involving informed, consenting adults has the potential to be healthy and mutually beneficial — or not, depending on individuals and circumstances.

I also bring my personal experience to this project. After many years in traditional relationships, I began to consciously explore unconventional relationships in 2001. I discovered that this suits me better than the Escalator ever did. Personally, I practice a form of consensual nonmonogamy called *polyamory*. I also know many people in various kinds of unconventional relationships.

I've seen the Escalator work well. I've witnessed the pain that can result when people ride Escalator mostly because they think it's the only way to love or to be loved. Similarly, I've also seen unconventional relationships work well, and not so well. I am motivated to do this project because I believe people should be aware of their options for relationships that can so profoundly shape their lives.

If reading this book affirms that the Relationship Escalator is indeed the best choice for you, that's great. Also, wouldn't it feel better to know you're making such a crucial life choice consciously, rather than by default?

Reading this book also can help you make the world a friendlier place. If diversity and fairness matter to you, then this book can help you find more ways to practice those values.

The Relationship Escalator enjoys substantial social visibility, benefits and privilege. Consequently, there is considerable prejudice against less-common approaches to love. In a December 2016 interview,[2] filmmaker Jackie Stone (creator of the fictional web series *Compersion*,[3] which is about being black and polyamorous) mentioned being surprised by the severity of this stigma:

> *The amount of fear that people have about talking publicly about [this show] has been amazing. Even monogamous people have a fear of saying "I watch this show," or sharing this show [on social media]. It really opened my eyes to the fact that just the idea of doing relationships differently is very scary and frightening.*
> *— Jackie Stone, filmmaker, writer, director and producer*

The stigma against unconventional relationships causes real harm, to real people, every day. Many people who took my survey reported facing discrimination, loss or invalidation when others learn about their unconventional relationships. Their jobs, housing or the custody of their children have been put at risk. They have sometimes been ostracized or vilified by friends, family and community. Sometimes their social status drops or their ethics or character are questioned. Their relationships sometimes become the subject of heightened scrutiny and invasive, inappropriate questions — or ignored entirely, as if they don't count or are shameful. Simply living in fear of these potential outcomes can be immensely stressful.

Furthermore, many people in unconventional relationships suffer from isolation and lack of guidance. They may have scant opportunity to learn from the relevant experiences of others. When their relationships are troubled, they can have difficulty finding appropriate support. Too often, counselors and confidantes assume that the cause of their problems is the fact that their relationship is unconventional.

Self-doubt is another challenge. Relationship norms are deeply ingrained and loaded with psychological and emotional triggers. As the stories in this book show, it can be tough to shake the feeling that doing relationships differently means you're doing it wrong.

Consequently, many people keep their unconventional relationships a secret, more or less. So: if you think you don't know anyone in an unconventional relationship, it's likely that you actually do. They're probably in the closet — perhaps because they're worried about what you might think, say or do if you knew the truth about their love life.

Ask anyone who's not 100% heterosexual: the closet can be an uncomfortable and scary place to live, and to love. Fortunately, there is less need for the closet when more people understand, accept and value relationship diversity.

Book 3 in the *Off the Escalator* series will address such concerns in detail.

The beauty of unconventional relationship options is that they can make more relationships — and thus more love, joy and support — possible. They can transcend obstacles that would be deal breakers on the Escalator.

This is, I believe, a good thing. This world could probably use all the love we can bring to it.

PART 1

WELCOME TO THE RELATIONSHIP ESCALATOR

1

WHAT IS THE RELATIONSHIP ESCALATOR?

"Is this relationship going anywhere?" If you've ever heard (or said) that catchphrase, then the Relationship Escalator may be something you already know quite well. When people think of what a "relationship" looks like, usually they mean something like this:

> **Relationship Escalator.** *The default bundle of societal expectations for intimate relationships. Partners follow a progressive set of steps, each with visible milestones and markers, toward a clear goal.*
>
> *The Escalator is the standard by which most people gauge whether an intimate relationship is significant, serious, good, healthy, committed or worthy of effort.*
>
> *The goal at the top of the Escalator is to achieve a permanently monogamous relationship: sexually and romantically exclusive between only two people. In addition, Escalator partners are expected to live together permanently, and to have their relationship legally sanctioned and publicly recognized — typically via legal marriage.*
>
> *Partners are expected to remain together at the top of the Escalator until death. Common related (but no longer heavily required) Escalator milestones include shared ownership of a home, combined finances and having kids together.*

The Relationship Escalator is what most people grow up believing, or at least assuming, that intimate relationships should look like and how they are supposed to work. This model typically is deeply ingrained at an early age, and it's reinforced through all stages of life. Because this model is so familiar to most people, traditional relationships often seem simpler or easier, as well as propelled along by their innate momentum. Thus, it's the Relationship Escalator, not the Relationship Staircase.

Furthermore, the Escalator is widely presumed to be what any emotionally healthy adult should want. Since Escalator relationships follow a key set of social norms, they usually are considered normal.

The Relationship Escalator is popular for a reason: it works well for many people. But it doesn't suit everyone.

> *Let's face it: At least half the relationships that people think are going somewhere are, in fact, not going anywhere good.*
> — *Nika, in a long distance open relationship*

Whether an intimate relationship is wonderful, healthy or mutually beneficial depends on the individuals and circumstances involved. This is true in Escalator relationships, and it is true off the Escalator, too.

As described in the introduction to this book, in 2013-14 I surveyed 1500 people about unconventional intimate relationships. Many participants reported that stepping off the Relationship Escalator allowed them to discover a sense of love, belonging, support, intimacy, fulfillment and authenticity that they hadn't been able to achieve otherwise.

> *The biggest benefit, for me? Happiness! That feeling of just being right, natural. Feeling okay and accepted for being who I am, for the very first time. Extreme feelings of love and support. Incredible closeness.*
> — *Yoni Wolf, queer and polyamorous*

> *A really big advantage is finding out firsthand that people will care for me — look after me, love me, want my company — rather than needing me (or some other interchangeable woman) in order to get to the top of that Escalator. That they will care for me because of, rather than in spite of, who I am and what I want out of life and relationships.*
> — *Amazon Syren, married, polyamorous, queer and kinky*

Unconventional relationships might be enduring, deeply emotionally invested, or strongly logistically entwined. Or they might be shorter-term, more casual or discontinuous. Or anything in between.

I am 66. I first married at 32 after living for seven years with my partner in a nonexclusive relationship. We continued our nontraditional marriage except for a few brief periods of monogamy. We were married for nine years until I was widowed.

My present partner and I have been living together now for 10 years and we will be married next May. Our relationship has always been polyamorous.

— Daniel, polyamorous

I have a few meaningful pause/play type relationships with loves who I only see at Burning Man festivals. One has been going on for 10 years.

— Lyndsay, nonmonogamous

Notably, off the Escalator there's far more room to value and savor relationships that might otherwise get dismissed as trivial, pointless or not real.

Here's the interesting element of my entanglements: they are often highly emotional, sweet and meaningful — but not necessarily romantic. They're also sporadic and don't seem to require much maintenance or upkeep.

They can involve a lot of time spent discussing other relationships (past and present) in a very friendly, not at all jealous manner. All integrated smoothly with playful flirtation and "Let me fill up your wine glass. No really, I am trying to get you drunk!" These are some of my favorite kinds of relationships.

— Siobhan, nonmonogamous

By far the biggest benefit is that I don't have to conform to social norms that would be actively damaging to me: specifically, the norm of having sex in a relationship. Being able to have the sort of committed emotional intimacy I want without the expectation of sex is important — and very hard to find.

I am part of a four-person relationship that isn't sexual or romantic. However, it is very emotionally intimate and long-term committed — in ways that don't really correspond to what's normally thought of as friendship or family-like bonds.

— Helen, asexual

Especially touching were stories where people shared how they felt profoundly empowered by letting go of Escalator norms and goals for their intimate relationships. They stopped seeing themselves as fatally flawed, or their future as devoid of joy.

> *I feel more myself. I trust myself more. I don't feel like I have to hide who I am or make excuses for feeling trapped. I no longer feel like there is something wrong with me, or that I was meant to be alone.*
>
> *I used to always dread the day when I would start to look at other people. I knew I still loved my partner but I felt... not right. I thought I was broken. It is great to know I am not destined to always hurt people. It is nice not to feel broken for thinking the idea of one true love is flawed or that "the One" is a ridiculous notion. Now things feel so much better.*
> — *Moni, polyamorous*

That said, no relationship style guarantees joy. Both traditional and unconventional relationships can sometimes be difficult, unsatisfying or painful. Off the Escalator, the hard parts of relationships can have unusual twists.

> *Once two of my significant relationships (including one which lasted nearly five years) fall apart in one week. That was intensely devastating.*
> — *Cherad, polyamorous*

> *Sometimes potential lovers think that since you're already in a relationship, you can't (or won't) have a deep relationship with them. Or that they don't need to treat you with the respect they'd give someone they were dating monogamously.*
>
> *This happened to me once, with someone I was dating for most of a year. I fell deeply in love with him, even though I knew we weren't 100% compatible. Our relationship seemed strong and deep, and I looked forward to maintaining a friendship even if our romance didn't last. However, when he met a woman he wanted to date "for real," he immediately cut off all contact and never spoke to me again.*
>
> *That breakup scarred me in deep ways and was incredibly painful. I mean, I really felt used! And since he completely cut off communication once he decided he didn't need me anymore, I had no way to say my piece.*
> — *Sabrina, nonmonogamous*

Steps on the Relationship Escalator

Relationships that follow social norms typically progress through eight stages. This is the "escalation" that occurs on the Relationship Escalator, and it is illustrated by the story of Chris & Dana in the preface to this book.

This progression is not always uniform. Some couples might skip some steps, or the order may vary slightly. For instance, these days, many people have children before getting married or perhaps before moving in together — and some Escalator couples never get legally married at all. But on the whole, this is how the Relationship Escalator typically works:

1. **Making contact.** Flirting, casual/social encounters, possibly including making out or sexual hookups.

2. **Initiation.** Romantic courtship gestures or rituals, emotional investment or falling in love, and usually sexual contact (except in religious or socially conservative circles).

3. **Claiming and defining.** Mutual declarations of love, presenting in public as a couple, adopting and using common relationship role labels (boyfriend, girlfriend, etc.). Having expectations, or sometimes making explicit agreements, for sexual and romantic exclusivity — and also ending other intimate relationships, if any, and ceasing to use dating sites or apps. Transitioning to barrier-free vaginal/anal intercourse, if applicable, except if that would present health or unwanted pregnancy risks. Once this step is reached, any further step, including simply remaining in the relationship, may be considered an implied intention to continue the relationship indefinitely.

4. **Establishment.** Adapting the rhythms of life to accommodate each other on an ongoing basis. Settling into patterns for regularly spending time together (date nights and sexual encounters, time at each others' homes, etc.). Developing patterns for keeping in contact when not together, such as email, phone calls, video chat or texting.

5. **Commitment.** Explicitly discussing, or planning, a long-term shared future as a couple. Expectations of mutual accountability for whereabouts, behavior and life choices. Meeting each other's family of origin.

6. **Merging.** Moving in together, sharing a household and finances. Getting engaged to be married, or agreeing to a similar legal or civil formalization of the relationship.

7. **Conclusion.** Getting legally married or making similar equivalent formal, recognized, legally binding arrangements. The relationship is now finalized; its structure should remain fairly static until one partner dies.

8. **Legacy.** Purchasing a home together, if possible. Having and raising children — not mandatory, but still strongly socially venerated. This part of the Escalator is no longer as obligatory as it once was. However, often couples may not feel, or be perceived as, fully valid until they hit these additional milestones post-marriage.

The preface to this book describes how a traditional relationship can move through all of these steps, and how this affects people's lives.

The majority of intimate relationships don't progress very far up the Escalator. In fact, it's typical for a relationship to not be deemed "real" until it gets to at least step 3 or 4. However, the early stages aren't necessarily fleeting.

> *I had one significant relationship which we both described as "no strings attached" and "just about sex" — even though we saw each other very frequently and were a major part of each other's lives. We slept together for over a year and even celebrated our anniversary.*
>
> *But we didn't call it a "real" relationship — I suppose because we weren't on the Relationship Escalator. It was perpetual, pointless dating.*
> *— Rose, polyamorous*

Traditionally, people who are dating usually seek to determine fairly soon whether a new connection has Escalator potential, and proceed accordingly. If at some point a partner or relationship becomes disqualified from the Escalator, usually it gets sidetracked to a less important status; or it ends or simply fizzles out.

If a relationship ends after about stage 4 or 5, this is usually deemed a breakup — or getting dumped or ditched, if it didn't happen by mutual choice.

The Language of Love, Off the Escalator

The very words that most people use to discuss intimate relationships tend to reflect Escalator assumptions. This can make it difficult to discuss, or even consider, unconventional relationship options.

For example, sexual/romantic relationships typically are distinguished from *friendship:* a potentially significant relationship that usually is defined by its lack of sexual or romantic connection, or of family ties.

In mainstream culture, relationships that include both sex and romance often tend to be emphasized and prioritized above friendships and other types of connections that one might have with other adults. The socially acceptable exception to this is obligations to family members who are dependents. (*Family* is usually construed as people who are directly related by blood, adoption or marriage.) This doesn't mean that people must always prioritize an existing or potential Escalator partner above friends on every occasion — but when they do, friends typically are expected to gracefully understand and accept it.

Here's one way that the traditional pecking order for relationships becomes apparent: relationships which do not include sex, romance or family ties tend to get a diminutive label: *"just" friends.* This can seem like a rebuff not only to the power of friendship but also to people who are asexual or aromantic, whose deepest relationships often are dismissed or devalued.

Furthermore, when people say that a relationship is *real* or *serious*, they usually mean that the couple in question appears to be riding the Relationship Escalator. This can have the unfortunate side effect of marginalizing people whose treasured intimate relationships somehow diverge from social norms.

> *Often, when surrounded by monogamous friends, I feel like they do not consider or take my loves or relationships as seriously as they do their own. Also, should I need advice or an ear to discuss my thoughts, it can be hard to get advice or have discussions that are applicable to nonmonogamy.*
> *— Jason, polyamorous*

Because of the limitations of traditional relationship vocabulary, many people have begun repurposing existing words, or inventing new ones, so they can more accurately and easily discuss unconventional relationships. For instance, *polyamory* means being willing to engage in more than one significant intimate relationship at a time — that is, deeply involved in a sexual, romantic or emotional sense, with the full knowledge and consent of everyone involved. *(See the Glossary)*

Knowledge Is Power

Knowing one's options is crucial when it comes to envisioning how intimate relationships might look and function. For some people, this has enabled them to finally have great relationships, as well as other rewarding and fulfilling intimate experiences.

> *Until discovering polyamory, my past relationships all fit on the Relationship Escalator perfectly. I never considered that this might be why I felt so unfulfilled by them.*
> *— Matt, polyamorous*

Until four years ago, I only ever had monogamous relationships — about a dozen, serially. Then my marriage ended and I went on a sex binge for two years. That was fantastic! I fucked close to 100 guys, totally on my terms, with respect and consideration on all sides. It was incredibly liberating and empowering.

I got that out of my system, learned about ethical nonmonogamy and started building the relationships I have today. I have a great life.
— Antipodienne, nonmonogamous

Several survey participants wish that they'd learned about relationship options much sooner. This knowledge might have spared them, and their partners, considerable distress.

The amount of heartache I could have skipped by not having to blunder into what I wanted by chance would have been incalculable.
— Allen, polyamorous and kinky

As an asexual, aromantic person in a poly relationship, it can be difficult to figure out how my relationships work. People like me are so far outside social norms that we don't have any norms or templates to base our relationships upon. It would help to have more relationship templates out there, as viable and widely known options.
— Indigo, asexual and aromantic

Story: Putting New Knowledge to Use

Jackson feels that he is probably polyamorous by nature, if not yet in practice. He described how he is putting his newly acquired knowledge of relationship options to use, to consciously renegotiate an existing relationship.

I am a man in a committed partnership of one and a half years. My partner and I live in different apartments in the same neighborhood, and we have been seeing each other almost every day for the past year. We have both had sexual experiences outside of this primary relationship — though generally carefully, and after much discussion.

At this moment, I am waiting for her to come over so I can explain that I would like to step off of this Relationship Escalator we've been on. I'd like us to think about taking a few steps... sideways? "Back" seems pejorative. Point is, I'd heard the term. In my search to find it so I could reference it as part of this discussion, I ended up here, at your survey. So...

I think the primary advantage of stepping off the Escalator would be the level of honesty and self-examination it requires, which I didn't experience in my previous life of serial monogamy.

Unfortunately, I'm not sure the two of us are secure enough yet to really make it work. Hence my interest in taking a step back so we can work on the independence part of interdependence.

2

FIVE HALLMARKS OF
ESCALATOR RELATIONSHIPS

How can you tell whether a particular relationship is mostly on or significantly off the Escalator? As I read through 1500 survey responses and saw why people consider their own relationships to be unconventional, this clarified the sometimes-vague conventions which collectively define what makes a relationship more traditional.

Five hallmarks of Escalator relationships became apparent. Each hallmark is a key attribute of how intimate relationships are expected to function, under current social norms. All five hallmarks are present in relationships that are firmly on the Escalator. Diverging from any of these hallmarks is how people step off the Relationship Escalator.

Once a relationship diverges from any Escalator hallmark to any significant extent, there are fewer social conventions guiding how that relationship should proceed or function. Partners must figure this out on their own, or seek guidance from other people in similarly unconventional relationships. Fortunately, the internet has made it much easier to find such support.

Here's a quick overview of the Relationship Escalator hallmarks. Each of these was evident in the example Escalator story of Chris & Dana, in the preface to this book. Parts 2-6 of this book explore in greater depth the types of unconventional relationships that can result by diverging from each of these hallmarks, or some combination of them.

1. **Monogamy.** Under current social norms, this means a closed relationship where sex and romance are shared exclusively between two partners. Monogamy is actually about who a person is *not* allowed to share sex or romance with. Sex and/or romance commonly wane in long-term monogamous relationships, so monogamy does not ensure access to sex or romance — but it does preclude seeking it outside a monogamous relationship. In contrast, *consensually nonmonogamous* relationships (where everyone involved understands that the relationship is not

exclusive) are the most visible way, and probably the most common way, that people step off the Escalator. Some popular approaches to consensual nonmonogamy are *polyamory, swinging, don't ask don't tell* or being *monogamish.*

2. **Merging.** Riding the Relationship Escalator means that partners eventually move in together and otherwise blend the infrastructure of their daily lives, such as sharing finances. Furthermore, Escalator partners also tend to merge their identities to some extent. Typically they start to view and present themselves as a unit — for instance, saying "we" more often than "I." Relationships where partners deliberately choose to limit or avoid this kind of merging may be considered more *autonomous.* This can include choosing not to live together at all, or not full time. It also can mean socializing separately, making big choices (like career moves) independently, or not treating an intimate partner as a default companion or sole/primary source of support.

3. **Hierarchy.** Traditionally, some types of relationships typically are presumed to be most important — which means they usually get to trump other relationships by default. Typically, an Escalator relationship is deemed more important than almost any other adult relationship someone might have, such as friendships. (Parenting, and certain other responsibilities to immediate family, usually are permissible exceptions to this pecking order.) In contrast, off the Escalator and especially in consensual nonmonogamy, hierarchy gets more complex and can become ethically and emotionally fraught. In *egalitarian* relationships, decisions about spending time, attention and other resources are made case-by-case, not based on a default or predefined ranking of relationships.

4. **Sexual and romantic connection.** People tend to assume that Escalator partners do (or at least, at some point, did) have sex with each other, as well as feel romantically "in love" with each other. Furthermore, it's widely assumed that if an Escalator relationship is healthy and strong, then partners should continue their sexual and romantic connection — barring considerations such as age, illness or disability. There's a subtle stigma that if partners never connected sexually and romantically, then something must be wrong with, or at least not fully valid about, their relationship. However, many people fall along the spectrum of *asexuality:* sex is not an important, necessary or desirable part of their intimate experience. Also, people who do enjoy and desire sex sometimes choose to form committed nonsexual relationships, even life-entwined partnerships, with people who are not sexual or romantic partners.

5. **Continuity and consistency,** at least as a goal. The Escalator is a continuous, one-way trip. Escalator relationships are not supposed to pause or step back to a less-merged state. Also, Escalator partners have defined, permanent roles — for instance, partners aren't supposed to shift between being lovers and platonic friends. (Well, actually this does often happen in long-term traditional relationships, but it's usually not overtly acknowledged.) And finally, the Escalator is supposed to last forever; death is the only way to end an Escalator relationship that isn't automatically branded a failure. Nevertheless, many intimate relationships are *fluid* (shifting form or roles over time), *discontinuous* (on/off, or pause/play) or *finite* (agreeably limited by time or context, such as a summer romance). These can be deeply meaningful and significant — even though by Escalator standards, such relationships can be dismissed as insignificant, unhealthy, a waste of time or a failure.

Degrees of Stepping Off the Escalator

Stepping off the Escalator isn't always a huge, obvious matter. For instance, someone might diverge slightly from one hallmark — say, by choosing not to get legally married, or by not treating attraction to others as a threat.

> *Our relationship is close to the standard Relationship Escalator; it is the center of my life. We live together, plan our lives together and plan to have kids in the next 3-5 years. We are known as a couple in our families, workplaces, etc. The only deviation is: we don't plan to get married.*
> *— Sarah, in a nesting relationship*

> *We are allowed to comment on how good or sexy others look.*
> *— Kevin, in a long-term relationship*

Or, partners might step off the Escalator in a bigger way, just rarely. Say, by occasionally sharing sex with others, with all-around consent.

> *My partner and I are now currently monogamous, aside from occasional threesomes with friends. We have explored nonmonogamy in the past, and we are not closed off to it in the future. We may still discover our nonmonogamous niche.*
> *— Annie, monogamish*

Steps off the Escalator get bigger the more they become an ongoing feature of someone's life or relationships.

> *My husband and I are swingers. We have sex with others, couples and singles. Sometimes we are together when we have sex with them, and sometimes we go off alone to have sex with others. We are both bisexual, so if we were in a monogamous relationship, we would have to suppress that side of ourselves.*
> — *Trudy, married swinger*

Finally, it's possible to diverge from several Escalator hallmarks all at once — for example, an intimate relationship that is asexual, nonmonogamous and long distance.

> *There are four of us in this asexual relationship. We're spread out over three different countries.*
> *Ideally, we'd all like to live together at some point. But we realize this is pretty unlikely to happen. One person moving to another country is tricky enough when they're in a traditional Escalator Relationship, with the option of marriage or civil partnership. Moving two or three of us to another country when we don't really have that option would be tough.*
> — *Helen, asexual and polyamorous*

Story: Married But Not on the Escalator

Just like you can't judge a book by its cover, you can't always tell whether a relationship is on or off the Escalator based on one or two characteristics. For instance, people marry for a variety of reasons, not just to ride the Escalator.

Sabrina's story shows why it's important not to make assumptions about any relationship — even a legal marriage.

> *For nearly five years I have been in a long-term, committed relationship with my partner. Throughout this time, we've had an open relationship. I've had two long-term dating partners, as well as the freedom to explore feelings with several others.*
> *My partner and I recently moved abroad. We got married for visa reasons. I never thought I'd get married. Adjusting to this new status, while keeping our true to our unconventional values, has been more of a challenge than when we were just dating. For instance, there's a lot of baggage that comes with the terms "marriage," "husband" and "wife."*
> *It's a struggle to feel pride in being married, even though I love my partner very much. I've been tempted to get a divorce once our residency papers go through. Not to break up, mind you. More as a statement of my personal devaluation of the institution of marriage.*

I understand the concept of a marriage-like goal at the top of the Escalator. However, as a poly person who recently married due to immigration concerns, I have an issue with this. Not all marriages are alike. Vilifying marriage as the bastion of 1.5 children, middle-class monogamy does people like me a disservice. Basically, it makes me feel shitty(er) about being married.

Some people arrive at marriage through the back stairs, not by riding the Escalator. I'd appreciate not being lumped in the aforementioned group simply because of a legal status.

— Sabrina, married and polyamorous

3

WHAT THE ESCALATOR IS NOT

Often when I mention that I write about unconventional relationships, people assume I'm talking about same-sex marriage. That is quite an important topic; however, same-sex marriage is mostly about riding the Relationship Escalator.

The Relationship Escalator does not hinge upon gender expression or sexual orientation. Many people who are queer (transgender, genderqueer, lesbian, gay, bisexual, heterosexual, pansexual, asexual, etc.) choose to ride the Relationship Escalator in terms of overall relationship structure. Also, with the advent of same-sex legal marriage in many nations, any two unrelated adults might (for the time being, at least, in the U.S.) ride the Escalator all the way to the top. Thus, a monogamous, married cohabiting lesbian couple would be as much on the Escalator as *Ozzie and Harriet*[4] and their nuclear family.

Unfortunately, this does not mean that same-sex relationships and genderqueer people are now free from stigma, in the U.S. or elsewhere. Too often, this stigma overshadows the privilege that queer couples might otherwise enjoy from riding the Escalator. As well as putting queer people at all sorts of risk.

However, anti-queer stigma, including the historic denial of social and legal recognition and privilege for queer relationships, has yielded an intriguing side effect. Being part of any demographic that is marginalized for diverging from social norms sometimes can create more freedom to explore additional unconventional approaches to life and love — at least, within subcultures.

Thus, people who are exploring unconventional or queer intimate relationships today — whether they're heterosexual and cisgender, or not — owe a profound debt to the many queer people who bravely stuck their necks out for the right to live and love as they choose. They helped foster many of the values and practices useful when stepping off the Escalator today, such as consciously negotiating the nature of an intimate relationship, with awareness of options.

These pioneers often faced dire personal risks for stepping out of the closet — including violence, death and ostracism. Many of these risks persist, today. However, as the 2015 legalization of U.S. same-sex marriage demonstrates, things can change.

> *In a few generations, maybe polyamory will be widely accepted, and people will be fighting for the right to get poly-married. Maybe protesters will be holding up pictures of lesbians in wedding gowns, and saying: "Remember when this was illegal? Don't be on the wrong side of history again!"*
> *— Siobhan, nonmonogamous*

Unconventional relationships are not necessarily queer. That said, many queer people do have unconventional relationships.

For instance, queer communities often recognize and value deeply emotionally intimate and committed relationships which involve neither sex nor romance in any traditional sense. Such *queerplatonic* relationships often go far beyond the traditional concept of friendship.

Many queer people did share stories of their unconventional relationships. Future books and other content in the *Off the Escalator* project will explore queer and other intersectional considerations that can affect intimate relationships.

> *I notice that your survey doesn't make any distinctions between same-sex couples, heterosexual couples, and couples with transgendered or genderqueer partners. There may be differences in the structure of unconventional relationships between these groups that might be worth looking at.*
> *— Amanda, polyamorous and engaged*

If you're kinky, you can ride the Escalator if you want to. *Kink* is an umbrella term for a vast array of unconventional practices, concepts or fantasies which hold sexual, erotic, emotional or psychological significance to individuals. This includes, but is not limited to, bondage, domination/submission and sadism/masochism. (*BDSM*, which is increasingly recognized as a potentially healthy outlet for sexual and emotional expression.) Kink also may involve various kinds of play: role playing, fetishes, sensation play, costume play, voyeurism, exhibitionism and more.

Kink may or may not involve sexual contact, but in some ways, it is akin to sexuality. As with sex, the meaning or significance of kink can vary. For some people, kink is highly emotionally significant, even essential to their experience of deep intimacy. However, kink can also be recreational, exploratory or cathartic. It's a very personal experience.

A couple in a relationship that bears all five Escalator hallmarks, including monogamy, might indulge in kinky sex or play just between themselves. Or they might agree that they can participate in nonsexual kinky play with others — for example, foot worship or domestic service. That wouldn't necessarily knock their relationship off the Escalator.

However, people in monogamous relationships might consider it cheating to indulge even in nonsexual kink with others. This is a gray area since there are many ways to practice monogamy.

> When I was married, I was involved in a secret Master/slave relationship with a married man. We were very happy with that for more than a year. To my knowledge, my now-ex-husband never knew about it.
> — Tana, poly, pagan and kinky

Of course, kink is often important or fun for people in unconventional relationships, too.

> I'm a male servant with a genderqueer master, and we are polyamorous. We don't have sex (my master is attracted to females), and we don't live together, but my master owns me and I obey everything my master orders.
> — Sonic, kinky and polyamorous

The Escalator Is Not a Straitjacket

There is plenty of variety on the Relationship Escalator, for lots of reasons. In fact, most relationships that are highly traditional (bearing all five Escalator hallmarks) don't look exactly like the Chris & Dana example in the preface to this book.

For instance, these days many long-term monogamous couples are choosing not to have children or get legally married. As society evolves, these are becoming acceptable options while riding the Relationship Escalator.

This is similar to how the concept of "family" has evolved well beyond the social norms. While the traditional *nuclear family* remains an influential social concept, today most families take other forms. [5]

Sometimes monogamous partners, even couples who are married and living together, retain a stronger focus on personal autonomy than is common in traditional relationships. They don't surrender too much of their individuality to a joint identity as a couple. Thus, they may socialize and vacation separately, maintain close friendships with people who are potentially sexually or romantically attractive, not consider each other to be default companions for support, and so on.

Even if someone is in a traditional pair-bonded, exclusive, committed relationship, this might not be their highest priority. Sometimes, people prioritize community, work, health, education, creative projects, life goals or spiritual pursuits above their Escalator relationship — either temporarily or permanently.

If someone does decide to step off (or on) the Relationship Escalator, they're not necessarily branded for life — or even for the span of a particular relationship. They might change their mind either way, at any time.

Some people who are currently off the Escalator are open to the possibility of riding the Escalator in the future — whether with a current partner or in a new relationship. Similarly, some people who are riding the Escalator today might be open to the possibility of stepping off someday.

> We don't have a shared goal to continue climbing the Escalator, necessarily — things like moving in together. But we're not completely closed to that, either.
> — Lina, polyamorous

> I would like to stay with my current partner as long as possible, which is why we're engaged. I would be fine with lifelong monogamy — but it might be possible that we could benefit from being open.
> There are some things I can't provide him (such as sex with a cisgender male body), and things he can't provide me (an outlet for my top/sadistic tendencies in kink). So who knows?
> — Pony, trans person in a monogamous relationship

The Escalator Is Not Easy to Leave Behind

Deeply ingrained social norms about relationships, reinforced by media, role models, legal and financial considerations, and external support and recognition, can make it quite daunting to step off the Escalator — or even to consider doing so. Several people reported conflicting feelings about stepping off the Escalator. Sometimes, it's unclear whether these emotions are authentic, or the result of strong social conditioning.

Filling out this survey gave me some serious food for thought — especially the question "What would your ideal intimate relationship(s) look like?" Typing out my response to that made it all seem so simple, and yet still unattainable.

I'm not going to lie: part of me still craves monogamy. It just seems so simple compared to what I'm trying to do. But it's not my current goal. I think even that feeling is part of the Escalator mentality.

I frequently feel off-kilter because I don't have a traditional path to follow. I've yet to find a fairy tale that gives me a clue to what's next. Escalator relationships are so embedded and assumed that the path is there without you even realizing it.

— Kate, divorcing from an open marriage

When people continue to have strong emotional reactions or personal crises triggered by lingering ingrained Escalator assumptions (particularly about monogamy) that they no longer believe in, some people call this the *monogamy hangover.*

Even years into exploring open relationships, lingering notions and assumptions can crop up in the ways we are approaching our nonmonogamous relationships. Sometimes they are internal dialogues, never spoken out loud. Or, they might appear in the ways we start to interact with our partners.

When this happens, it can be jarring. It can feel like a friction emerging from the inside of our being: the outer form of things does not match the internalized societal programming, and therefore we might act from spite, anger, or jealousy. Or, paralyzed by shame and self-judgment, we might suddenly change from being very present and forthcoming, to absent, reticent, even fearful.

Our partners may be perplexed by our actions, and they may feel pushed away by the monogamy hangover that threatens to destabilize a relationship they were embracing.

— Relationship coach Mel Cassidy[6]

The Escalator Is Not a Problem

Monogamous, life-merged partnerships that are intended to be lifelong do work quite well for many people. Traditional relationships often help many people be who they want to be, have a good life, and engage with others in ways that make sense and feel right to them. Yet, this does not reduce the value of understanding and appreciating unconventional relationships.

> *Ultimately, I want the old-fashioned husband, wife, kids. But as a society, we need to start accepting that not everyone wants (or ends up with) the old-fashioned way of marriage.*
> — Betty, monogamous

> *It's not that normative relationships are the problem. The fact that they are considered normal is the problem.*
> — Shannon, currently monogamous

In my own life, I've known many people who are in traditional relationships. More often than not, this makes them genuinely happy — or at least, happy enough.

> *It would be disheartening to see this book turn into a negative tirade against monogamy. I hear it works for some people.*
> — A, polyamorous, in a long distance marriage

Playing the Field and Cheating: Part of the Escalator

Casual dating and cheating are two popular ways that people often bridge the gap between Escalator ideals, human nature and real life. In fact, they are so conventional that they can be considered complements to the Relationship Escalator.

Casual dating (often called *dating around* or *playing the field*) is a popular way to share a lighter level of intimacy, attraction and companionship, and often some sex, without the life-altering expectations and obligations of an Escalator relationship. What makes these connections "casual" is the lack of significant emotional investment, or any intention beyond having fun or killing time, or any expectation that the relationship will continue beyond the current encounter.

Generally, casual dating is not monogamous; it's common to casually date a few people simultaneously. Nonmonogamy is usually assumed, not overtly disclosed or discussed.

> *Once I figured out that I was poly in college, I made sure to explain to anyone I dated that I believed in being able to have long-lasting loving relationships with more than one person at a time. In high school, I was open to this as well — but I had difficulty finding other partners who could be honest with everyone involved.*
> — Winona, married and poly

Casual, uncommitted dating has become thoroughly normalized in Western cultures. Long gone are the days when it was expected that someone's first and only intimate relationship should be lifelong monogamous marriage. (Or, as Dolly Parton sang, *"He's done kissed me on the mouth, he's gonna marry me."*[7])

Thus, casual dating does not conflict with riding the Relationship Escalator — as long as it is strictly a temporary phase "between" Escalator relationships, or a preliminary step in auditioning potential Escalator partners. Eventually, people are expected to find their way to the Escalator.

> *There's a big myth about "hookup culture" on college campuses. Everybody is talking about it, but nobody is doing it. That makes for some interesting dynamics regarding how the Escalator is addressed in college life.*
>
> *Does the temporary acceptance of casual relationships reinforce the Escalator in the long run, or does it expose more people to alternative relationship styles?*
> — *Eva, unattached college student*

Similarly, cheating is another popular approach to nonmonogamy. People in monogamous relationships often *cheat* — which means engaging in clandestine or unauthorized sex, flirtation or romance, despite agreeing to exclusivity in these things. Research statistics on infidelity vary, but in most research, half of all adults[8] (or more) admit to cheating at some point in their life.

When someone violates their agreement to monogamy, typically this transgression gets viewed as riding the Escalator badly, not actually stepping off by abandoning allegiance to the socially venerated goal of monogamy. In effect, cheating has become an acknowledged, if not socially acceptable, backchannel which attempts to reconcile monogamy and human sexuality. This point was emphasized in a 2010 study of cheaters' attitudes toward cheating. [9]

> *Data suggest that participants who cheat do so not because of lost love. Instead, cheating represents an attempt to rectify conflicting desires for monogamy and recreational sex.*
> — *Eric Anderson, University of Bath, England*

Cheating often does trigger the end of Escalator relationships, since it transgresses the weightiest Escalator hallmark. Still, cheating is pretty conventional: most people understand what it is and how it works. It can generate considerable shock and drama — but usually, not much confusion.

41

In fact, it's common for cheating to be considered more socially acceptable than consensual nonmonogamy.

> *People accept married people having affairs more than married people swinging. Something seems off there.*
> — *Arthur, married swinger*

Cheating commonly sparks public and private shame, scandal, fear and moralizing. Thus, it effectively reinforces Escalator norms, as long as people contend that cheating is intrinsically wrong.

However, cheating isn't always kept secret or considered a serious transgression.

> *I'm currently married unhappily, with a known lover.*
> — *Cicely, married*

> *Throughout our 10-year relationship, my ex and I struggled with monogamy. There were slip-ups and "cheating" once every year or so. Neither of us was bothered by it. We didn't discover the conceptual framework of polyamory for several years.*
> — *Ryan, polyamorous*

Perpetually perfect monogamy can be incredibly challenging. Consequently, from a practical (if not moral) perspective, cheating can be what enables some Escalator relationships to survive intact across decades. Rationalizing this choice often entails some ethical gymnastics.

> *Often lies can save more than one relationship. Truth is so much better and easier, but not when you have to deal with someone who cannot control their emotions.*
> — *Vanessa, in a clandestine relationship*

Story: Gray-Area Cheating

Cheating is probably more common than unconventional relationships — and it's by no means a black-and-white issue. Usually, complex reasons yield behavior that might be called cheating.

Thus, it isn't always clear what's cheating and what's not, or whether a specific instance of cheating is unethical or immoral. Sex advice columnist Dan Savage[10] often says: "Sometimes you do what you need to do to stay married and stay sane."

Runner52's story is just one example of how it can be hard to judge people who choose to pursue other intimate relationships without the express knowledge and consent of their existing monogamous partner.

> *I am a married man. My wife has early onset Alzheimer's disease and cannot participate in the marriage. I am also in a relationship with a woman who is in an open marriage. I know her husband and consider him a friend.*
>
> *Prior to my current extramarital relationship, I had another relationship with another married woman. She was in an open marriage, but her husband did not know me and I did not know him. In a way, I viewed this as cheating.*
>
> *As my wife's illness progressed, my needs and wants changed. That's what got me to the point of looking for love and connections outside of my marriage.*
>
> *I am where I am. Life sometimes just happens. I am happy in my relationships. My wife is cared for, and my kids are coping as best they can. I am happy with my girlfriend and get along well with her family and spouse.*
>
> *I think it's important to just talk about these kinds of relationships. Be honest. I have begun the conversation with my children so that when they come visit they will recognize that just having connections is both lovely and loving.*

4

CAN UNCONVENTIONAL RELATIONSHIPS WORK?

It's common for people ask some version of this question almost as soon as the topic of unconventional relationships arises. Because, according to conventional wisdom, trying to do anything too different or radical with intimate relationships is borrowing trouble.

> *Open relationships that work well with no one getting hurt: do they really exist?*
> *— Christine, monogamous*

But what do "work" and "success" mean in the context of intimate relationships? The Escalator story of Chris & Dana, in the preface to this book, exemplifies the social ideal of "till death do we part." Increasingly, this ideal is being questioned.

> *I want to challenge the notion of what a "successful" relationship looks like. I was about to write that we need more models of successful off-the-Escalator relationships, but then I could find no definition for success without succumbing to Escalator-esque values.*
> *— Michelle, polyamorous*

> *I think we should stop seeing relationship issues in terms of failure and success.*
> *— Tahni, in a long distance monogamous relationship*

An important indicator of the success of an intimate relationship might be: how do the people in that relationship feel about it? Are they benefiting from it?

In my survey, I asked how generally satisfied (or not) people were in their unconventional intimate relationships. Nearly 75% of the people who took my survey answered this question — and the majority said they are generally pretty happy. Specifically:

- 43% Mostly happy or satisfied
- 33% Very happy or satisfied
- Far fewer reported less-than-positive experiences:
- 16% Strongly mixed feelings
- 4% Mostly or somewhat dissatisfied
- 2% Very unhappy or dissatisfied
- 2% Neutral

Thus, success is possible off the Relationship Escalator, At least, it's common for people to consider their unconventional relationships successful, on their own terms.

> *Speaking overall about my open relationships: I really love that I can be in love, but still not have the nagging thought, "If this relationship works out, I may never have sex with any new men ever again."*
> — *Aphrodite, polyamorous*

The catch is that when people inquire about the success of unconventional relationships, usually they aren't really wondering about happiness or satisfaction.

Does Longevity = Relationship Success?

Through many conversations over the years, I've learned that when people inquire about the "success" potential of unconventional relationships, typically they're mostly concerned with longevity. Specifically, they want to know whether unconventional relationships might endure as long as Escalator relationships.

> *How have people made polyamory work in the long term? There is help out there for how to make unconventional relationships work in the now, but not many actual success stories.*
> — *Didi, married and polyamorous*

Here's what people have told me about why they believe relationship longevity is such an important benchmark:

First, most people prefer some stability and reliability, or at least predictability, in their most important relationships. They'd rather not be dealing with lots of change or disruption, especially in areas of life where they might feel especially vulnerable.

This is understandable since, under current social norms, an Escalator relationship is supposed to form much of the foundation of one's life. This goes beyond securing access to emotional connection, sex and companionship. It also typically involves how people approach finances, housing, family, social status and a personal sense of identity and purpose. Plus, there's the need for support through misfortune, age, illness and other trying circumstances.

Loading so much onto any relationship can trigger considerable fear, uncertainty and doubt. If you don't manage to get and keep an Escalator relationship, will you suffer from lack of support? Will you have enough resources to realize your goals? Will your life have meaning? Might you die alone and unloved? Will other people judge you harshly, or pity you? Will you "lose" at life, or at least at adulthood?

Second, there's the deep-seated social assumption that a successful relationship should last a lifetime. This presents a logical quandary. Most people know that the majority of intimate relationships end short of a partner's death. Nevertheless, most relationships still manage to be mutually rewarding and valuable while they exist. Is that really failure?

In contrast, some couples continuously maintain monogamy, cohabitation and other Escalator hallmarks until death do they part — all the while making each other, and the people around them, utterly miserable. Is that really a success?

> *If a relationship lasts forever, there are costs associated with that.*
> *— Rhiannon, married and polyamorous*

> *The only way you can be sure you've succeeded on the Escalator is when neither of you has sex with anyone else, and then someone dies.*
> *— Mari Helena, solo poly*

Due to such commonplace beliefs, relationship "failure" typically means either that the partners did not ride the Escalator all the way to the top, or that the relationship ended or substantially changed after arriving at the pinnacle. Occasionally, even people who voluntarily step off the Escalator express this sentiment.

> *I've had some relationships that were more or less on the Escalator, but they all ended within a few years. I'd like to be in a stable relationship, one that might last a lifetime.*

> *Ideally, I'd also like to feel loved and cared for — but I'm not sure if I could feel this in polyamory. Since most of my relationships ended, I feel like I'm unfit somehow.*
> *— Amande, in a poly relationship*

But usually, people in unconventional relationships strongly reject the premise that longevity equals success.

> *You can view intimate, soulful interactions as worthwhile on a case-by-case basis, as opposed to failures or false starts when they did not lead to marriage.*
> *— Chloe, nonmonogamous*

> *In terms of long-lasting, my mom and stepfather swore "as long as love shall last" — and that's about as far as I want to go.*
> *— Kaia, polyamorous*

Successful Afterships

At one time, it was almost uniform practice that if an Escalator relationship ended, it had to be totally over. Former partners would exit each other's lives as completely as possible — often with considerable acrimony and social ripple effects.

Severing all ties with former intimate partners can avoid the awkwardness of learning new ways of relating to them. It may also reduce perceived barriers to a new intimate relationship since former partners are a common jealousy trigger under social norms. However, this practice also commonly yields considerable personal and social disruption.

Stark, harsh breakups still happen, but they are not quite as common as they once were. These days, it's increasingly common for former lovers, partners or spouses to conclude their intimate bond while retaining strong mutual respect and affection, and perhaps even an enduring friendship and substantial involvement in each other's lives. Some people call such post-intimate relationships *afterships*.

Afterships defy historic social norms. Traditionally, when an intimate relationship ended, one-time partners tended to exit each other's lives as much as possible, often with considerable acrimony. Or at most, they would be merely cordial to each other. The assumption was that making a "clean break" is the healthy way for people to "move on" and find new Escalator partners.

In my own life, I've maintained a very close relationship with my former spouse. Taken in its entirety, this is the most significant and enduring intimate relationship of my life, having lasted nearly three decades as of this writing.

After our divorce nearly a decade ago, my former spouse and I remained close and visited often. Since then, sometimes he has shared my home, as a guest or temporary housemate. Also, all along we've shared our vacation cabin, where we stay together several times a year. (In fact, that's where I'm writing this right now, as he's grilling up dinner.)

Throughout our relationship, he and I have always remained in daily contact, and we are each other's go-to support person for big news, changes and challenges. Currently, our homes are fairly close so we hang out a few times a week. We're still very affectionate and cuddly, although no longer sexual or romantic with each other.

Indeed, getting unmarried is what allowed us to preserve and nurture all these wonderful parts of our relationship. Being married, even in a poly marriage, never really suited us well. It created too much friction and pressure, and led us to chafe at each other. Our aftership has proved to be the most peaceful and mutually fulfilling phase of our entire relationship.

This experience isn't unusual. Off the Relationship Escalator, it's fairly common for people to transition from being lovers or partners to platonic friends — or at least on very good terms, able to socialize with or be around each other easily. In part, this happens because communities of people in unconventional relationships tend to be small and close-knit. In that setting, harsh breakups can trigger relatively more damaging ripple effects across social circles or entire communities, especially where nonexclusive relationships overlap.

People who connect with such communities are likely to witness the peaceful, considerate, amicable transformation of intimate relationships. Seeing positive role models in everyday life can have a powerful influence on behavior. This is fortunate, since framing relationships as failures rarely seems to make anyone happy.

> *As my partner and I de-escalate our relationship, we've faced a lack of understanding about how to navigate changes in relationships. This has caused both of us emotional pain when trying to work out how to accept these changes without feeling that we've failed.*
>
> *I wish there was more understanding that all ties don't have to be cut if a relationship changes. It is normal for relationships to change form — and not a sign of failure.*

> *I need to start discussing with my friends the benefits of unconventional relationships. I need to get over my fear that this will be seen as proof that I am trying to excuse what others might see as my failure in relationships.*
> — *Karen, polyamorous*

Furthermore, longevity isn't what it used to be. Average lifespans continue to rise around the world, while social stigma associated with divorce or other relationship endings has largely disappeared in many cultures. Consequently, now people usually perceive longevity in terms of whether a relationship lasts for a few years, at least.

How many years qualifies as "long term?" That depends on who's counting. In anecdotes and research, this can range from two or three years up to decades. Mostly, the perceived value of longevity appears to depend on whether someone views intimate relationships as a wonderful part of life, or as an essential foundation for long-term plans, goals and life structure.

In my survey, several people described unconventional relationships that have lasted for many years — including some which have endured for decades:

> *I'm male, and my female partner and I have been in a V-type relationship with another man for nearly 25 years. They are married to each other; I'm not married.*
> *We're like a water molecule: two hydrogen atoms, one oxygen. I'm pretty good with this. A quarter century of a stable relationship with flexibility is hard to beat.*
> — *Ted, polyamorous*

> *I am still in an extremely intense, and even more loving and genuine, open relationship with the same person who I partnered with 42 years ago. It isn't slowing down.*
> — *Charlie, polyamorous*

My survey did not ask people how long their relationships have lasted. That's because, off the Escalator, this can be a surprisingly complex question. People might have more than one relationship at a time, or different ideas about what an intimate relationship is, or whether a relationship has a clear beginning or ending. Also if a relationship is discontinuous, do the gaps count?

For instance, Rejoice lives a nomadic life, spending different parts of the year with different partners. She notes:

One of my central partners is a trans lady on the west coast. We've been romantically and sexually involved intermittently for the last 12 years. For the last three years, I have been spending 4-12 weeks per year with her. She and I have a loving but zero-expectation relationship.
— Rejoice, solo poly

In my own life, my longest-lasting intimate relationship has spanned nearly three decades, as of this writing.

My former spouse and I met as we graduated from college. We fell in love and progressed through dating and living together all the way up the Escalator to a dozen years of legal marriage. At first, our marriage was monogamous; but a few years after we got married we decided to embrace polyamory. We each had other intimate relationships. For a few years, we were even part of a quad relationship with another married couple.

Over time, he and I realized that we wanted to move forward in different directions. Our sexual and romantic connection had gradually faded, but our love had deepened. So we got unmarried and separated our households. However, we have remained extremely close. Today, we are affectionate and cuddly with each other, we support each other emotionally and sometimes logistically, and we still spend lots of time together.

Our relationship did end when we ceased to be monogamous, or even when we got unmarried. Rather, we view this as one continuous relationship. We allowed the form of our relationship to shift, in order to accommodate our changing needs.

Major Pros and Cons of Stepping Off the Escalator

If a successful relationship is mutually rewarding, then it helps to clarify what rewards an intimate relationship can offer. On this point, my survey did yield some clear answers.

I asked participants to list the most important benefits and drawbacks which they have personally experienced by stepping off the Escalator. I deliberately did not provide a checklist of possible benefits; people wrote whatever they wanted.

According to my survey, here are the 25 most commonly mentioned benefits of unconventional relationships. The percentages indicate the portion of participants who mentioned each category.

Note that most of these benefits might also be realized on the Escalator. Very few (such as sexual variety) would be difficult or impossible to realize in a traditional relationship.

- More love, intimacy, belonging or acceptance (30%)
- Sexual variety, thrills or exploration (29%)
- Freedom (28%)
- Greater personal authenticity, integrity or self-expression (26%)
- Less pressure or expectations (24%)
- Better communication (23%)
- Personal or interpersonal growth, discovery or insight (22%)
- More honesty (20%)
- Fewer norms or defaults (20%)
- Less codependence (20%)
- Novelty: new experiences or people (19%)
- Accommodating differences (17%)
- Making existing relationships better or stronger (15%)
- Feeling more secure, safer or trusting (14%)
- Emotional support enhanced (14%)
- More autonomy and personal space (14%)
- Less guilt, shame or worry (13%)
- Appreciating the uniqueness of relationships (13%)
- Stronger ties with family, community and friends (11%)
- More satisfying or fulfilling life (11%)
- More needs met (11%)
- Ethics and values: more consideration and practice (11%)
- Customizable relationships (10%)
- Sex or touch, more or better (10%)
- Enhanced stability or continuity (10%)

Inevitably, stepping off the Escalator has some downsides, too. Here are the 25 most commonly mentioned tradeoffs of unconventional intimate relationships.

Again, the percentages indicate the portion of participants who mentioned each category. Many of these challenges might occur in traditional relationships, but a few (such stigma and closeting) are primarily off-the-Escalator problems.

Also, note that some issues (such as communication and personal growth) were frequently mentioned as both benefits and problems off the Escalator.

- Stigma, judgment or discrimination (29%)
- Being closeted (27%)
- Communication, too much or harder (26%)
- Jealousy or envy (24%)
- Emotional stress or pain (23%)
- Time management (23%)

- Family, trouble dealing with (21%)
- Social norms: navigation or pressure (20%)
- Lack of support, understanding or acceptance (17%)
- Assumptions and expectations (16%)
- Insecurity or inadequacy (15%)
- Hierarchy and couple privilege problems (12%)
- Worry or fear (12%)
- Relationship imbalance or inequity (11%)
- Complexity (11%)
- Can't satisfy everyone (11%)
- Too much work (11%)
- Loneliness, isolation or feeling left out (11%)
- Personal growth is hard (11%)
- Work, insurance, financial or legal concerns (10%)
- Ethical quandaries (10%)
- Trouble changing or ending relationships (10%)
- Frustration or resentment (10%)
- Metamour or network problems (9%)
- Conflict (9%)

Story: Complex But Successful Relationships

Based on my survey and additional research, it is evident that unconventional relationships can succeed. Happiness, stability, mutual benefit and even longevity (if that matters to you) can be found in almost any kind of unconventional relationship — just as they might be found in traditional relationships, too.

This can be true even in relationships that might seem hopelessly complicated by Escalator standards. Liz described her long-term polyamorous network:

> *My partner M. and I are life-entangled. We live together, have shared finances and investments, and expect to stay together for the long term. We are also poly, and we each have other relationships.*
>
> *I have two other partners. My girlfriend J. and my partner D. are both not life-entangled, but emotionally important to me. J, D and I are also in a triad.*
>
> *My life-entangled partner has two girlfriends and one occasional play partner. Roughly twice-a-month he also has dates with each of his girlfriends, and "when they can schedule it in" dates with his play partner. Both of his girlfriends are currently only dating him, I believe.*

However, they are open to other relationships, and have had other relationships in the past, while dating M.

This structure has been stable for a number of years. M and I have been together for almost 15 years. J, D and I have been together for over five years. M has been with one girlfriend for nearly six years. M's other relationships have each lasted for approximately two years.

I feel more secure in my poly relationship since I have multiple people to go to for support. I'm also able to explore attractions to new people without fear of losing my life-entangled partner. I have the security of knowing that even though my partner may be interested in other people, they are actively choosing to stay with me as well.

The way we're living is pretty damn awesome for us.

5

WHY PEOPLE RIDE THE ESCALATOR
AND STEP OFF

People ride the Relationship Escalator for many reasons. Sometimes, this happens because the Escalator is the only potentially viable option that they know of for experiencing love, intimacy and connection in a deep or enduring way. But that's definitely not the only reason.

People often choose the Relationship Escalator quite deliberately, not by default. The traditional approach to intimate relationships can align well with innate needs and preferences. It can be an authentic expression of love and commitment.

In such cases, partners tend to consciously consider and negotiate steps they take up the Escalator. They don't just automatically do whatever is "supposed" to come next. Rather, their authentic desires happen to match the traditional approach to intimate relationships. Sometimes, these partners also are aware of — and perhaps have considered, discussed or explored — less conventional relationship options.

Still, the pressure that social norms can exert on personal choices should not be underestimated. It's common for people to assume that if they feel a strong emotional bond with an intimate partner, then they must keep riding the Escalator if that relationship is to continue at all.

> In many ways, my spouse and I always were extremely good friends. The problem was, the Escalator model told us that because we were such good friends, we needed to get married. Riding the Escalator did a lot of damage to our friendship, and we are in the stages of rebuilding.
> — Rei, divorced

Even when someone consciously disagrees with the assumption that "serious" relationships must follow a traditional trajectory, it can be surprisingly hard to ignore the weight of the Escalator, compared to other approaches. This is not surprising, since the Escalator is so prominently touted in society and media as the best, and perhaps the only, path toward achieving several common goals:

- Creating a stable structure for having and raising children. Or building a family beyond one's family of origin, for those who don't have or want children.
- Obtaining reliable help and support in daily life, including emotional support.
- Care in old age, disability or illness.
- Reliable access to sex, affection and touch.
- Companionship, including having a default companion for gatherings and special occasions.
- Gaining family or social recognition as a full adult.

Also, some people ride the Escalator (or keep riding it) for logistical or economic reasons, at least in part. It might be someone's best or only option to access or maintain health insurance, affordable housing (or perhaps any housing at all), childcare, household help, support for disability and aging, etc.

These are all valid, compelling reasons; but they are not the only forces nudging people toward the Relationship Escalator.

The Escalator Can Feel Simpler or More Natural

Most people understand how the Escalator works at a subconscious level. This is why traditional relationships can feel like they "just happen." They might seem to naturally flow from one step to the next — with relatively less effort, introspection or negotiation, compared to other types of relationships.

The perception of being carried along by the Relationship Escalator is, in fact, an illusion. In any intimate relationship, partners always make choices every step of the way — even if it's merely the choice to stick with an established course.

Thus, everyone who rides the Relationship Escalator is really taking the stairs; they just don't necessarily deliberate about every step they take. Nor are they necessarily aware of the many external and internal forces which help to propel the Escalator. It can seem much simpler to assume that as long as an intimate relationship looks a certain way, then it should meet people's needs and make them happy. Sticking to popular patterns of relating generally supports such assumptions.

In contrast, not making lots of assumptions about how relationships work can seem like an onerous burden. Clear, frank, discussion of what intimate partners each truly want or need in life (or within a specific relationship), and negotiating how to customize relationships in light of this information, is sometimes viewed not normal — and perhaps even risky or threatening.

The Escalator Can Feel Safer or Less Awkward

The human mind tends to equate familiarity with safety. People often instinctively assume that something new, unfamiliar or unusual is more likely to prove dangerous or inferior. This is why "weird" usually does not imply "good."

Thus, it may feel daunting merely to contemplate exploring an unusual or new path, even if a less popular approach might end up working much better.

It's like the joke that compares Linux (a collaboratively developed, highly customizable, freely available computer operating system) was an airline:

> *When you board a Linux Air flight, someone hands you a seat, four bolts, a wrench and a copy of the seat HOWTO document.*
>
> *But once you settle in, your fully adjustable seat is very comfy, and you have exactly as much leg and elbow room as you need. Plus, there are no baggage fees on Linux Air, and you never have to make a connecting flight, no matter how obscure your destination. The plane departs and lands precisely on schedule. The in-flight meal is delicious and free, and the free WiFi is screaming fast.*
>
> *You try to tell your friends — who fly, and complain loudly about, other airlines — all about your excellent Linux Air experience. But all they can say is: "You had to do what with the seat?"*

Even when people are aware of (or perhaps practice) unconventional relationship styles, sometimes they still assume that traditional relationships must be safer — or at least, less prone to risk and trouble.

> *Sometimes all this freedom does feel a bit unsafe and unconnected.*
> *— Lottie, polyamorous*

> *It can be difficult for my partners to come to terms with me not being monogamous. Often, they try to limit their emotional connection with me because they assume that it's an unsafe and unstable relationship, with a higher risk of jealousy.*
> *— Kissobelle, solo poly*

Unconventional relationships definitely are not risk-free. However, in the big picture, all intimate relationships are inherently risky, to some extent. As author Susan Piver[11] notes, *"Love can never be made safe. It is the opposite of safe."*

The Relationship Escalator comes with its own set of risks, pressures, stresses and complexities. People usually take these tradeoffs in stride, like accepting the everyday risks of driving a car. But these risks are quite real, and they can end relationships.

> *I really like some traditional relationship goals: owning a home, having a family, etc. But they don't necessarily figure into my relationship-making lexicon.*
> *They have figured into my relationship-ending lexicon, however.*
> *— Josef, polyamorous*

Then, there's social awkwardness. Stepping off the Escalator can alter the fundamental geometry of common social situations.

> *My husband and I used to go out with another couple, where mostly I talked to the other woman, and the two men talked together.*
> *Now the five of us, including my other male partner, go out together. However, it's uncomfortable figuring out how things can fit together.*
> *— Catherine, in an open relationship*

Social norms exist, in large measure, to reduce uncertainty or friction in everyday life. When people venture beyond social norms, others often feel unsure of how to interact with them. This can feel uncomfortable for everyone.

> *It's awkward to tell someone I'm attracted to that, although I have a boyfriend, I'm still available. That is really difficult to work into casual conversation.*
> *— Joanie, in a sexually open relationship*

> *I was very comfortable meeting my girlfriend's new lover and chatting away with him — but it turned out my friend who was also there was squirming inside!*
> *— Keir, nonmonogamous*

Extra Support for the Escalator

Traditional relationships often benefit from many types of support that unconventional relationships typically cannot access. This social exoskeleton may not always be easy to see; people tend to take it for granted. However, it can help buffer Escalator relationships from difficulty or help keep them intact. The desire to gain these advantages can lead people to rush to the Escalator. Similarly, fear of losing them can discourage Escalator partners from splitting up when things get rough.

When two people visibly ride the Relationship Escalator together, this fact alone often yields some increase in their security, prestige and comfort. These advantages spring from social *couple privilege:* the assumption that people who are coupled up are more important, and worthy of greater consideration and reward, than other people. If their relationship is also sexually and romantically exclusive, cohabiting and otherwise life-entwined, this phenomenon is significantly amplified.

Consequently, all else being equal, people who are coupled up Escalator-style (or who appear to be) often receive more respect, validation, support and recognition than people who are unpartnered, or unconventionally partnered. Understandably, many people desire and seek this advantage.

> *I would definitely like to be married someday. I like the feeling of being in a couple, and I like the social benefits of being in a couple.*
> — Clare, queer and asexual

Couple privilege is a subtle but powerful social force. It offers tangible and intangible benefits[12] and opportunities — from better access to health insurance, to a better chance of being considered likable, competent or trustworthy.

One of its biggest advantages of riding the Relationship Escalator is that it can reduce many common social and logistical obstacles. Generally, people in traditional intimate relationships tend to face less suspicion, scrutiny, resistance and prejudice. *Singlism*[13] is rampant: the common stigma associated with adults who are entirely unpartnered — or at least, who do not appear to have a "committed" (potentially Escalator) relationship. Furthermore, the stigma associated with consensual nonmonogamy can be even more pronounced than singlism — because this choice is widely deemed taboo, not merely undesirable.

In the preface, the example Escalator relationship story includes several common markers of couple privilege that arise in the course of everyday life. For instance:

> *...Chris & Dana display each other's photo at work, and they feel free to note the existence of their relationship in casual conversations, even with coworkers or strangers. This is not considered oversharing, even though everyone assumes that Chris & Dana have sex with each other.*
> *...Flashing their new rings, they publicly announce their engagement with much excitement, and they are unanimously congratulated. They*

easily acquire a marriage license. Their wedding, which is announced in the newspaper, is held in a church and is attended by many friends and family, who all bear gifts.

...When they have children, there is no question about their right or ability to parent. They feel immense pride in having created a real family. Their relatives show respect for, and take pride and interest in, Chris & Dana's marriage and family.

...Overall, their life together feels fruitful. Its patterns feel familiar and comforting, and not just to them. Other people easily understand how to interact with Chris & Dana; they know what to expect from the couple, and what's appropriate.

Despite the social benefits of couplehood, any type of privilege is always a mixed bag. This is what makes privilege such a controversial and fraught topic. For instance, couple privilege is often mitigated by more well-known stigmas related to class, sex, race, age, ability, sexual orientation, gender expression, etc.

Thus, a monogamous, cohabiting, married couple may not feel very privileged if they are also poor, black, elderly, disabled lesbians. This doesn't mean they completely lack couple privilege; just that it probably would be overshadowed by the stigma they experience due to those other personal attributes.

Thanks to couple privilege, Escalator couples often gain automatic access to tangible benefits, especially if they get legally married. In many countries, this includes tax, insurance, hospital visitation, housing, immigration, financial and inheritance benefits, and more. Legally sanctioned relationships also entail default obligations (such as shared responsibility for debt), but typically people accept this.

There are many social benefits of couple privilege, as well. These may include public recognition, the expectation that others will spend money and time celebrating Escalator couples (i.e. the vast "wedding industrial complex"), maintaining good standing with one's family of origin, or getting invited to more dinner parties.

"Privilege" may sound heavy-handed in the context of relationship styles, but it's just part of life. Most of us are privileged, or not, in some way. Privilege is socially conferred whenever someone appears to possess certain socially desirable characteristics. Privilege is not optional; people get it whether they want it or not. It affects the treatment some people receive and the opportunities they are offered.

The benefits currently associated with couple privilege need not come at the expense of others. This is especially important when it comes to tangible benefits. For instance, financial, legal and healthcare benefits can be accorded to individuals, regardless of relationship style or status — a practice more common in Europe and Canada than the U.S.

Couple privilege does have a potential dark side for the couples who possess it. The fear and shame commonly associated with losing couple privilege often keeps people in Escalator relationships which have ceased to be joyful — and which may have even become toxic or damaging.

Then there's stigma. This is not merely the absence of a socially conferred privilege. Rather, *stigma* is an active disadvantage — an intrinsic strike against a person or relationship, right off the bat.

Stigma breeds obstacles, stress and self-doubt or self-loathing. Many common negative stereotypes about unconventional relationships boil down to stigma. It was quite telling that in my survey, the most common disadvantages (by far) associated with being in unconventional relationships all related to stigma — especially dealing with judgment and discrimination, and the stress and difficulty of being *closeted*.

The active stigma against unconventional relationships surfaces in myriad ways: being casually treated with suspicion, housing and child custody discrimination, alienation from family and community and much more. Or having to explain your relationships more than other people seem to need to.

> *Often others can't or won't understand our relationship setup. I get tired of being expected to justify it.*
> — Nic, polyamorous

Such stresses can accumulate to fracture unconventional relationships, or prevent them from being considered or explored.

No relationship exists in a vacuum. On the Escalator or not, all relationships are affected by the world around them. Consequently, if an unconventional relationship appears to be unhealthy or struggling, it may be facile to blame this on its structure, without deeper inquiry.

Conversely, if a traditional couple is struggling, don't dismiss the Escalator as a possible cause of their woes. Dig deeper, and look at the whole picture — including how relationships are supported by social privilege, or not.

> *Poly relationships are no more or less likely to end than monogamous ones. However, it might look slightly more impressive when a poly relationship does last.*
> — Suzanne, polyamorous

Why Step Off the Escalator?

Since the Relationship Escalator works so well for so many people, and since it offers more benefits and prestige, then why would anyone want to step off of it?

In the real world, the Escalator does not work for many people — either at all, or for some relationships, or during some portion of their lives. In my survey, people noted many reasons for stepping off the Escalator.

Too much pressure, and too many expectations, were commonly cited as reasons for avoiding the Escalator.

> *A lot of pressure comes from the all-or-nothing convention of monogamy. Positive experiences like the flutter of new chemistry, as well as negative ones like the ennui that comes and goes in any long-term relationship, all must be framed as potentially major life decisions. "Did I pour all my energy into this relationship for years just to throw it away? Is it throwing it away to leave it behind? Will I regret this in six months?"*
> *— Richard, married and monogamish*

> *Quite simply, it's a big relief that we do not expect to meet all of each other's needs. The expectation of perfection, of being everything the other needs, is a huge weight that has been lifted.*
> *— Lidaria, polyamorous*

Notably, monogamy doesn't suit everyone. Some people feel actively oppressed by monogamy; others simply never liked it.

> *Actually, monogamy doesn't feel natural to me. Having a few different partners who I'm committed to, connected to, and loving — relationships that go beyond friends-with-benefits — that feels good.*
> *— Loretta, polyamorous*

> *Monogamy made me feel trapped, and I would often cheat.*
> *— Ms. LT, polyamorous*

Similarly, some people feel stifled by the merging of life and identity that occurs in traditional couplehood. They need more autonomy.

> *I've never wanted to have children, get married, or cohabit. That made it hard when I was dating under the monogamous model. Most people seem to want to eventually move in or get married.*
> *— Melanie, solo poly*

Some people found that the Escalator tended to exacerbate, rather than solve, common relationship problems.

> *In my monogamous relationships, jealousy was a problem. So was fighting to suppress my desire for others. I never cheated, but the desire would sometimes be there. Jealousy kills relationships. It destroys trust.*
> *— J.H., in an open relationship*

> *In monogamous relationships, communication seems to be a barrier.*
> *— JustinMH, swinger, engaged to be married*

Experience and observation are powerful teachers. Some people figure out, by riding the Escalator, that they never wish to do so again. Also, some people look at the Escalator relationships around them and see nothing they care to emulate.

> *Five years ago I wrote in my diary that I knew monogamy and life-entwined partnership were not for me. I was once engaged and in a very traditional monogamous relationship with a cisgender man. I would have nervous breakdowns and sob uncontrollably when I would think about my life and future. I knew it was deeply wrong for me.*
> *— Jenny, solo poly*

Story: Dying to Get Off the Escalator

In a few cases, dire experiences are the catalyst for abandoning the Relationship Escalator. John William is now happily polyamorous, with three partners at the time he took my survey. But he found this path the hard way, through a painful ending to his monogamous marriage.

Despite considerable trauma and life disruption, he and his former spouse have ended up in a good place. They retain a strong, active friendship — something also somewhat contrary to prevailing social norms.

> *She and I were married for seven years. We had a close and strong relationship. People thought we were a great couple.*
> *In many ways we did, and still do, have a great relationship. But while we were married, she discovered that she is asexual. We had sex every month or two, but that was too much for her and not enough for me. I read many books, we tried various approaches, but eventually we chalked it up to personality differences.*

Then I read up on relationships where one partner is monogamous but the other isn't, by mutual consent. I was trying to find a non-divorce route that would allow me to have sex without giving up the friendship of my asexual spouse.

It didn't work. That wasn't the relationship we'd agreed to and signed up for at the altar. We felt like failures. The only way to win a wedding is for someone to die. She almost did, because she does not like failure. That was one of the scariest parts of my life.

Today we're both alive, divorced, and it isn't as bad as either of us imagined. Fuck Disney.

Our separation was a horrible emotional mess. But now that we've gone through the crucible, we still respect each other and meet up about once a week. It's okay, I think it is better that way. I still feel very attached to her.

6

MONOGAMY AND
THE POWER OF SOCIAL NORMS

The most obvious and popular way that people can step off the Relationship Escalator is to let go of monogamy, with mutual consent. This is when partners agree to be open to sharing some amount of sex, romance or deep emotional intimacy with more than one person at a time — while also being transparent about this with everyone involved.

For various historical reasons, the conventional wisdom has been that monogamy is "natural," at least for women. However, extensive research in the sciences of biology, anthropology, sociology and paleontology generally does not support this conclusion. [14]

Since monogamy is such a powerful social hot button, it is rather surprising that consensual nonmonogamy has been steadily growing in popularity and visibility. In fact, the strong stigma against consensual nonmonogamy, plus social and legal structures favoring monogamy, are so prevalent that they can make monogamy seem compulsory.

> *Despite the widespread desire for more than one sexual partner, and despite relatively widespread nonmonogamy, most people do not engage in polyamorous relationships. But neither do most people affirmatively choose monogamy: Laws and norms exert strong pressure on people to promise monogamy, and most people simply succumb to this pressure.*
> — *Elizabeth F. Emens, Columbia Law School*[15]

Compulsory monogamy is the simple idea that in our culture, monogamy is somewhat less than optional.

> *...Modern systems of cultural conformity perform the miracle of allowing us to think that we are making a choice, when the choice we are making is really not much of a choice at all.*
>
> *Monogamy is one such choice.*
>
> *On the surface, it seems like something we choose. Indeed, people moving into a relationship often have the "we should stop seeing other people" conversation as evidence of this choice. But in actuality, when a person attempts to choose something other than monogamy, they run into numerous forms of resistance.*
>
> — *Pepper Mint, queer and poly essayist, activist and educator*[16]

Not only is there a strong social taboo against intimate partners making any agreement to relax or eliminate existing sexual or romantic exclusivity; it's also taboo to agree to never be exclusive in the first place. That's because nonmonogamy is broadly presumed to be unreasonably risky for the people involved — and perhaps even threatening to social order.

Want to test this? Try mentioning consensual nonmonogamy, or even just not assuming monogamy, in an everyday conversation — as if that were normal. *"You're engaged? Great! And how are your other relationships going?"* Or, *"I know that restaurant, one of my boyfriends used to work there."* Watch how people react; this almost never goes without notice or comment. Often, reactions are rather negative: confused, prurient, offended, skeptical, distancing or scandalized. But even a positive reaction (*"You have three partners? Right on!"*) indicates how much monogamy is presumed in mainstream society.

Casual, automatic suspicion and disapproval is a key enforcement mechanism of social norms. This can make it much harder for people to consider the option of consensual nonmonogamy, let alone try it.

> *It hurts when you hear strangers, friends and family casually stating the impossibility of your love and relationships. Personally, I have found it nearly impossible to build a strong foundation for nonmonogamous relationships when faced with questions and challenges from coworkers and close friends.*
>
> — *Grace, nonmonogamous*

Oddly, when it comes to consensual nonmonogamy, the consent part is generally considered more taboo than sharing sex or romance with more than one person. That's because cheating is an acknowledged aspect of social norms.

It's common for people to discuss cheating as something that unfortunately happens. In contrast, *knowing* that one's partner is having sex with, or falling in love with, someone else, and being okay with that? *Negotiating* nonmonogamy? *Agreeing* to it? Maybe even *meeting or befriending* their other partners? That's where the shaming and freakouts tend to start.

> One of my friends refers to my poly relationship as though it's seedy, despite the fact that he knows it involves total honesty among all people involved. And despite the fact that he himself has cheated on partners in monogamous relationships on numerous occasions.
> — Bob, polyamorous

> My husband and I are considered the perfect couple because we've managed to have a very long seemingly-monogamous relationship. Dunno what other people may think if they knew we're poly now! If they knew he has a permanent lover and I have a Master, and that we're both into BDSM!
> Society as a whole wouldn't accept that — even though pretty much everyone breaks their socially-accepted apparent monogamy. But doing so with everyone's consent? Satan at work!
> — Subkat, kinky, poly and married

What Is Monogamy?

To understand consensual nonmonogamy better, it helps to understand the practice of monogamy more clearly.

Under current social norms, *monogamy* typically means that for the duration of their relationship, two people agree to mutual exclusivity in sharing three types of intimacy:

- **Sexual or sensual.** At a minimum, monogamous couples typically refrain from sexual contact with others — specifically, physical contact involving the genitals, anus or breasts. For many monogamous couples, kissing and cuddling other people (at least, potentially attractive people), or other kinds of affectionate touch (such as holding hands), are also considered out of bounds. Likewise with phone or webcam sex, sexting or erotic emails. In its stricter forms, monogamy also can mean that partners are not allowed to flirt with or compliment others, look appreciatively at attractive people, mention that they find other people attractive, spend time alone with or perhaps even talk to potentially attractive people, visit strip clubs or enjoy pornography.

- **Romantic feelings and expression.** In monogamy, often partners are not permitted to exhibit toward others the behaviors commonly associated with seduction, crushes/infatuations, courtship and falling in love. Nor are they allowed to respond to romantic or flirtatious overtures from others. In some cases, monogamy also forbids having romantic emotions, desires, or fantasies about others, even if these are never acted upon.

- **Emotional bonding.** Some monogamous partners consider it out-of-bounds to share deep emotions, or emotionally laden experiences, with others who might be romantically or sexually attractive or available. This can include confiding with such people about emotionally sensitive topics such as one's relationship challenges or unmet needs. Turning to potentially attractive others for emotional comfort, reassurance, validation, advice or to share joys and triumphs can be considered a significant betrayal. Sometimes, this practice is called an *emotional affair*[17] and it may be considered more of a betrayal than sexual infidelity.

I have not officially had a nonmonogamous relationship, but I consider one of my dearest friends to be my partner in everything but name. Knowing and being emotionally close to him has caused a lot of strain on my marriage.
— *EssGee, married and curious about nonmonogamy*

Monogamy Is Open to Interpretation

Not all people who prefer to ride the Relationship Escalator, or who simply consider themselves monogamous, adhere to all three types of intimate exclusivity. And even if they do, their interpretation need not be draconian.

For instance, in many cultures and social circles, it is completely acceptable for people in monogamous relationships to spend time alone with potentially attractive or available people, to flirt with or fantasize about others, to cuddle and kiss others, to indulge crushes, or to share deep emotional intimacy with others.

Sometimes, monogamy comes down to how someone defines sex. Most famously, President Bill Clinton[18] implied that he had not violated his marriage vows. In a press conference, he said, *"I did not have sexual relations with that woman."* Whether his spouse agreed with this interpretation, in light of later revelations of extramarital fellatio, was never publicly clarified. However, it's possible that, like many couples, Bill and Hillary Clinton had their own private agreements and definitions regarding sex, and sex with others.

One surprise in my survey was that some people believe monogamy means emotional or romantic exclusivity, but not necessarily sexual exclusivity. For this reason, some swingers consider themselves monogamous.

> *My wife and I are monogamous in the idea that our love is only for each other. Sexually we are nonexclusive. We each have lovers on the side: one-on-one boyfriend-girlfriend relationships, plus swinging in group settings. We still consider ourselves monogamous in the idea that our primary relationship is on such an elevated status above others.*
> — *Mr. Wilson, sexually nonmonogamous*

> *Our hearts are monogamous but our sex life is not. We have an open relationship that is built on trust and love for each first. Playing with others is an added bonus for us.*
> — *Anita, swinger*

Who Gets to Say Whether You're Cheating?

The strong social taboos against consensual nonmonogamy make it difficult for some people to grasp the concept that intimate partners might be able to consent to nonmonogamy. This choice is sometimes interpreted as an intrinsic moral violation, or perhaps even a logical impossibility. Thus, consensual nonmonogamy is often labeled "cheating" — just with "permission."

This illustrates the power of social norms to deny personal agency. Many believe that it's not up to partner(s) to decide for themselves whether they might be cheating.

> *I live with my poly boyfriend and his monogamous wife. Everyone thinks my boyfriend is cheating or otherwise being awful to his wife.*
> — *Suzanne, polyamorous*

> *People tend to assume you're a terrible person (i.e., cheating) before they assume that your relationships are all consensual. I hate that.*
> — *Anastazie, polyamorous*

Story: Getting Curious About Nonmonogamy

Despite the pressure of social norms about monogamy — or perhaps because of them — it's common for people in monogamous relationships to be curious about nonmonogamy.

Belinda explained her own curiosity, and how it was stifled by the stigma against even considering nonmonogamy:

> *I have only ever been in monogamous Escalator relationships, and I am happy with my current one. But I would be open to occasionally sexually involving a third person from time to time. Right now I'm not sure what that might look like. I would also be fine with it never happening, but I am curious.*
>
> *I know from experience that feeling left out is one of the things that makes me feel most upset. So while I am interested in experiencing nontraditional sexual scenarios, I feel that I would enjoy them much much more if my partner and I took part in them together.*
>
> *I definitely would not want my partner to have other partners in my absence. However, I am interested in the idea of sharing a third partner.*
>
> *I'm not interested in having affairs or cheating on a partner, and I would be crushed if my partner cheated on me.*
>
> *The last time I was single, I was very interested in taking part in non-Escalator sexual experiences, particularly with another couple. However, I had absolutely no idea how or where to go about this safely. I felt that I did not have anyone to talk to about my feelings.*
>
> *In fact, I was terrified that my friends or family might find out about what I was considering — despite the fact that I pass no such judgment on others for their non-Escalator relationship choices.*

Part 1 Questions to Consider and Discuss

- Does this book's description of the traditional model for intimate relationships (the Relationship Escalator) seem fairly accurate to you? Why or why not? Did it surprise you in any way?

- Do you believe that you're riding the Relationship Escalator, or wish to? Why or why not?

- Have you ever stepped off the Relationship Escalator in your relationships, or considered doing so? How and why?

- What do you believe makes an intimate relationship successful or unsuccessful?

- Which topics in Chapters 1-6 would you like to read more about, and why? What questions did these first few chapters spark in you?

Share your answers or your own story online*

OffEscalator.com/resources/book1questions

* By answering any of these questions or sharing other personal information via the Off the Escalator website, you agree that the Off the Escalator project may quote your responses in our books, web content and in other material. You can answer anonymously if you like.

PART 2

BEYOND COUPLEHOOD:
NONEXCLUSIVE SEX AND ROMANCE

7

WHAT IS CONSENSUAL NONMONOGAMY?

Roughly 90% of people who took my survey mentioned that they are consensually nonmonogamous, either in practice or by inclination. That is, they are, or prefer to be, free to engage intimately with others, even if they also are in existing relationships.

What distinguishes *consensual nonmonogamy* from other kinds of nonmonogamy is, well, consent. That is, partners clearly discuss and agree to this feature of their relationship. Ironically, the "consent" part is often viewed as more taboo than the "nonmonogamy" part.

> *For some people, the thrill of nonmonogamy depends on it being*
> *forbidden and secret, i.e., deceptive. For these people, consent takes all*
> *the fun out of it. I don't get it, but there it is.*
> — *Martin, polyamorous*

Usually, consensual nonmonogamy also means that additional people who might be involved (other intimate partners, or their other partners) also know what's going on. This gives everyone the opportunity to consent to this arrangement, or to decline to participate.

Consensual nonmonogamy may not be socially accepted, but it has become fairly common, at least in the U.S. In a 2016 study[19] of data from 8718 single adults, 21% acknowledged that they have dated under consensually nonmonogamous terms. An article summarizing these findings noted:

> *Study authors clarified that nonmonogamy was defined to the*
> *participants as "any relationship in which all partners agree that each*

*may have romantic and/or sexual relationships with other partners."
Other demographic data wasn't made clear, but interestingly, the study
found that the prevalence of nonmonogamy stayed steady among most
identity groups.*

*Researchers wrote of the 21% figure, "This proportion remained
constant across age, education level, income, religion, region, political
affiliation, and race, but varied with gender and sexual orientation."
Specifically, men and LGB-identified folks practiced non-monogamy at
higher rates than women and the straight population, respectively. But
the race and class data flies in the face of media portrayals which often
paint polyamorous folks as rich, white, and highly educated.*

*In our Tinderella-saturated dating culture, it's easy to imagine that
plenty of folks who are casually dating — especially those on a dating
service like Match — would remain nonexclusive. But there's no reason
why nonexclusivity can't also accompany a more serious relationship if
all parties can set good boundaries and maintain open lines of
communication. Which is precisely why the study concluded that
polyamory is sufficiently prevalent that it needs to be regarded as a
legitimate relationship model in social science circles.*

— Mariella Mosthof, writing for Bustle[20]

There are many ways to do consensual nonmonogamy. Often these approaches get
lumped under a popular label: *open relationships*. However, in this book, I've chosen
not to rely on that simple, common term. That's because people tend to have very
strong — and quite contradictory — ideas about what "open relationship" means.

For instance, some people assume that an open relationship must necessarily be
an established couple whose "outside" intimate encounters are strictly transient,
recreational or otherwise far less emotionally involved or important.

Others are equally adamant that open relationships can accommodate concurrent
intimate connections of any depth, without predefined limits.

Interestingly, a few people even believe that an open relationship need not involve
all-around informed consent; all that matters is that the partners are not sexually
exclusive. Under this interpretation, cheating could be considered a type of open
relationship — just, not everyone in that relationship is aware that it's open.

*Her boyfriend doesn't know about me. This bothers me more at some
times than at others, but I usually disregard it as "not my problem."
I disown their relationship, preferring to see it as unrelated to our
relationship. Of course, they're quite related, aren't they.*

— Siobhan, nonmonogamous, in a clandestine relationship

It's true that "consensual nonmonogamy" is more of a mouthful than "open relationship."[21] However, I'm choosing to use the longer term in this book, since it refers only to relationships where everyone involved knows, and overtly consents to, the fact that that their relationship is not sexually or romantically exclusive.

Since cheating is extremely common in mainstream society, the "consent" part appears to be far less common than nonmonogamy. Thus, consent is what makes these relationships not simply unconventional, but especially intriguing.

Roots of Stigma Against Consensual Nonmonogamy

There is a strong social stigma against consensual nonmonogamy — but where does it come from? It appears to draw on two ancient, deep-rooted beliefs that are common in many cultures:

- **Social territoriality.** The belief that people can — and in certain contexts, particularly intimate relationships, should — be treated as a kind of territory. This is crucial subtext when intimate partners say or believe that they "belong" to each other. It's also why, in an intimate relationship, partners might feel somewhat entitled to surveil, judge or restrict each other's behavior, associations or choices. Such controlling behavior is especially likely for anything they believe might lead their partner to have sexual or romantic connections with others. This gets to be dicey territory; a socially acceptable level of monitoring and limits can easily shade into an abusive relationship. Furthermore, people sometimes believe that failing to exhibit territoriality toward their intimate partner might indicate weakness or a lack of care or commitment.

- **Sex negativity.** The belief that sex and sexuality are intrinsically evil and/or dangerous. Therefore they must be restricted to protect the safety of individuals, relationships, families, communities or even society at large. This tends to be most visible in attitudes toward female or queer sexuality, but it can apply to anyone.

I would like to see more people speak up when others try to enforce social norms and sex-negative attitudes.

When people claim that anything outside of traditional marriage-based monogamous relationships is immoral or wrong, we should ask why they think that is the case and keep asking why until they realize there really is no logical basis for those views.

> — *Beth, considering nonmonogamy*

While monogamy is a valid and potentially healthy relationship option, it does not challenge these ingrained beliefs. This might help explain the extraordinary social prominence and privilege that monogamy enjoys, as well as the strong stigma against consensual nonmonogamy.

To be clear, this does not mean that people who prefer monogamy are insecure control freaks, terrified by the power and diversity of human sexuality. Nor does it mean that consensually nonmonogamous relationships are necessarily free of territoriality or sex-negativity.

> *I have certain types of partners I "forbid" her from sleeping with, and she likewise.*
> — *Paul, in an open relationship*

Since monogamy is strongly socially privileged, it tends to have a *halo effect.* That is, individuals and relationships tend to be viewed in a generally more positive light because they happen to be monogamous. This was demonstrated in series of studies at the University of Michigan.

> *As a nonnormative sexuality, it is predictable that consensual nonmonogamy (CNM) is valued less than monogamy. Still, the depth and pervasiveness of bias and stigma toward nonmonogamy are surprising.*
>
> *...People perceived monogamous relationships to have wide-ranging benefits at the individual, family, and societal levels. ...Participants assumed that people in monogamous relationships were happier in their relationships, sexually more satisfied, and simply better citizens than those in CNM relationships.*
>
> *...Monogamy clearly seems to be privileged in contemporary U.S. culture, and this privilege extends across a broad range of domains. ...We hope that researchers will empirically scrutinize the construct of monogamy and its relative benefits to assess whether this rosy perception is warranted.*
> — *Terri D. Conley et al, University of Michigan*[22]

Myths About Consensual Nonmonogamy

Thanks to monogamy's halo effect and nonmonogamy's stigma, myths and misconceptions abound regarding consensual nonmonogamy. For instance:

- **It's just about having lots of sex,** especially group sex, casual sex, attending sex parties, having sex every day (perhaps several times daily), or having many sex partners to relieve boredom. This belief not only presumes that sex for its own sake is wrong or inferior; it's also simply not true. Many consensually nonmonogamous people have a small number of sexual partners, or sometimes none at all. They might dislike group or casual sex. They might even be asexual. That said, consensual nonmonogamy does offer more room than the Relationship Escalator for sexual exploration, expression and recreation. Sex is rarely the main reason why people choose consensual nonmonogamy, but it can be a considerable benefit.

Asexuality and polyamory actually go awesomely together.
— Ben, asexual and solo poly

I dislike that I'm often misunderstood as only wanting casual sex. In fact, I'm seeking deeper emotional connections in a poly/open context
— Angelita, nonmonogamous

- **There must be one "primary" or "official" relationship,** with all other intimate connections relegated to a lesser status. Strongly hierarchical arrangements are common, but they are far from mandatory. In some styles of consensual nonmonogamy (notably swinging, monogamish and don't ask don't tell), hierarchy can be a defining characteristic. However, more egalitarian approaches are possible. And in polyamory, they are increasingly popular.

- **It's only for kinksters and weird subcultures.** Many consensually nonmonogamous people are not at all kinky or geeky. That said, kink communities and certain interest-based subcultures (such as science fiction fans or Burning Man festival attendees) do tend to be more aware and accepting of alternatives to traditional monogamy. Consequently, gatherings of these communities tend to be safer spaces, where people feel less need to hide their consensual nonmonogamy. However, sometimes such stereotypes can become a problem even within these niche communities.

I wish people knew that there is a difference between polyamory and kink/BDSM. My boyfriend and I are not into any kind of bondage or fetishes, but sometimes it seems very expected of poly people.
— Candace, polyamorous

- **It's contagious.** Not exactly. People don't "catch" nonmonogamy. However, learning that someone you know is nonmonogamous, or simply learning that consensual nonmonogamy exists as a viable relationship option, sometimes confers motive and a sense of tacit social permission to learn more. Learning can lead to exploration. Thus, the knowledge that consensual nonmonogamy is a potentially valid choice is kind of a forbidden fruit; encountering it can feel profoundly unsettling. This may make it tempting to paint the transmission of this knowledge as a contagion.

"Once people become aware that there is a middle ground between monogamy and cheating, they have grasped the polyamorous possibility, and can never unthink it again. They might reject the idea or decide to explore it further. But the potential for them or their partner to initiate discussion of polyamory exists in a way it had not before."
— *Elisabeth A. Sheff, Ph.D.*[23]

- **They're just kidding themselves.** It's common for people to automatically dismiss the idea that consensually nonmonogamous relationships might be happy or healthy. When people do mention their healthy, happy nonmonogamous relationships, often this elicits responses of disbelief, or at least second-guessing. Similarly, consensual nonmonogamy is often dismissed as "just a phase," a temporary state to be followed by the inevitable need to "grow up and settle down." This is similar to the dismissive trope that bisexual people simply "haven't chosen a side yet."

People assume, annoyingly often, that my decision to be poly is because I fear commitment and am lying to myself. This makes them feel all superior and intelligent for figuring out my deep, dark psychological secret. Assumptions, assumptions, assumptions!
— *Kissobelle, solo poly*

If you're young, it's almost impossible to escape the "It must be a phase" conversation whenever anyone who's not poly (or poly-friendly) finds out that you're poly.
— *D, polyamorous*

- **It's beginning of the end.** When partners agree to open up a previously exclusive relationship, often this gets seen by others as a portent of doom, foretelling an inevitable, messy breakup. As if the only reason why partners would pursue nonmonogamy is that their relationship must be fatally flawed, or already dying. Or as if monogamy guarantees relationship success or survival.

People assume that opening up is the start of a failing relationship. Or that my boyfriend is not good enough for me, or there is some problem in our relationship.
     — Darla, in an open relationship

- **Watch out, they're coming after your partner!** Or you! Often people view sex, love, family, stability or privilege as scarce resources — and monogamy as the key to securing access to them. From this perspective, it's tempting to perceive consensually nonmonogamous people in one's social circles as an imminent threat. Gossip about consensually nonmonogamous people often implies that they are perpetually on the prowl: predatory, greedy or at least an unwelcome temptation.

Understand that we are not trying to steal your partner when you are in a monogamous relationship.
     — Jeff, polyamorous

People feel that I'm being unfair by having two partners, while they only have one. The moral condemnation is exhausting.
     — Catherine, polyamorous

- **They must hate monogamy.** Or, that nonmonogamous people must believe that monogamous people are stupid or prudish. Or that they believe nonmonogamy is superior, so everyone should want it. In my survey, it was vanishingly rare that a participant trashed monogamy wholesale. However, it is common for people to explore nonmonogamy after having unfulfilling or negative experiences with monogamy. When people share why monogamy hasn't worked for them, this does not constitute a wholesale attack on monogamy. Nor does it necessarily mean that they believe monogamy is a bad idea for everyone, or that they're attempting to persuade others to try nonmonogamy.

- **It's abuse.** This is perhaps the most pervasive troubling myth about consensual nonmonogamy. In particular, people often conflate polyamory with patriarchal religious polygamy, which has a notoriously checkered history. Sadly, abuse can happen in any kind of relationship, even on the Escalator. Active, all-around consent and empowerment are essential to preventing abuse. Truly consensual nonmonogamy is not a plot to coerce women, or anyone, into accepting an exploitative relationship structure that they do not desire and that does not benefit them. Furthermore, it's worth noting that domestic violence shelters are filled with people who mostly are fleeing monogamous relationships — yet that does not mean monogamy is intrinsically abusive.

I'm often asked how we got into this relationship. Many people perceive swinging as something my boyfriend pushed on me. That is not the case. It began when we first got together, since our relationship was long distance for the first six months. After we moved in together, we discussed the subject extensively.
— Whitney, swinger

Diverse Approaches to Consensual Nonmonogamy

In consensual nonmonogamy, there's no requirement that people must have multiple partners at all times. Also, partners need not practice the same style of nonmonogamy or have precisely the same preferences or boundaries.

Blended relationships are fairly common in consensual nonmonogamy. This is when partners have different approaches to consensual nonmonogamy, and they negotiate their common ground.

I consider my husband to be polyamorous, and myself to be nonmonogamous. He tends to form deeply emotional and psychological relationships with his secondary partners, who he calls his girlfriends. So far those outside relationships have lasted 1-3 years.

In contrast, I am not looking for a boyfriend. I prefer having friends with benefits — basically, shag buddies. At times I seek the emotional rush of new relationship energy, but I prefer not to fall in love with my outside partners. Nor do I engage in any kind of regular activity that might make them more than a friend with perks.
— Rosalyn, married and nonmonogamous

Consensually nonmonogamous relationships also may include individuals who consider themselves to be monogamous.

I can only be seriously romantically attracted to one person at a time, but I don't care how many people they're seeing. I would only ask them about their other partners if they wanted to stop using condoms (health reasons) or if I suspected they had a significant other who might not know about me. Cheating is a betrayal of trust, and I have no intention of being someone's down-low. Primary partners should be aware of my existence.

— Eva, unattached college student

People in blended relationships are free to make agreements that feel right to them. Such agreements can be consensual and mutually beneficial without being symmetrical. When everyone involved is being true to who they are, and is satisfied with their arrangement, blended relationships often work out fine. This even applies to agreements that might superficially appear unfair.

After nine years with my male partner, I came to question the necessity of monogamy. I informed him that he is free to have sex with anybody he wants to. And we agreed that I am free to do what I want — but with women only.

I have been satisfied with this arrangement. As a feminist, I sometimes feel conflicted about it. But I have no practical qualms about it since I have moved towards being more sexually interested in women anyway. The gender differentiation of my partner's boundary is arbitrary, but who said feelings have to be rational?

— River, pansexual and polyamorous

Why Informed Consent Matters

Informed consent can apply to any intimate relationship style, monogamy included. This takes work: specifically, introspection, inquiry and negotiation.

The catch is, social norms encourage assumptions. This can create dilemmas about consent. When people rely on assumptions, they often sidestep communication and negotiation. Making choices that impact others can seem less risky when you don't expect them to object or raise questions. However, not giving people a fair chance to voice their wishes impairs their ability to consent. The stakes can be extremely high.

I like the Escalator except for the monogamy part. My boyfriend doesn't like the Escalator but would be fine with monogamy. This makes it so difficult to plan my life — especially deciding whether or when to have children.

I wish I could just believe that if we are together for more than seven years, that he should want to have children with me.

— Lea, in an open relationship

In general, one's preference for monogamy, or children, or anything that might involve or affect people in a relationship is something that probably warrants discussion. Simply assuming that partners want the same things from a relationship rarely yields dependable results.

The book *More Than Two*[24] includes a "Relationship Bill of Rights"[25] that outlines several ways that informed consent can apply to intimate relationships or networks.

Explicit consent need not feel unromantic or daunting. Done right, it can be another form of intimacy, or at least friendliness. It need not be an inquisition. It can be a conversation; ideally, an ongoing conversation rooted in mutual appreciation and care, and revisited periodically.

> *In polyamory, the "define the relationship" talk happens more frequently. If you are not comfortable with that, it can be hard to create healthy relationships with your partners.*
> — *Kess, polyamorous*

Introspection is a vital part of informed consent. This means getting to know oneself well enough to be able to clearly express wants, needs and uncertainties; as well as what one can offer or accept in intimate relationships.

> *Learning how to articulate my expectations has been key. "Happily ever after" means connecting with people who need what you have to offer, and who offer what you happen to need. This is something that nobody freaking talks about in Escalator-land.*
> — *Amazon Syren, married, poly, queer and kinky*

Is all-around 100% informed consent absolutely necessary? Is it possible to have a healthy intimate relationship without it? For instance, what if:

- You start dating someone new, and you don't mention that you're already involved with someone else.

- You're intimately involved with someone, perhaps dating for some time, but you haven't clearly discussed with them whether this relationship is exclusive or not.

- You don't inform people you date that, after a certain point, you will only continue an intimate relationship if it becomes exclusive.

- You tell your partner, "I don't care if you sleep around sometimes; I just don't want to hear about it from you or anyone else."

- You are intimately involved with more than one person, but you don't disclose this to one of your partners because you don't think they could handle it, or because you believe it's none of their business.

...Sure, it's possible. People do such things all the time, especially very early in relationships. It doesn't invariably trigger a relationship apocalypse.

That said, it can be a quite risky to neglect to inform intimate partners about how one really plans to operate in a relationship, as well as what one expects from a partner. The potential for perceived disrespect, entrapment and betrayal are huge.

Therefore, even though it may initially feel weird or scary to break the subtle taboo against being completely forthcoming and honest about nonmonogamy, many people believe this skill is worth cultivating.

> *I want people to understand that the effect of discrimination against some forms of unconventional relationships is to make consent a taboo.*
>
> *Many people have urges to have sex with multiple people, or to engage in rough sex, or to dominate or submit to others. When we make such things taboo, we take away the only way that people can act on these urges healthily: with consent.*
>
> *The results are the nonconsensual forms of these things: infidelity, sexual abuse and assault, and emotional abuse.*
>
> *— Sonic, kinky and polyamorous*

Story: Bridging the Gap, Monogamy and Nonmonogamy

A key benefit of prioritizing consent is that it creates more opportunity to accommodate differences in relationships. Because unless someone is dating their clone, intimate partners always have substantial differences.

Mashed Potatoes, a monogamous person in a poly relationship, explains how this kind of accommodation can work, and the benefits it can offer.

> *My partner is polyamorous. I am 18 and new to sex and relationships in general. However, I'm pretty confident that my commitment is monogamous — as in, I haven't felt any desire to explore other romantic interests, for as long as I have been involved in this one.*
>
> *I am comfortable with my significant other's multiple interests. In fact, I am very fond of their two other partners whom I have met.*

My relationship also differs from social norms in that my significant other is 10 years older than me. This relationship is a challenge for me to navigate since general societal wisdom doesn't give me a lot of great advice about this kind of experience.

Fortunately my partner has made me more comfortable by always being available to answer my questions (and specifically making a space for my questions), and by reminding me to take things at the pace that works for me.

Comparing Consensual Nonmonogamy to the Escalator

Consensual nonmonogamy departs from the first and most weighty Relationship Escalator hallmark: *monogamy.*

As illustrated in the example Escalator relationship story of Chris & Dana (see the preface), some common indicators of monogamous relationships include:

...Of course, their commitment involves monogamy. They stop dating others, having sex and flirting with others, and frequenting bars alone. Their online dating profiles vanish.

...Chris & Dana never consider having other sexual partners, even though [after many years together] their sexual connection sometimes feels a bit stale. Fidelity is important to them, so they remain faithful to each other, even after many years together.

Furthermore, consensual nonmonogamy diverges from the Relationship Escalator specifically because it involves the informed consent of all participants. This differs from cheating: a highly conventional and socially acknowledged form of nonmonogamy which lacks the informed consent of at least one partner.

The Chris & Dana story also hints at the kind of stigma that consensually nonmonogamous people are commonly subjected to. For instance, if Chris & Dana were not a monogamous couple, and if they did not conceal this aspect of their relationship, then these parts of their story would probably not be true:

...They display each other's photo at work, and they feel free to note the existence of their relationship in casual conversations, even with coworkers or strangers. This is not considered oversharing, even though everyone assumes that Chris & Dana have sex with each other.

...When they have children, there is no question about their right or ability to parent. They feel immense pride in having created a real family. Their relatives show respect for, and take pride and interest in, Chris & Dana's marriage and family.

...Other people easily understand how to interact with Chris & Dana; they know what to expect from the couple, and what's appropriate.

...At Dana's funeral, everyone ...praises their perfect marriage.

8

PLAYING AROUND:
RECREATIONAL AND CASUAL NONMONOGAMY

Consensually nonmonogamous relationships often require work — but they can involve plenty of play, too.

Some styles of consensual nonmonogamy are mainly focused on fun, excitement, variety, comfort or adventure. People who approach consensual nonmonogamy this way are not necessarily open to fostering deep emotional involvement or a sense of commitment with more than one partner at a time.

Lighter or less-involved intimate connections can be a valuable part of life. Social norms tend to trivialize or denigrate such connections — as if they're worthless, perhaps even harmful. However, when everyone involved is treated with consideration, forthright about where they're at and what they want, and checking in to make sure they're all on the same page, there's less chance that people might feel used or misled by a strictly recreational or compartmentalized approach to consensual nonmonogamy.

Typically, more recreational styles of consensual nonmonogamy are favored by couples in established, life-entwined relationships who are otherwise mostly riding the Relationship Escalator. Sex educator Tristan Taormino has broadly categorized this as *partnered nonmonogamy.*

> *Partnered nonmonogamy is a style for committed couples who want a relationship that is erotically nonmonogamous, where each partner can be involved with other people for sex, kink, or other erotic activities.*

> *...Experiences with other people may occur once or be recurring, but they are generally considered temporary, casual, commitment-free and nonromantic. The primary focus of your time and energy is your committed relationship, not entering a serious relationship with anyone else.*
>
> *If you have fantasized together about bringing a third person into your bed for a night, if you want to have a casual fling (or two) while you're out of town, then this style might be your ideal form of nonmonogamy.*
> — *Tristan Taormino, author of "Opening Up"*[26]

People who are not in life-entwined relationships also may participate in recreational types of consensual nonmonogamy. If they consider themselves single, then this kind of playing around has become socially acceptable and thus is no longer very unconventional — unless it involves sex parties/clubs or group sex, which are still more taboo than one- on-one casual sex hookups.

People who practice consensual nonmonogamy that does allow for more than one emotionally bonded relationship at a time, such as polyamory, also may indulge in more recreational erotic encounters; these styles are not mutually exclusive.

> *My intimate partner of seven years and I are both poly. We have never expected either of us to be anything but what we are — so there is a lot of fluidity to our relationship.*
>
> *For instance, we sometimes operate as a couple for swinging activities. We maintain a profile as a couple on several swinger sites.*
> — *Lanikino, polyamorous*

There are many reasons why people might prefer a more recreational approach to consensual nonmonogamy. Most commonly, they find it simpler and easier to manage. It allows for sexual variety and new experiences while minimizing potential disruption to their life, emotional balance, or existing relationships.

Concern about the strong social stigma against consensual nonmonogamy also can drive this preference. It's usually easier to keep mostly-recreational nonmonogamy fairly compartmentalized and private.

This chapter offers a brief overview of some common types of consensual nonmonogamy that aren't all about sharing "Big-L Love" with multiple partners — although it often strengthens the bond within an existing relationship.

My wife and I are swingers. We like to watch each other with other people. We also play very safely. We are closer now than ever before. We always had fantasies but never acted upon them. Then one day we did — and our bond has never been stronger.
— *Cixelsydster, married swinger*

Swinging: The Lifestyle

Some people are pretty organized about recreational sex.

Swinging is usually associated with the well-established "Lifestyle" subculture. People within this community tend to connect via through local clubs, networking sites (Kasidie[27] and others), as well as numerous resorts, conventions and parties.

In Lifestyle culture, as well as other kinds of recreational nonmonogamy, sex is commonly called play — because it's supposed to be fun.

Lifestyle culture has grown established, and quite large, over many decades. According to *The Lifestyle: A Look at the Erotic Rites of Swingers*[28] by Terry Gould, swinging began among U.S. Air Force pilots and their wives during World War II.

Statistics about how many people swing are hard to come by. This is not surprising since most swingers prefer to keep this part of their life very private. Still, it's usually not hard to find swingers and Lifestyle gatherings in most parts of North America. This is true even in more socially conservative regions, such as the Midwestern and southern U.S.

Despite the general social stigma against consensual nonmonogamy, the demographics of swingers heavily represent social privilege. In researching swingers, psychologist Edward Fernandes found:

> *The demographic profile of swingers suggests that they are white for the most part, between 36 and 55 years of age, mostly college educated, married for at least 11 to 20 years, and with an average household income between $40,000 and $200,000. Many professions and occupations were represented, from blue-collar and white-collar workers to individuals with advanced professional degrees.*
>
> *...The men in my two studies were, for the most part, heterosexual, although about 20% did consider themselves bisexual. The majority of the women considered themselves bi-curious, with a small minority fancying themselves as pure bisexual. Female bisexuality is accepted within the swinging lifestyle; however, male bisexuality is discouraged and not welcomed.*

> *...Most of the swingers in my sample were married or cohabiting, the great majority had been in a relationship for well over 10 years, and for most this was their first marriage.*
>
> *...Swingers are not a politically homogenous group. Rather, swingers hold disparate political ideology, from social conservatism to liberalism and socialism with a certain percentage holding no political views at all. However, it is interesting to note that of all political categories, Republicans held the majority.*
> — *Edward Fernandes, Ph.D.[29]*

Most swinger communities strive to be welcoming and non-intimidating. They usually host periodic informal, nonsexual meet-and-greet gatherings. Here, people new to or curious about swinging can talk to more experienced swingers and ask questions about the Lifestyle — without anyone getting naked.

Only about 7% of people who took my survey called themselves swingers. However, roughly one-third of all survey participants indicated a desire to participate in swinging — either with a partner or as an individual.

Lifestyle culture is a structured and generally hierarchical approach to consensual nonmonogamy. It's mostly intended to enable established, life-entwined heterosexual couples (usually married) to enjoy sexual variety, without additional romantic bonding or ongoing relational entanglements.

Swinging isn't only about physical contact. For instance, at swinger parties and clubs, exhibitionism and voyeurism (within etiquette guidelines) often are accepted aspects of sexual expression.

Most couples who swing make clear agreements with each other about which kinds of sex they are allowed to have with other people, under which conditions — although often these rules relax as a couple gains experience and trust in this setting.

Swingers tend to be very frank about their sexual practices and boundaries.

> *As a swinger couple, we engage in group sex as a couple with other men, women and couples. We also have a standing "hall pass" to engage in same-sex encounters without our primary partner present.*
> — *Oltima, swinger*
>
> *My partner and I have foursomes with other couples, without any man-on-man action.*
> — *Howard, swinger*

Unpartnered individuals can participate in swinging, but this varies by gender. Single women are generally welcomed, especially if they are bisexual. In contrast, unaccompanied men usually must work hard to gain trust in this setting. Typically, single men pay much higher fees and often must be personally vouched for by established community members in order to access swinger gatherings or networks.

For instance, as of this writing, Scarlet Ranch[30] (an adults-only Lifestyle club near Denver, Colorado) listed the following pricing for annual "Gold Pass" membership:

- Single females: $250
- Couples: $1750
- Single males: $3500

Some swinger settings are reserved solely for couples. For instance, as of this writing, Desire Riviera Maya,[31] a Lifestyle resort in Cancun, Mexico accepted bookings only for parties of two.

The role of women in swinging is widely misunderstood. This may be because Lifestyle culture commonly projects the kind of female sexual expression common in mainstream pornography geared toward straight men, which tends to objectify women. However, women are largely in charge of how swinging works.

Specifically, the consent, pleasure, safety and comfort of women are typically top priorities at swinger gatherings and encounters. If the women don't feel safe and aren't having fun, then the entire dynamic collapses pretty quickly.

> *It has often been said in the swinging community that women control what happens in swinging. Research validates that suggestion. After the initial nervousness wears off, it is the women who have the final say on who "parties with whom" and how (couples only, girl on girl, threesomes, group sex, including the enforcement of safe sex rules).*
>
> *If a woman is not interested in an individual or couple, then a polite excuse is given. Usually, the man abides by the decisions of his female companion.*
>
> *...Women in swinging score very high on the self-determination scale, meaning, they are in absolute control of their decisions and are unlikely to be easily swayed by others.*
> — *Edward Fernandes, Ph.D.[32]*

Not all swinging happens at parties, clubs, resorts and conventions. Swinging also can happen informally, between friends. While swingers often first connect via organized Lifestyle gatherings or networks, after personal connections are established, it's common for swingers to carry on privately.

> *Swingers are particularly picky about who they choose to play with. This is because you have to satisfy the wants of four people instead of two, and conform to both relationships.*
>
> *Usually, swingers have a few close couples that they play with; they don't often venture outside that circles. It is hard to find a compatible couple. Once you find them, it's better to stick with them instead of starting the hunt all over again.*
>
> *— JustinMH, swinger and engaged*

Also, informal swinging is becoming more common. That's when groups of friends simply decide that it's okay to mess around with each other for fun. They may or may not label this activity "swinging," and they don't necessarily rely on organized Lifestyle communities, networks or gatherings to find each other.

Swinging often isn't only about having fun; it also can be a path toward personal growth and fulfillment. Several swingers emphasized their belief that swinging is essential to the health of their established relationship, and to their sense of personal integrity. Also, it's becoming more common for swingers to develop close ties of friendship or love with their play partners — blending aspects of polyamory and swinging.

> *I've been with my primary partner for almost 23 years. He is straight and I am bisexual. We are not married, no children, but we own a house together and have run two businesses together over the years. To most of the outside world, we appear to have a heteronormative relationship.*
>
> *We've been active swingers for nearly our entire time together. We often host and attend play parties, and we occasionally each have play dates with women from our swinger circle.*
>
> *Within the swinging world, we mostly have some connection with our partners (as couples who play, but we also socialize in vanilla ways). But occasionally we'll meet a couple/person in a club, play, and never see them again.*
>
> *I've recently organized a group of women who gather regularly for play dates. We have sex, but we also do a lot of talking and learning from each other.*
>
> *We've also dabbled in polyamory and are currently expanding our boundaries with several different types of secondary relationships. I currently have two secondary boyfriends.*
>
> *I can't imagine having a traditional relationship. The lack of integrity with my nature would cause so much stress, it'd make my head explode.*
>
> *— Sonia, swinger*

Being Monogamish

Monogamish is a term coined by sex advice columnist and podcaster Dan Savage[33] that has caught on widely in mainstream culture. It refers to a relationship where an established couple is mostly riding the Relationship Escalator. However, they explicitly agree or acknowledge that occasional minor sexual excursions with other people are allowed.

It's very common for monogamish couples to engage together in group sex — occasionally including a "special guest star" for threesomes or moresomes.

> *My partner and I have had outside liaisons, including threesomes and foursomes. We would consider them again if the right person and circumstances came along.*
> — *Hawkeye, monogamish*

However, some monogamish couples prefer dating or sex with others separately.

> *We are a committed gay male couple, with an arrangement. If we aren't doing anything together, it is okay to have sex with other people.*
> — *Markus, monogamish*

In practical terms, being monogamish usually amounts to an occasional feature to spice up an otherwise fairly traditional relationship — strictly for entertainment, curiosity, experimentation or sexual revitalization. For this reason, many monogamish couples prefer to keep their sexual excursions private. They may not even consider their relationship unconventional.

> *We are socially monogamous, but not sexually monogamous. We each have sex with other people — sometimes the same people, sometimes different people.*
> *Anyone who didn't know about our temporary sexual relationships with both opposite and same-sex partners would think we were monogamous. The relationship I've got is my ideal.*
> — *Tracee, in a sexually open marriage*

Don't Ask Don't Tell

Some people are fine, or mostly fine, with their partner(s) engaging intimately with other people — they just don't want to hear about it, or negotiate it in detail. Typically, they don't want anyone else to know about this arrangement, either.

Don't ask don't tell relationships are nominally open, at least under some circumstances. However, the partners agree to specifically avoid asking for, or volunteering, most/any information about their other intimate encounters. It's effectively consensual nonmonogamy with agreed-upon limits on disclosure.

Some people feel quite peaceful and satisfied in don't ask don't tell relationships.

> *We are free to have sex with other people outside of our relationship, and we don't expect to share that information with each other. When we met, we both shared the need for privacy in our lives. To that end, we don't share every moment of our days with each other — and specifically, we keep any other sexual and romantic friendships private. I know a lot of poly people look down on this type of relationship, but so far it's really working for us.*
>
> *Because this is don't ask don't tell, I don't have to negotiate seeing others or process feelings and agreements with her. We get to just really enjoy each other while knowing that our private lives are ours alone.*
>
> *I've been in many relationships over the past 30 years. This one feels the most right to me in terms of respect, ease and fun. Don't ask don't tell gives both of us the sense that we don't "belong" to one another. It makes me feel more in control of my own body than a monogamous relationship does — but without the drama that can come with new lovers and romantic interests.*
>
> *I'm not interested in polyamory anymore, it just didn't work for me, even though I really wanted to be that person. I'm happy I've found something that suits me, and her too. I feel lucky.*
> *— Sidney, in a don't ask don't tell relationship*

Don't ask don't tell agreements seem more common among people in established relationships who are brand new to consensual nonmonogamy. Since this approach tends to require less negotiation, and mostly shields partners from information they might find discomforting, it can initially feel less emotionally challenging. However, when partners decide to continue along the path of consensual nonmonogamy, they often progress into styles that support greater disclosure.

But sometimes, don't ask don't tell is a permanent relationship feature.

> *Our seven-year relationship has been nonmonogamous since day one. We both have other relationships. The deal between us is that we don't talk much about them with each other. So if one of us is out and sees the other with someone else, we say hi and that's about it.*
> *— Moonwoman, nonmonogamous*

> *We don't require monogamy from each other. We don't ask. We don't
> tell. And we talk as if there are others, even if we don't know.*
>   — *Kittypush, solo nonmonogamous*

Usually, people in don't ask don't tell relationships use this freedom mostly to enjoy casual sex or short-term flings, especially if their relationship began on the Escalator. But sometimes, more committed or long-term relationships are conducted on this basis.

> *I have a nonprimary, long distance relationship in addition to my
> primary one. My nonprimary relationship is significant to me, but we
> keep it in the closet. Our respective primary partners know our
> relationship exists, but they have chosen not to know any more details.*
>   — *Jessica, nonmonogamous*

One of the most popular reasons participants cited for having a don't ask don't tell relationship is that they see it as a way to experience variety while managing jealousy or other uncomfortable emotions.

> *My partner and I have a one-way don't ask don't tell policy. He is not
> at the point where he doesn't get jealous and insecure if I'm intimate
> with someone else. However, he believes strongly that his feelings should
> not interfere with my desires, and that he has no right to limit me in such
> a way. So he thinks: what he doesn't know, won't hurt him.*
>   — *Sloane, nonmonogamous*

Under don't ask don't tell agreements, it's usually impossible to confirm whether a potential partner truly is in a don't ask don't tell relationship; verifying this directly with their existing partner would constitute a kind of asking/telling. This can raise questions: might someone who claims to be in a don't ask don't tell relationship really be cheating? Many people prefer to avoid that situation, and thus are reluctant or unwilling to get intimately involved under these terms.

Some people in don't ask don't tell relationships reported feeling conflicted about keeping secrets from a partner — even though this happens by mutual agreement.

> *Before having committed partners, I was in open relationships. My
> primary partner expressed the desire for us to be in a don't ask don't tell
> open relationship, which I respected for over 30 years until she decided
> she wanted to know. During that time I had relationships of various
> degrees with nine women.*

> *The most difficult part of being in that sort of don't ask don't tell relationship was keeping my other relationships secret from my primary partner. I never kept anything secret from my secondary partners, nor have I had to keep any secrets from anyone for the last four years and more.*
>
> — *Charlie, polyamorous*

Story: Compartmentalizing: Not Always as Simple as it Sounds

Many nonmonogamous people prefer compartmentalized intimate relationships or encounters, where little or no information about relationships is shared between relationships. Often, this is done with the intent of keeping things simple. It can seem easier, at least initially, to mostly ignore the existence of other relationships, or to assume that overlapping relationships don't really affect each other. Also, compartmentalization can be a strategy to minimize jealousy or insecurity.

Compartmentalization tends to be most feasible in consensual nonmonogamy that is more casual or recreational. However, compartmentalization sometimes does work well even where a person has more than one concurrent relationship that feels fairly deep and committed.

However, compartmentalization is not without its complications. In particular, don't ask don't tell agreements usually require partners to effectively keep secrets from each other, and sometimes even to lie. While some relationships accommodate don't ask don't tell smoothly, it's common for this practice, over time, to end up fueling the very suspicion, jealousy and insecurity that it was intended to mitigate.

Furthermore, when the additional relationships conducted under don't ask don't tell terms grow to be more than casual, everyone in the network might start to feel the stress of subterfuge. In my survey, several people in don't ask don't tell relationships mentioned this problem. For instance, Na'ama recounted mixed feelings about keeping their relationship a secret.

> *I am in a secondary long distance relationship with a woman who is also in a long-term cohabiting relationship with a man. They abide by a don't ask don't tell policy.*
>
> *My partner's live-in partner is aware that she pursues additional emotional, romantic, and sexual relationships. However, he does not want to know anything about her lovers, or what we do together, and does not want to be involved in any way.*
>
> *He and I interact and speak on occasion. I believe he is unaware that I am involved with our shared partner. But I could be mistaken.*

On occasion, when she and I meet up, her live-in partner is traveling with her. I like him as a person. But it is incredibly uncomfortable to feel like I'm sneaking behind his back to kiss her. Although I know they have a don't ask don't tell agreement, it does almost feel shameful and dishonest to engage in sexual or simply romantic acts (like holding hands) when he is around — even when he's out of sight.

I do experience jealousy when I am around both him and her together. Since they are an established couple, they sit together, stand together, and do everything as a couple — while I become relegated to "friend in the group" status. Does this bother me? Of course. But I understand why it is the way that it is, and accept it.

The hardest part about my relationship is keeping secrets from him. I have always firmly stood by open disclosure in open relationships. However, it is his preference to not know. While I respect this, it has been difficult for me to adjust and completely be at peace with his decision. It goes against every bone in my body to keep my fully consented relationship a secret!

≈

9

POLYAMORY: HEARTS ON THE LINE

In polyamory, people are open to engaging in more than one significant intimate relationship at a time, with the full knowledge and consent of everyone involved. This form of consensual nonmonogamy has grown fairly popular in the past two decades.

What distinguishes polyamory from more recreational consensual nonmonogamy is its potential for depth and commitment in more than one concurrent intimate relationship. That is, in polyamorous relationships, people typically are open to the possibility that more than one of their relationships at a time might develop a strong sense of emotional investment or commitment, and perhaps also some level of logistical entwinement.

In my survey, a majority (55%) of participants called themselves polyamorous or indicated that they effectively practice polyamory.

The word *polyamory* was coined in the early 1990s[34] but has been widely adopted. It mixes Greek and Latin roots to mean "multiple loves." And yes, this neologism can sound a little awkward. (To be honest, many poly people aren't really crazy about this term, but usually, they roll with it.)

Still, even in polyamory, not every intimate connection must blossom into a major romance or life commitment. Many poly people also enjoy lighter, short-term or recreational connections, as well as deeper ones. Similarly, many intimate relationships evolve toward polyamory after starting from swinging or other more recreational types of consensual nonmonogamy. These lines all get quite blurry.

Polyamory has gained substantial visibility in recent years. Mainstream media coverage[35] has increased general awareness. Also, online discussion forums and resources, such as the *Polyamory Weekly*[36] podcast. And books such as *More Than Two*[37] and *The Polyamorists Next Door*[38] have played a key role in increasing awareness and exploration of polyamory. These days, in nearly every major U.S. metro area, and even in many smaller cities, it's often easy to find a local polyamory group via Meetup.com.

Networks and Metamours

In practice, polyamory is about forming networks of overlapping intimate relationships. Yes, relationship networks exist in all kinds of nonmonogamy, consensual and otherwise. However, since polyamory tends to emphasize informed consent across the board, poly people usually are quite conscious of not just their own relationships, but of the other relationships in their network. Often, they also have a sense of the shape and functioning of their network as a whole — sometimes called a *polycule.*

The simplest form of a polyamorous network is a "V." In this arrangement, one person (the *hinge*), has two intimate partners, and those partners are not intimately involved with each other.

> *I'm a woman who's in love with, and committed to my long-term romantic relationship with, another woman. She is married to a man.*
> *— Grebe, polyamorous*

Within a polyamorous network, it's possible for many kinds of relationships to overlap — not all of them necessarily sexually or romantically intimate.

> *I am in a polyamorous relationship with two guys who are best friends. I also have a casual male partner. It is all out in the open; everyone knows about everyone else.*
> *One of my partners lives with his other girlfriend. She is also in a relationship with his best friend, as well as one of his ex-girlfriends.*
> *My other partner lives with one of his other girlfriends. In addition, he's also dating my other partner's live-in girlfriend, his ex-girlfriend and another girl — plus a casual girlfriend.*
> *— Scarlet, poly*

Within a poly network, people who both have an intimate relationship with the same person (such as the two ends of a V) also are recognized as having their own connection. They are *metamours* to each other. This is rather like being lovers-in-law.

Metamours are definitely not a new phenomenon. They have always existed, despite the powerful social norm of monogamy, via cheating and other less-than-socially-validated intimate connections. Sadly, such delegitimizing context tends to set metamours up to treat each other very badly — from automatic hostility and attempts to sabotage each other, to violence.

In contrast, polyamory creates room for metamours to enjoy positive, mutually supportive relationships. Often poly metamours become friends, sometimes even close friends — however, friendship is definitely not required. Also, in polyamory, metamours occasionally develop their own sexual or romantic connection. Of course, not every metamour relationship in polyamory lives up to this rosy potential; some are quite toxic.

In most poly networks, metamours at least know about each other, and that they share a partner. Typically metamours meet each other or directly communicate at least a bit. However, in some cases, polyamorous relationships involve only indirect metamour communication; the shared partner acts as a go-between.

Being a metamour has some things in common with family ties. For instance, siblings are people who have an important relationship in common: they share the same parents. However, it's up to siblings to shape their own relationship. Siblings may or may not like each other or be close, but they're still family — and "family," after all, is just another kind of relationship network.

In some poly networks, metamours spend time around each other quite often — whether with their shared partners or on their own. Together, a polycule might go out to parties, stay home and watch TV, work on collaborative projects, discuss their relationships, etc. Some people call this *kitchen table polyamory*: the kind of network where people in overlapping relationships would feel very comfortable sitting around the kitchen table together, involved (if not necessarily entwined) in each other's lives.

> *I like spending time with my partner's other partner. We occasionally*
> *go out and do things as a group.*
> *— Jade, solo poly, with a partner in a long-term nesting relationship*

> *I love discussions like this:*
> *Man: "Hey, I was thinking of having Suzy Q come spend the night*
> *while you're visiting your mom."*
> *Me: "Sounds good. She makes a mean split pea soup, think you could*
> *get her to leave some here for dinner the night I get back? Also, the kids*
> *have been asking about Norway and I think she visited there last year.*
> *Maybe she could answer some of their questions."*
> *— Gwendolyn, nonmonogamous*

Other poly networks are more compartmentalized: metamours are cordial when they happen to be together, but they don't make much effort to interact on their own. Such overlapping relationships are conducted mostly separately; matters concerning each relationship in the network are mostly kept private within that relationship.

They don't become a topic of discussion throughout the network. Sometimes this is a transitional phase, but it can become a permanent aspect of the network.

A few people even practice polyamory under don't ask don't tell terms: they are aware that their partner may have other significant relationships, but they prefer to hear nothing about their metamours. This can happen for a variety of reasons; it doesn't necessarily indicate stonewalling.

> *I am not married to my partner, but we live together part time. His wife is aware of our relationship and is trying to become more accepting of it — but our network is a work in progress.*
>
> *He works in my town, owns a home in another so he's at each home 50% of the time. I am not part of his life on the other side, she is not part of ours here.*
> — *Kayla, poly and kinky*

> *I have been the hinge in a long-term term "V" network. My partners were my husband and another male partner. Neither of them had any other partners. These relationships were don't ask don't tell and not publicly acknowledged since my husband was a military officer and wanted "discretion."*
> — *Lynn, polyamorous*

In my survey, many poly people shared how their metamour relationships feel special and important to them.

Metamours can be a valued source of camaraderie and support.

> *I value my partner's girlfriend as a person and am happy to have her in my life.*
> — *Gwen, polyamorous*

> *Our other partners have offered us support through hard times. I once was ill for several months, and our partners rallied round to support with things like bathing and night shifts.*
> — *Raheem, married and polyamorous*

Constructive interaction with metamours is a unique skill that mainstream culture does not tend to foster. In particular, learning to communicate with metamours can feel rather awkward. Some people avoid this challenge; others embrace it.

I am recently separated from my spouse, and seriously dating a man who is poly and married. I am only dating him. His wife doesn't want any real contact with me. I would have enjoyed being her friend.

This has a big effect on our relationship. I'd like to be able to go over to his home and hang out, watch a movie together. So far, he nearly always comes to my place.

— *Cible, single and poly*

Polyamory does sometimes lead to awkward conversations, such as having to involve my metamour in my partner's and my decision on whether to stop using condoms. But it also leads to us teaming up on some seriously awesome pranks.

— *Bette, poly and kinky*

Similar to family relationships, metamour relationships aren't always sunshine and roses. Where more people are involved, the potential for personality clashes and conflict increases.

I am not friends with my metamour (my primary partner's lover). I don't dislike her, but she is very shy and hard to talk to. This is hard for me; it makes situations where she and I are both present very awkward.

— *Gabrielle, poly*

Some metamour relationships get quite contentious or strained. Competitiveness, insecurity, jealousy and power plays are common problems.

Resentment can make metamour relationships difficult. It's hard having a partner who is less available, or to see them give more (in any respect) to another relationship.

— *Dan, in an open relationship*

Often couples don't realize how intimidating it can be — having to consider someone else (or multiple someone elses) when getting involved with someone new. If your partners don't get on, that makes it very tough to talk about them to each other — such as when trying to arrange things, or simply report on your day.

I've also had trouble with being treated poorly by my partners' partners. Specifically, my Master's girlfriend has sometimes been pretty disrespectful to me, if not downright bitchy. I let it roll off my back and pretended not to notice for Master's sake — but it did hurt.

— *Trix, poly, queer and kinky*

Polyamory that Kind of Looks Like the Escalator

Some styles of polyamory substantially resemble Escalator relationships, just with more people involved.

For instance, *family-style polyamory* is usually an expanded nuclear family: more than two adults in a poly network who live together and consider each other family. Or at least, they live near each other and spend a lot of time together as a group.

> *I'm married to my male partner, and I have another male partner who is equally important to my marriage. My husband has a girlfriend, who is also my boyfriend's girlfriend and the mother of his child. We currently live together as a family: four adults and one toddler.*
> — *Ravyn, polyamorous and married*

> *Our poly family includes eight adults and five kids (mostly now-adult) over five different households. The family, in its currently configuration, has been together a bit over a decade. Some individual pairs or groups within it have lasted up to 30 years. There are various configurations of intimacy within the family.*
> *I love the sense of family, of having a group of people that I can count on to be there for me in worldly, sexual and spiritual ways. When our children were young, I loved having co-parents. You could call time out, and have trusted partners step in.*
> — *Roszinha, polyamorous*

While cohabiting family-style polyamory attracts a fair amount of media attention (perhaps because it tends to be easier for mainstream audiences to comprehend), such arrangements are relatively less common in polyamory. This approach requires a high level of mutual compatibility, which can be exceedingly challenging to establish and maintain.

A more common (but still probably not the most common) approach is *couple+ polyamory*. Here, the Escalator hallmark of hierarchy is paramount. That is, the most established or life-entwined couple is considered the most important and influential part of the network.

In couple+ polyamory, usually each partner in an established couple has separate relationships with other people. Usually this assumes the form of *primary/secondary hierarchy*. That is, established (and usually life-entwined) *primary* partners may date others, with the potential to establish ongoing deeper relationships. However, the newer relationships are clearly *secondary,* and thus subordinate in many ways to the primary relationship.

Many people who approach polyamory by "opening up" a formerly monogamous Escalator relationship feel threatened by the idea of pursuing new relationships separately. They'd rather do polyamory together, so they prefer to date "as a couple." Their goal is to find someone who will be sexually and romantically involved with them both, and perhaps with no one else. Often this is motivated by a wish to avoid jealousy, feeling left out, and male sexual competition.

Thus it's incredibly common to see personal ads from newly poly couples seeking a "third" partner — nearly always a single bisexual woman, a.k.a. *unicorn*. Here's a typical unicorn hunting[38] ad from Craigslist:

> *Couple Exploring Polyamory Seeking Third: We are a stable couple in a long-term relationship, consisting of a bisexual female and a straight male. Our life is very fulfilling and we are excited to share that with another. We are seeking a third: a bisexual single woman....*

Triads, Quads, Polyfidelity and the "Poly Escalator"

Triad and *quad* poly relationships arise when three or four people share deeper intimacy. There also can be larger intimate groupings, such as quints or sextets, but those are exceedingly rare.

A defining feature of poly relationships that are a group (not merely overlapping couples) is a strong, clear, mutual sense of commitment to that group. Also, usually, all partners hold equal power within the group, or they have a goal of creating a level playing field within their group.

Many people desire a poly relationship with three equal partners. But in practical terms, it's notoriously hard to deliberately manufacture a triad. It's rare that a new partner feels equally attracted to both members of an established couple. Also, there's usually some mismatch between what an established couple wants or can offer, and what a prospective new partner might want or need from a triad.

Thus, it's common for both established couples and prospective third partners to end up feeling frustrated and discouraged by efforts to forge a triad. But occasionally, deliberately designed triads do develop quite happily.

And of course, triad relationships can also arise organically.

> *My husband and I didn't set out to find a third or form a triad. It just sort of happened. We actually met our girlfriend at a house concert we were hosting. From the beginning, we all just got along famously. We all felt mutual chemistry and attraction.*
>
> — *Margaret, polyamorous*

Four-partner quad relationships most commonly arise when two existing couples become intimate with each other. This doesn't always mean that every member is sexually involved with everyone else in the quad, but it usually does mean that they all feel emotionally (if not necessarily romantically) invested in each other, and in the quad as a whole.

> *I'm married to my husband, and we have a boyfriend and girlfriend who are married to each other. This gives us sexual variety, emotional support from more than one person, and deep friendship with more than one person. Logistically it's awesome: four people to clean up after dinner, put kids to bed, etc.*
>
> — *Jennifer, in a polyfidelitous quad*

Polyamory isn't always open to new partners. In *polyfidelity*, relationships include more than two people, but these relationships are otherwise closed to intimate connections with others.

> *I am currently in a poly quad relationship with a married couple. I am dating the husband, and the wife also has a boyfriend. While I and the wife's boyfriend are welcome to date others, we currently choose to be exclusive to our partners. I am very happy with polyfidelity, with a little kink tossed in.*
>
> — *J., polyfidelitous*

Some polyfidelitous relationships allow the entry of new partners, as long as all existing partners agree. This usually presents a considerable barrier to entry.

And then, there is the poly version of the Relationship Escalator, at least in terms of trajectory. In this approach, a newer relationship is deemed serious or successful only if it progresses toward Escalator-ish merging of identity and life infrastructure — for instance, having a goal that "serious" partners should eventually move in to create or expand a group household.

> *I am part of a live-in poly family: three women and one man, plus another man who just moved out. We're all free to have other partners.*
>
> *All of us have a tendency to give more priority to partners who live here, than to those who do not. We all tend to assume that if an outside partner works out, the thing to do is invite them to move in.*
>
> — *JY, polyamorous*

Freeform Networks: The Most Popular Approach to Polyamory

While many people practice couple+ polyamory — and fewer are in triads, quads, or polyfidelitous networks — usually polyamory is not so rigidly structured.

Based on my survey, and on my nearly two decades of active experience in the poly community, it seems to me that freeform, continuously evolving networks of overlapping relationships represent the most common approach to polyamory.

That is, most of the time, poly networks form naturally as one-to-one relationships (dyads) arise. These networks tend to shift over time, as existing relationships wane or end, and as new ones form. In any freeform poly network, some relationships are likely to be deeper or more entwined than others.

> *I have one long-term lover who is in an open marriage. I have one girlfriend who is dating someone besides me. I have another girlfriend who is just starting her exploration in polyamory and open relationships. And I have a casual fuck buddy who I see only occasionally.*
> — *Rich, polyamorous*
>
> *I am married. I also have other kinky and romantic relationships, with two women and one man. My wife has one additional relationship with a man.*
> — *Antonin, married and polyamorous*

Some freeform poly networks can get pretty complex.

> *Oh God, we usually need to draw a graph on the whiteboard to explain this...*
> — *Theresa, polyamorous*

Many people who prefer polyamory also strongly value their personal autonomy, sometimes to the extent that they prefer to avoid Escalator-style merging of life or identity with partners, even in very deep or long-lasting relationships. Such solo polyamorists tend to find their poly niche within freeform networks.

109

I live by myself, and I am in several sexually intimate, romantic relationships. I am in the process of establishing a second home base geographically. However, I will not be living with anyone I'm sexually intimate with.

My multiple sexual/intimate relationships are not headed toward marriage or even cohabitation. Each relationship developed to be what it will be. My relationships started at various times and some are more than a decade in duration at this point and continuing.

— CG, solo poly

Story: A Poly Family of Choice

The fluidity of freeform poly networks may make these relationships sound fragile or ephemeral. However, in practice, this approach to polyamory often proves quite resilient. There's more room to adapt since there's less pressure to maintain a specific configuration. All of the relationships involved get to find their own level.

Sometimes freeform poly networks evolve to function as a family of choice — providing much of the emotional and logistical support that, under social norms, people usually expect from family ties of blood or marriage. This can be especially valuable because sometimes people are rejected by their family of origin due to the stigma against polyamory.

Andrea, who is kinky as well as poly, offers one example of how polyamory isn't just about sex and romance — that it can be about fostering deep emotional ties, shared support and a profound sense of commitment. Also, this story shows how the nature of shared intimacy between members of a poly network may shift, while a sense of family endures.

I have been partnered with my Boy for going on six years now, and we have been nonmonogamous from the get-go. Currently, we're in a triad with our partner, the Old Man, who does not live with us.

We're a D/S poly family — with myself at the head, the Boy and the Old Man in service to me, and the Sailor in service to the Boy. I also have a long-distance Houseboi who occasionally visits, and a Pet Librarian who comes by two or three times a month for cataloging and cuddles. We're all queer and express a range of genders.

We don't believe in marriage, but we sure do believe in family and commitment! We're committed to a vision of queer family. This concretely manifests in several ways:

- *Our triad supports a young queer person emotionally and financially.*

- *We support members of our family who are sex workers via safecaller help and similar work.*[40]

- *We support our housemate in her pursuit of a budding career via flexible rent and other things.*

- *We maintain an open-door policy if anyone connected to us needs space to crash or a hot meal.*

- *We maintain family traditions such as regular dinners, an annual brunch, a solstice celebration, and a range of other things.*

For the most part, we're all free to engage romantically or sexually with whomever we please. Our queer poly family's kink structure (domination/submission) imposes certain technical constraints. Our sole requirement is that we must talk about everything openly and regularly.

Also, each of us also has had significant relationships outside our triad. The Boy, for instance, has been involved with the Sailor for the better part of a year now. The Sailor takes turns living with us and living with the Old Man.

We're looking for a place big enough for the three of us, plus another housemate or queer family member.

10

NOT "JUST" FRIENDS:
THE FRIEND-LOVER SPECTRUM

People often discuss friendships and intimate relationships as if these are distinct categories which are, to some extent, mutually exclusive. But in the real world, they exist along a spectrum of personal connection.

In mainstream culture, friendships are generally considered close (or at least, somewhat close) personal relationships between people who do not share sex or romance. Nevertheless, it's quite common for friendships to include some sex, affection and/or romance, at least at some times, in a mutually rewarding way. This can even be true for people who consider themselves fundamentally monogamous.

Before delving into the gray area between friends and lovers, it's worth taking a closer look at friendship — specifically, how friendship is commonly perceived and discussed. Grasping friendship's potential for significance and intimacy can clarify many aspects of unconventional intimate relationships that might otherwise seem confusing or challenging.

The Language of Friendship

Words get very, very interesting when it comes to friendship.

It's common for people to discuss friendships as if these relationships are inherently less important than sexually or romantically intimate relationships. For instance, people usually don't count platonic friendships as "real" relationships — even though friendships might be some of their most enduring, meaningful and intimate personal bonds.

Consider this: once past teenage or college years, many people believe it sounds odd to call someone their *best friend.* Often, adults lack the vocabulary to clearly acknowledge the depth and intensity of very close friendships.

> *I am very intimate with my two "best friends" — not my favorite term but most apt out of the usual terminology. However, we don't have sex and aren't in a traditional relationship.*
> *— Grace, nonmonogamous*

Furthermore, social norms implicitly assume that if there's any chance that two people might share sex or romance, then they must default to having a sexual or romantic relationship. This is why, when mentioning a potentially attractive friend who happens to not be a sexual/romantic partner, people commonly volunteer this clarification: *"Oh, we're just friends."*

...That diminutive "just" is telling. It indicates how society prioritizes sexual romantic relationships or above others. It also implies that whether people are sexually or romantically involved is always relevant — even to people who are not involved.

> *People may assume I'm "just friends" with someone when really our relationship transcends "just friends." I recognize this is often because they've been conditioned to think a certain way about relationships, but it's still frustrating. There's nothing "just" about friendship in the first place. With that someone, I feel home.*
> *— Em, aromantic asexual in a queerplatonic, open relationship*

In my survey, many people described friendships as some of their most significant and meaningful relationships. They often noted a strong dislike for how friendships tend to be undervalued, and also for how unusually close friendships are often treated with suspicion.

> *I have a few friends who I wish could be more like life partners. I have romantic ideas about living with them, creating a home and possibly a family. I would like to raise kids with nonsexual life partners, whether we are romantic with each other or not. I have not felt this way about the people who I date and am sexual with.*
>
> *My past monogamous partners were uncomfortable with my close or romantic friendships. Now I'm poly, and it works for me. It is amazing to connect in ways that feel natural, unhindered by social strictures.*
> *— Emma, queer and nonmonogamous*

114

> *I think it's completely bogus that people are taught to value their sexual and romantic relationships above their friendships. I should not be less important to anyone because I'm not fucking them.*
> — *Clare, queer and asexual*

Such commonplace devaluation of friendships is a bit odd, considering how strong, enduring friendships are venerated in popular media. Substantial same-sex friendships are widely celebrated in TV shows, movies and books — the *bromance* or *womance* plot device. For example:

- Batman and Robin[41]
- Thelma and Louise [42]
- Captain Kirk, Mr. Spock and Dr. McCoy[43]
- Cagney and Lacey[44]
- Butch Cassidy and the Sundance Kid[45]
- The four female stars of Sex and the City[46]

The nonsexual, nonromantic deep bonds shared by these characters are quite central to the story. Certainly, none of them would ditch the others in favor of an Escalator partner.

> *No, those two people might not be dating even if they've been close for years and cuddle sometimes. They might be intimate friends. Frodo and Sam are life partners; that doesn't mean they're boning. You get the drift.*
> — *Ety, in an undefined, long-term open relationship*

That said, the socially perceived value of a friendship doesn't automatically rise if it starts to include sex, or perhaps some overt flirtation or affection. Quite the contrary. Under current social norms, if friends develop a sexual or romantic connection that isn't heading toward the Escalator, this is often perceived as foolish or dangerous — or at least, as a sure way to ruin or cheapen that friendship.

> *I enjoy crushes and flirting, the rush of infatuation, and occasional making out with friends — all of which are things I cannot safely indulge from within monogamy.*
> *Human relationships don't fit well into simple boxes. There's a lot of gray area between friends, lovers and life partners. I enjoy being able to take each relationship for what it is, not imposing a structure on it.*
> — *K, polyamorous*

Sexual Friendships

Sexual friendships are a popular, if often underestimated or overlooked, approach to sharing intimacy. This is when friends enjoy sharing sex, either occasionally or regularly — even though they may not especially share romantic feelings or consider themselves to be in love.

Roughly 15% of responses to my survey clearly indicated a current or past sexual friendship. Probably this was significantly underreported since I inquired about intimate relationships — and under Escalator-influenced concepts, people often do not count friendships (even ones that include sex) as "relationships."

> *I once had friends-with-benefits relationship that lasted three years. Most people don't understand that. They think that if you get on well enough to keep having sex for years, surely you'll naturally drift into a more traditional romantic relationship? But it worked for us.*
>
> *I never had any interest in being his girlfriend, and vice versa. Still, we were excellent for what we were to each other — great sex and an affectionate friendship.*
>
> *It would have been awful if I'd felt pressured to start getting lovey-dovey with him. That was just not what I felt for him; we'd both have been miserable. I have no regrets, even though we had some tough times.*
> — *Melinda, nonmonogamous*

Mutual affection, respect, attraction and erotic compatibility are hallmarks of sexual friendships. Sexual attraction isn't always what brings these friends together. Sometimes the sex happens first, and sometimes the friendship.

It's not unusual for people to discover that exploring sexual friendships expands their capacity to deepen any friendship.

> *In the last five years, I've had a lot of casual sexual connections. Increasingly, most of these have also had some element of friendship. I've also found that my nonsexual relationships have gotten more intimate; I've become more emotionally open to them as well.*
> — *Katharine, polyamorous*

The main advantage of sexual friendships is that they generally allow a high degree of autonomy, enjoyment and satisfaction, without a lot of the overhead commonly associated with intimate relationships.

Common drawbacks of sexual friendships include awkwardness, mismatched emotions or expectations, miscommunication and the hard-to-unlearn effects of social norms.

Where Sexual Friendships Fit in

In consensual nonmonogamy, often sexual friendships are enjoyed in addition to more intense, committed, or entwined relationships.

> *Since I got married, I've had a few friends with benefits relationships. They range from friendly acquaintances I see a couple times a year and maybe have sex with a few times, to friends I see often and specifically get together with to have sex.*
>
> *For whatever reason, not even counting the fact that I'm already in one primary-type relationship, we wouldn't work well as committed romantic partners.*
>
> *— Jen, married and polyamorous*

However, for some people, or at some points in life, enjoying sex with friends might actually be a healthier choice than having more intense love affairs or strong commitments. Deeper, more committed ongoing intimacy often involves substantial effort and emotional turmoil — especially when relationships are new and shiny (perhaps heading toward the Escalator), or when they are troubled or changing. Deeper relationships also tend to consume considerable time, energy and attention, which can hinder progress on other fronts in life.

Just because someone might not want a major romance or life partnership right now doesn't mean they must remain celibate or without romantic spark, or that they must resort to one-off hookups with strangers. Sexual friendships can help people feel happy, more comfortable or less stressed.

> *I've frequently had relationships of various types evolve into what I categorized as "friends with whom I occasionally have sex." This means we care about and support each other, without the pressures or expectations of being in a romantic relationship. And we still enjoy physical intimacy when the mood strikes us.*
>
> *I have found this type of relationship actually suits me best, and plan on having only this type in the foreseeable future.*
>
> *— Dragon Fox, polyamorous*

Swingers often establish ongoing sexual friendships with their play partners — as do people who consider their relationships open, monogamish or nonmonogamous, but not necessarily polyamorous.

> *We fall somewhere between being swingers and strictly polyamorous. We are both allowed to have sex with anyone we want, apart or together. By choice, both of us really only want to sleep with people we feel a connection with. So far, that has meant sex with friends.*
> *— JH, swinger/poly*

> *We were monogamously married, but have since opened up our relationship to include sexual and emotional connections with other people. My wife and I have a group of friends who we are sexual with.*
> *— Cecil, in an open marriage*

Friends with Benefits: Mainstream Sexual Friendships

The now-popular term friends with benefits (FWB) grants an acknowledged, if not always respected, place in mainstream culture to sexual friendships — while still reflecting cultural presumptions about what's supposed to differentiate friends from lovers or partners. For many people, sexual friendships provide comfort and joy between "real" (Escalator-bound) relationships.

> *Our friends with benefits relationship worked for us. It ended because he found someone to settle down with, in a 100% conventional, monogamous, cohabiting Escalator relationship — currently at the stage of buying a house and planning kids.*
> *That was never going to be my thing, but he's ecstatic — and hardly because he's unaware of any alternatives. Takes all sorts!*
> *— Melinda, nonmonogamous*

Sexual friendships occupy an interesting social niche since monogamy is rarely assumed in these relationships. In particular, sexual friendships often happen among people who may wish to ride the Escalator someday — but until "The One" comes along, they're open to sharing sex with some friends.

This makes sense: it's now generally considered acceptable for adults to have sex, whether they're partnered up or not. So while one is waiting for the Escalator, having some regular or familiar sex partners, especially friends, can feel more comfortable and safer than hooking up with strangers or leaping into relationships. And often, the sex is better, too.

In such cases, people usually wish to remain available to potential Escalator relationships. Therefore, their sexual friendships cannot be exclusive. Typically in sexual friendships, the norm is to cease having sex with friends once someone decides to jump on the Escalator. Sometimes people discuss these expectations with their sexual friends. They might even make agreements about it early on. And sometimes this intention is just assumed — which can lead to misunderstandings.

However, there is a big potential disadvantage to how sexual friendships are commonly perceived. In mainstream culture, people often view friends with benefits arrangements as strictly casual. In turn, *casual sex* is commonly construed to mean no emotions involved, no strings attached, sex-only hookups. Hence, another common and sometimes derisive label: *fuck buddies.*

Friendships, whether they include sex or not, involve real people with real feelings — and ideally, some level of mutual appreciation, consideration and respect. Also, strictly recreational, no-commitment sex is fine, with mutual consent.

That said, social presumptions that devalue casual sex sometimes lead people to treat their sexual friends with stunning inconsideration. When one person sincerely values the "friends" part, while the other is solely focused on the "benefits," hard feelings can result — even if no one wanted to ride the Escalator.

> *Sex with someone you're not committed to doesn't have to be empty.*
> *It is a sharing. It's a way to grow closer.*
> *— Slyph, in an open relationship*

Romantic Friendships

Less common, but no less valid, is when friends harbor romantic feelings for each other. They may flirt, express overt affection, use terms of endearment, exchange love notes, cuddle, etc. They may or may not also share sex.

Romantic or passionate friendships are well known in history, especially between women. Although they're often assumed to be a thin cover for an unacknowledged sexual relationship, that often is not the case, especially in the online age.

> *I have an online romantic friendship with a demisexual guy who lives*
> *in another country. We haven't met in person yet, but are open to doing*
> *so in the future.*
> *— Cynthia, asexual and polyamorous*

> *I tend towards monogamish relationships because of time, trust and habit — but ultimately I would like to feel comfortable expanding into other areas of loving. Romantic friendships are also a category I tend to fall into. There are so many ways of being in a relationship, I am open to suggestion and dialogue.*
>
> — *Jenn, nonmonogamous*

Story: Experimenting via Sexual Friendship

People embark upon sexual friendships for many reasons, including a desire for sexual variety and exploration. This can provide a sense of safety for people taking their first uncertain steps off the Escalator. As long as everyone's feelings and needs are treated with consideration, these forays can work out well for all involved.

H shared this story:

> *Our relationship is heterosexual, but we are both bisexual. My male partner had little same-sex experience at the start of our relationship, and I had none. Both of us wanted to explore same-sex attraction while maintaining our relationship, and neither of us wanted to keep the other from doing so.*
>
> *We have invited a close female friend of ours (also bisexual) into our shared bed. While she is not part of our relationship, sex has become an aspect of our friendship, when she is not in a relationship of her own.*
>
> *My partner and I are currently discussing where our comfort level would be if we invited a man in. We would ideally involve a close friend again, although we have no close male bisexual friends. If it is to be someone who is not a close friend, then I would not be involved. However, my partner could possibly have same-sex encounters with my prior knowledge. This is still in early discussion, so boundaries have not yet been properly established.*
>
> *I think I could comfortably explore polyamory, but he is less certain. So for now, our external relationships stop at close friendships.*

Part 2 Questions to Consider and Discuss

- What are your personal beliefs or opinions about consensual nonmonogamy and the people who choose to practice it?

- What do you see as the likely pros/cons of the types of consensual nonmonogamy covered in Part 2? (Swinging, polyamory, sexual friendship, monogamish and don't ask don't tell)

- If consensual nonmonogamy was more widely recognized and accepted, how might this affect society as a whole? How might it impact you or people you know?

- Which topics in Chapters 7-10 would you like to read more about? What are your questions about consensual nonmonogamy?

Share your answers or your own story online*

OffEscalator.com/resources/book1questions

* By answering any of these questions or sharing other personal information via the Off the Escalator website, you agree that the Off the Escalator project may quote your responses in our books, web content and in other material. You can answer anonymously if you like.

PART 3

PRESERVING AUTONOMY

11

LOVING, BUT NOT LIVING, TOGETHER

In many cultures, but especially in North America, there's an odd tug-of-war over autonomy. On one hand, it's generally considered a good thing to value and express one's personal independence. However, when it comes to intimate relationships, often "too much" autonomy is viewed as suspect, problematic or even threatening — not only to a relationship or family but to society.

Despite this, many people strongly prize their ability to function as autonomous individuals, even while they maintain significant or committed intimate relationships. In fact, some people believe that they cannot be healthy, happy or fulfilled without maintaining more autonomy than might be acceptable in a traditional relationship.

The need for individual autonomy within the context of an intimate relationship can be expressed in many ways. Most visibly, sometimes long-term partners maintain separate households.

Apartners: Together but Living Apart

Being together, even as committed life partners, doesn't necessarily require living together. Many intimate partners are actually *apartners*,[47] people who feel committed to their relationship despite choosing to live separately. A 2010 study indicated that one in 20 U.K. couples chooses to live separately. [48]

Nesting (sharing a home and otherwise combining the infrastructure of daily life) is a key marker of Escalator-style merging. Today, partners typically move in together before their relationship gets legally sanctioned via marriage or civil union; but not too long ago, it was common for couples to marry before cohabiting. Times change.

However, it's still generally assumed that if partners feel strong mutual love and commitment, then eventually they must move in together — and keep living together until death do they part.

Nesting is also an important part of many unconventional relationships. However, Off the Escalator, it's definitely not mandatory. Many partners are deeply committed to each other, even though they do not live together, or plan to ever do so.

> *My life partner and I do not live together or share finances. We chose to buy two homes in the same neighborhood. We share many activities, including our spiritual life. We support each other with instrumental assistance and occasional financial collaboration.*
>
> *— Channing, polyamorous*

> *My partner and I reside in different states. While we may resume residence in the same city at some point, I don't know that we'd live in the same physical structure together.*
>
> *— A, polyamorous, in a long distance marriage*

Noncohabiting relationships can be quite deep, committed and enduring.

> *Our relationship is committed, long-term and monogamous, but we do not share the same household. We see each other on weekends and talk to each other during the week.*
>
> *We hold vacation property jointly, vacation together, and share vacation expenses. We alternately share expenses for entertainment (the person who suggests the experience pays). We have designated each other as the beneficiary on our retirement accounts.*
>
> *I prefer living alone because, when we argue, I have someplace to escape to. I feel this freedom preserves the balance of power between us. I am not forced to deal with unreasonable conflict.*
>
> *On another level, I can decorate my home the way I want, while still keeping some stuff at my quasi-husband's home. I like having down time during the week when I don't have to talk or interact with anyone. I like having my friends visit without worrying whether he enjoys their company. We talk on the telephone every evening to recap our day and stay connected.*
>
> *We spend the night together every weekend (Friday through Sunday night). A pesky disadvantage is always forgetting something at my house, and missing my pets on the weekends.*
>
> *We are together because we want to be, not because a piece of paper says we should be together and it's just too inconvenient or expensive to get a divorce.*
>
> *— Susie, monogamous*

Some intimate partners effectively live together part-time. But unlike people who are riding the Relationship Escalator, this is not merely a transition step toward eventually moving in together.

> *I spend half of the week living with my wife and the other half with my other partner.*
> — *Peter L., poly and married*

> *I live full-time with my son. My partner lives with me part-time. His younger son lives with me during the school year, since I'm close to his college campus. Is this living alone or with a partner?*
> — *Lynn, polyamorous*

Living apart from intimate partners doesn't necessarily mean living alone. People who choose not to live with any intimate partners often do reside with children, housemates, friends, family or within an intentional community.

In my survey, one in five participants reside with friends or roommates, or in an intentional community — but not with an intimate partner. Vanishingly few indicated that they would prefer living with an intimate partner. Additionally, 10% live with their kids or family, but not an intimate partner. Sometimes living with other people is a matter of choice; sometimes it's a necessity.

> *There's so much work to living with a partner. Just living with my kids, I get to focus on the needs of myself and my family without having to add another person to my family environment.*
> — *Polychrohm, solo poly*

> *If I did live with someone, I'd prefer that we not be sexually involved, to avoid falling into norms I do not like. I know that it is easy to do.*
> — *Storm, relationship anarchist*

Options are increasing for adults who wish to live together and pool resources to some extent, in ways that do not hinge upon family or romantic ties. These might include intentional communities, group households, cohousing, housing cooperatives, communes or spiritual communities — and, of course, housemates.

Also, some people are nomads, connecting and reconnecting with partners as they roam. For instance, Rejoice lives a nomadic life. Throughout the year she spends time alone or with various lovers and partners around the U.S. In addition, she often spends long stretches with one partner who lives in a farm-based intentional community — where she is considering settling down if she can avoid losing her autonomy in the process.

> *Part of what makes my romantic life ideal is that I'm nomadic. I love my partner on the farm dearly, but I'm glad I only live with him an average of six months a year. The longer we spend together, the more I feel in myself a sense of jealous attachment that I associate with primary relationships in my past. I begin to try to anticipate what he's going to do in the future and how my life fits into it.*
>
> *We're going to have to sit down and talk about this a lot in the future if I end up living on the farm full-time. Unassociated with my romantic relationship, I'm starting to realize that I'd like to live at the farm full-time. They'd give me health care and other benefits. I would feel more connected and "at home" when I'm staying there. I'd be a full member of the collectively-owned business, capable of participating in decisions that affect the group. And I'd be able to take on long-term responsibilities that would make my life feel more satisfying.*
>
> *Ideally, if I stayed in one place, I'd like to have romantic and sexual relationships with several friends, with fluctuating levels of time-spent-together and new-friend-sexual-excitement and my-goodness-we're-too-cuddly-for-words. I feel as though I artificially create this by moving three times a year and coming back to relationships that are different but still good.*
>
> *— Rejoice, solo poly*

Choosing to nest with someone other than an Escalator partner can be daunting since mainstream society tends to devalue other types of important relationships. This norm can encourage to people to treat housemates rather disposably.

> *I've dithered a lot on the question of my living situation, as I've lived alone for nearly 10 years. I am starting to long for something different. However, right now I think I'd rather share a household with friends.*
>
> *The downside is that friends are seen as less important. This makes it harder to find a long-term situation since folks tend to move in with their romantic partners over time. One of my biggest fears is getting stuck alone with a lease.*
>
> *— Avory, solo poly*

Some partners first try living together and later move apart because they discover this is healthier for them and their relationship. This can be challenging since in mainstream culture, moving apart is strongly equated with relationship failure. But for some people, moving apart is exactly what makes their relationships work.

> *My partner and I once lived together for a year and a half. As it turned out, we have vastly different views on politics, healthy eating, smoking/not smoking, excessive alcohol use, participating in organized religion, communicating information about daily events or schedules, expressing emotional needs/feelings, etc.*
>
> *We experienced a significant amount of tension when we lived together. We both would tiptoe around each other, to not rock the boat. We were both trying to be "good guys." This became very stressful, and it adversely affected our sex life.*
>
> *Now we live apart and see each other only a few times a week. This has given us the freedom to pursue the different kinds of activities we enjoy separately.*
>
> *The fact that we no longer live together has actually made it much easier for us to be totally open with our feelings. There is a relaxation factor that has settled into our relationship because we no longer have expectations that our relationship should move forward at any particular pace, just because we are sharing a home, finances, food, etc.*
>
> *— Kimberly, monogamous*

Interestingly, a few people who do currently live with a partner emphasized that they really would prefer to live alone.

> *Currently, I live with my partner. He is an ideal home-sharer: respectful, kind, considerate, gentle, responsible and all that. I honestly can't think of any major criticism for his living-together habits. (I mean, there are the little things like sometimes leaving hair in the sink...)*
>
> *But ultimately I've realized that I'm just not cut out to live with someone. I need a lot more solitude, personal space, and absolute control of my environment in order to relax and enjoy my home.*
>
> *It wouldn't be fair for me to absolutely control the environment that we share, so I try really hard not to do that. It is just very stressful for me to overlap space with someone on a daily basis; to realize that he could interrupt me at any time.*
>
> *— Agnes, nonmonogamous*

> *I am seeking ways to be financially independent of my spouse, so I would be able to have my own household. I do not function well in our current setting. I will not be any less in love with my partner, but I will be a darn site happier for losing their mess!*
> — *Helen, nonmonogamous*

Benefits of Not Nesting with a Partner

In my survey, the vast majority of people who do not live with an intimate partner like it that way. Sometimes, their reasons are simply a lifestyle preference or a matter of comfort.

> *I love sleeping alone and going to bed alone. I never have to share a bed again if I don't want to.*
> — *Laura E., solo poly*

For more introverted people, living alone can be essential for maintaining mental and emotional health.

> *I like having more space and time to myself. As an introvert, this is very important to me. I love not having the heavy emotional and time commitment required of a primary live-in relationship.*
> — *Nina, solo poly*

> *Continuous diluted contact with a partner makes me crazy.*
> — *Agnes, nonmonogamous*

Living apart from intimate partners can enhance overall life stability. Notably, when intimate relationships end, get rocky or significantly change, then living apart can minimize life disruption — although a breakup might still be emotionally rough.

When someone lives with one or more intimate partners, the stability of their housing — and perhaps also finances, child care, support networks and social ties — often hinges largely on the stability and continuity of that intimate relationship. This is a big reason why people sometimes remain for years, or for life, in life-entwined relationships that have become unhealthy, toxic or dead.

> *I have only lived with one partner, and that was ultimately one of the factors in our breakup. It made our breakup much harder.*
> — *Violet, polyamorous*

> *I like being able to leave, or they leave, and we go on with our lives.*

— J., solo and nonmonogamous

Not living with lovers can help keep relationships fresh and vital, by encouraging partners to never take their shared time for granted.

> *I spend considerable time with my female lover, but she and I choose not to live together. We both cherish our times of solitude and having our own space to be alone. It has an added bonus: it always feels special when I see her again.*
>
> *I have no intention of living with my male partner either.*
> *— Sandee, polyamorous*

Tradeoffs of Choosing to Live Apart

Of course, living apart from intimate partners can create some challenges, especially with logistics.

> *My partner has "two homes," so they are always dragging their stuff back and forth.*
> *— Cluckwerk, nonmonogamous*

Can it get lonely living alone? For some people, sometimes, yes — even if, overall, living alone is what they prefer.

> *At times, not living with a partner leaves me feeling lonely and makes time management much more difficult.*
> *— Mandy, poly*

Sometimes, not living with intimate partners triggers vulnerability and fear.

> *The fear of being sick and old and living alone is the most difficult part for me. I have become disabled during the last few years and, at age 55, I am facing the likelihood of disability retirement.*
>
> *It is scary to envision my future life if I don't move in with my primary partner and his family.*
> *— Sonja, poly in a non-cohabiting relationship*

Deciding whether to nest with a partner can be fraught. It's almost impossible to navigate this choice without facing daunting questions about what it might portend for one's identity and relationship(s).

> *I have reached a point with one of my partners that I'd like to mix our lives somewhat. However, it's hard to express why this is important since I am already living with another partner.*
>
> *I don't feel I can talk freely about my excitement over my relationship with the partner who I am not yet living with. Also, that partner may fear progressing our relationship in this way, since that might push his other partners away. (He has a few friends with benefits.)*
> — *Darla, in an open relationship*

Logistics and finances are important considerations that might constrain one's ability to sustain both a significant intimate relationship and a separate household. Conventional housing options generally don't support this choice well.

Consequently, when people begin to question whether it's necessary or desirable to share living space with intimate partners, they often express an interest in alternative housing options, especially cohousing.

> *Style of household is an open question for me right now. My last primary relationship ended in large part due to attempting to cohabiting with incompatible housekeeping styles. While I like the idea of living with a partner(s), I don't know if it's a good idea.*
>
> *Perhaps my ideal is some sort of cohousing situation where my partner(s) are co-located, but we have separate spaces (more than just bedrooms — those are already an absolute requirement).*
> — *Cheyenne, polyamorous*

Unfortunately, the current reality of cohousing options, at least in North America, is that there are relatively few cohousing communities, and they tend to be fairly costly. In the U.S., buying into a cohousing community can cost 30-40% more than comparable conventional housing. [49]

Similarly, maintaining separate households also tends to be more expensive than living with one or more intimate partners. Also, there's the issue of whether partners who wish to live apart can each find housing in locations that support how often and how easily they wish to spend time together.

Story: Living Apart Helps Some Relationships Thrive

Some people noted that if they felt obliged to nest, the very relationships that bring considerable reward and meaning to their lives might not be able to exist.

For instance, decoupling the concept of living arrangements from commitment is precisely what enabled Old Pandora to grow and deepen her intimate relationship.

For three years I've been partnered with a man I love who is diagnosed on the autism spectrum. He is an introvert who needs a substantial amount of alone time.

I have a nine-year-old child from a previous marriage, and I live alone with my child. I always have to put my child first; I don't want someone deciding for us what will happen. I am too independent to have others make choices for me. I fear getting involved with someone who's a bad choice. I prefer living alone. My partner and I mingle for entertainment and emotional support, but not financial or logistical support.

I have a sleepover date at my partner's home once per week, and he stays over at our home one night on the weekend. He is not able to handle day-to-day living with another person, let alone in a household with a child since kids have constant uncensored demands for attention.

I don't think we would have been brave enough to speak up and negotiate for what we really need if we hadn't been nonmonogamous. If we had gone with social norms that said, "This won't work because you can't live with me," I would have missed out on the most satisfying emotional and sexual connection of my life. That would have been terribly sad.

12

PERMANENTLY LONG DISTANCE LOVE

Love doesn't always follow geography; long distance relationships happen. In my survey, roughly 12% of participants reported being in some kind of long distance intimate relationship.

Long distance relationships are increasingly common in the internet age since people now often meet or develop personal connections online. Furthermore, the revolution in communication technology — especially options such as video calling, chat apps and internet telephony — has given people more, and more affordable, options to continue existing relationships after a partner moves far away.

Most long distance relationships are autonomous by necessity. When partners don't see each other much because they live far apart, it's almost impossible to get very deeply merged, at least logistically.

> *My boyfriend and I are somewhat long distance. We don't expect to hear from each other every day, and we see each other every two weeks.*
> *— Kendall, solo poly*

> *I live in the U.S. My nonprimary partner's wife is European, and they live in Europe. I usually see them once every year or two. The three of us often Skype, text and chat.*
> *— SK, polyamorous*

Many, perhaps most, long distance relationships don't start out that way. They start out as local relationships, but then someone moves away. This notoriously challenging transition fundamentally alters how partners relate to each other. Many relationships, monogamous and otherwise, do not survive it.

> *I spent many years living with a primary partner, who then had to move for work. That relationship dissolved over the distance.*
> — Sydnie, genderqueer, asexual and polyamorous

However, some enduring relationships are long distance from the start.

> *I'm in a long distance relationship that started online, and we've only seen each other in person once. It's been going on for years, we talk every day. It feels significant and wonderful. However, we aren't in any hurry to try to make it go somewhere — moving to live closer, coming out to our shared friends, or declarations of anything.*
> — Nika, in an open relationship

The challenges of maintaining a sense of intimate connection across distance are obvious. However, these arrangements can offer advantages.

> *We live on opposite sides of the world. Eventually, we think we'd like to move closer to each other — but we're happy with long distance for at least the next few years.*
>
> *Long distance makes everything extremely flexible. Spending time together is as easy as turning on the computer, and getting some space is as easy as turning it off. We can turn to each other for support anytime, but we also avoid burdening each other with our problems.*
>
> *I have anger problems, and being able to mute the microphone and go yell and break things off-camera lets me blow off steam without being threatening and abusive.*
> — Leonard, nonmonogamous

Long Distance Love: Bug or Feature?

On the Relationship Escalator, long distance love is usually framed as a problem to be solved: a bug, not a feature.

Consequently, monogamous relationships that are long distance nearly always involve plans to eventually move closer — and usually, to live together. Without this goal, long distance monogamous partners, and others, commonly start to doubt the relationship's viability.

> *I have been dating the same man exclusively for nearly seven years. We met on the internet. I live in New York and he lives in England.*

> *In the beginning, I expected a resolution. But during an in-person discussion over a year ago, he said something about fearing that. I was bummed; I figured we'd have to break up.*
>
> *Fortuitously, I met some poly people for the first time. So I began considering the idea of keeping what we had without the Escalator.*
>
> *Loneliness is a problem in this situation. It is very, very hard.*
> — *Kim, in an intercontinental monogamous relationship*

Yes, loneliness can be a big challenge in monogamous long distance relationships. If it's difficult, rare and costly to spend time with one's sole intimate partner, that usually leads to missing them more than just emotionally. This particular situation also means going without physical sexual contact.

> *Going long periods of time without sex is difficult. But the flip side of that is the long-time-no-see sex, which is something akin to make-up sex!*
> — *Tahni, in a long distance monogamous relationship*

For these and other reasons, sometimes long distance relationships exist only until someone finds a local partner. Typically this happens without prior negotiation; those awkward, painful, "Well, I've met someone here..." conversations.

However, long distance partners can be conscious about this possibility, and even make agreements about it.

> *I have only one partner. He is in California and I am in Pennsylvania. We met online and have many, many other online friends. I have made it clear to him that I want him to remain open to others who may be a better match for him.*
> — *Graham, gay and nonmonogamous*

Nonmonogamy Creates Options for Long Distance Lovers

Consensual nonmonogamy can help make long distance love more feasible, especially over the long haul.

> *Nonmonogamy made my long distance relationship easier. Obviously, it was still difficult, but it helped a lot that we could both seek physical and emotional comfort from others.*
> — *Rei, nonmonogamous lesbian*

Of course, simply agreeing to nonmonogamy doesn't automatically make long distance love easy.

> *The more partners I have, the more likely it seems that at least some of them will be distant. Having some partners close while others are distant doesn't really lessen the pain of missing them.*
> *— Anna, polyamorous*

Disclosure is a consideration for nonmonogamous long distance relationships. Some participants noted that what makes their relationships work well is the fact that they can discuss with partners what's going on in their other relationships.

> *My eight-year relationship with my boyfriend has always been long distance. I doubt it would have lasted if we weren't poly and didn't talk about everything.*
> *It would be hard to trust someone to stay monogamous when months go by without seeing each other so much of the time — and without talking through our other attractions thoroughly.*
> *— Candace, polyamorous*

But for some people, the choice not to hear about a long distance partner's other intimate connections is what allows them to feel comfortable in that relationship.

> *I am involved in an ongoing, committed relationship where I live eight hours from my partner. We have adopted a don't ask don't tell policy about lovers outside of our relationship.*
> *This has been a very satisfying experience because it keeps me from obsessing about what my partner is doing, or who he is seeing. My partner and I are then able to just enjoy the time we do have together.*
> *— Janeane, nonmonogamous*

Several people in consensually nonmonogamous, long distance relationships observed that it helps to have at least one local intimate partner.

> *I would like at least one of my relationships (preferably my primary partner) to not be long distance. Currently, I live in Portland and my main squeeze lives in Brooklyn. It's rough. I have another sweetheart in Montreal, and one other in Germany.*

I feel too emotionally maxed out to start dating someone new, but I definitely feel affected by the lack of physical contact in all my emotional connections. Visits are wonderful, but I'd rather have a partner who lives in the same city.
— *Lindsay, polyamorous*

I would like it if I had a partner who lived closer to me, with whom I had a strong connection, who could spend time with me regularly.
— *Corey, polyamorous, with several long distance partners*

That said, it can help to have local friends or community where cuddling or other kinds of affectionate physical contact are acceptable and easily available.

My boyfriend and I attend different colleges in different states. Knowing that I can cuddle with friends without worrying that my boyfriend might freak out and say I'm cheating — that is an incredible help when I get lonely or touch-starved.
— *Sarah, in an open relationship*

Story: Immigration and Long Distance Love

Sometimes, immigration issues make long distance the only option to continue an intimate relationship.

For instance, Tahni and her partner are trying to make the best of transoceanic love. As if immigration hurdles weren't enough, social disapproval of their choice not to marry increases their stress.

I'm currently in a committed monogamous relationship with long distance complications: my boyfriend is American, and I'm British. We spend more than half our time apart due to visa restrictions. When in the same country, we live together and are completely committed.

We get pressure from friends and family to "just get married" so that we can be together. But we have only been together for less than two years. My boyfriend was previously married and divorced, and we feel that it is too soon to get married. We want to pursue our relationship without putting that pressure on it — despite the possibility of this becoming an eventual necessity.

Our friends often comment on the nonconformity of our relationship, and their discomfort that he and I spend so much time apart.

Trying to build a life with someone who is only there part time can make you constantly question whether it's worth it. That can be overwhelming and a bad thing.

But it can also be good if the answer is: "Yes! it's worth it!"

13

GOING SOLO:
AUTONOMY IN AND OUT OF RELATIONSHIPS

Independence can be a matter of identity: who you are, not just how you navigate situations.

People who consider themselves *solo* tend to prioritize personal autonomy: their own, and that of others. Typically solos maintain a strong identity as an individual, eschewing the merging that the Relationship Escalator encourages. They prefer not to need anyone's permission or approval to make their own life choices. Usually, they also accept that others don't need their permission or approval, either.

> *I prefer to make my own decisions and live alone. I don't want to have to answer to another person about financial, job or any other decisions.*
> *People in traditional relationships always seem to have to discuss these sorts of decisions with their partners and come to an agreement.*
> *— Melanie, solo poly*

Many people choose solohood due to an ethical or emotional aversion to treating people like territory. Prioritizing personal autonomy may be the key to feeling good about their relationships.

> *I am more likely to act ethically and be honest with my partners if none of us are tied to each other. Then, my attitudes towards them are more consistent. It doesn't hit any triggers or feelings of obligation and confinement, so I am more stable in malleable relationships.*

> *If it's clear that you can always leave, you become much more aware of the reasons why you don't want to.*
>   *Also, consent is more obvious. Everyone pays more attention because they don't assume they already know everything about the person they're having sex with.*
>   *— Finn, queer and nonmonogamous*

> *I don't like feeling "owned."*
>   *— Kay, solo poly*

Solohood does not hinge upon relationship status. A solo person might have only one significantly intimate relationship, several, or none. Also, they might be monogamous, nonmonogamous, or uninterested in significant intimate relationships.

For many people, being solo means prioritizing one's internal relationship with oneself. Some people have called this *"being your own primary partner."* This focus need not preclude consideration of others, or making commitments to others, or even putting others first in certain situations. It just means refusing to lose or sacrifice oneself within any relationship. Thus, solohood can be precisely what empowers people to share love, intimacy and support in profound, healthy, enduring ways.

> *Taking care of yourself is not a crime. It's a right — and it makes you make a better partner.*
>   *— Siobhan, nonmonogamous*

Being solo is different from being single. In mainstream culture, *single* is largely circumstantial: the condition of having no significant intimate relationships at the moment. As soon as a single person develops at least one romantic relationship with any level of mutual commitment, then they're not single anymore.

Furthermore, in mainstream culture, people who consider themselves single typically hope to ride the Escalator someday — or at least, it's presumed that this is their eventual goal. Less commonly, conventional singles prefer to avoid "serious" relationships altogether. These things are rarely true of people who consciously adopt solohood as an identity.

In fact, thriving as a solo usually demands considerable attention to relationships. It's common for solos to carefully nurture a diverse range of deep ties with friends, intimate partners, family, communities and more. In part, this is because solos generally don't get the kind of automatic validation and support that visible couplehood often provides. Solos usually must build and maintain their support networks very consciously, so they can count on support in times of need.

Solohood can be expressed in many ways that influence how intimate relationships work. For instance:

- **Not living together** *(nesting)* with intimate partners.

- **Taking a fair amount of alone time,** or at least time apart from partners, without guilt, apology, justification or asking permission. The default becomes "me time," not "we time."

- **Prioritizing oneself in key life decisions or commitments,** such as whether to move to another state, rather than prioritizing a relationship or partner when making such choices.

- **Socializing or going out alone,** at least sometimes, by choice, rather than only as a last resort if a partner or date is not available.

- **Having and enforcing clear personal boundaries.** Being sure about which kinds of relationships or situations one is not willing to engage in. Also, being willing to communicate one's boundaries, and being able to withdraw or renegotiate should these be crossed.

- **Presenting oneself primarily as an individual,** not as part of a couple, family or other relationship group. For instance, saying "I" more than "we," even when discussing things that might be shared with an intimate partner.

- **Exercising personal efficacy.** Avoiding or leaving relationships where conditions would restrict or undermine one's ability to make independent choices or to negotiate effectively with partners. This can make relationship hierarchy a poor fit for many solos.

- **Respecting other people's autonomy.** Not limiting or controlling choices made by others, including intimate partners or metamours. This means avoiding rules, manipulation or ultimatums, and trying to respect other people's boundaries.

Living arrangements tend to be a key consideration for solos. Most solos prefer to avoid life-entwined intimate relationships, especially living with or marrying sexual or romantic partners. This tends to support independent decision making, fostering clarity in personal choices and relationship negotiations.

However not all solos live alone. Many reside with friends, family, housemates or an intentional community.

A few people consider themselves solo by mindset, even though they choose to entwine lives with an intimate partner, such as through nesting or marriage. Such people usually still receive couple privilege from society, despite their efforts to preserve their individuality within their relationship. They don't face the same social landscape that people who do not nest with a partner would face.

Roughly one-third of survey participants considered themselves solo or chose solohood during some portion of their adult life. About half of these people lived alone at the time of the survey; nearly as many resided with friends or housemates who were not their intimate partners. About one in ten lived with their family of origin or their children. Less than 1% lived with an intimate partner.

Benefits of Going Solo

Some solos emphasized that their autonomy is essential to their ability to grow and change, as well as to maintain their sense of personal authenticity or integrity.

> *Because I have spent years only in nonprimary relationships (and, in the last year, not in any relationship at all), I've been free to simply experiment with my life in ways that few people around me can do. I do not answer to anyone about how I spend my time or who I socialize with.*
>
> *I am responsible for keeping some contact with my lovers when we are apart, for being fully present when we are together, and otherwise taking care of myself (and my home and my cats), in whatever form that may take on any given day. If I decide to take a new lover, or to play with somebody at a party, nobody is in a position to second guess my decision.*
>
> *It's very important to me that I am absolutely free to explore and to recreate my life in any way I like. I have changed my gender identity and sexual orientation. I'll be physically transitioning to whatever degree I think is appropriate. I have moved and I have moved back. I have shifted my worldviews.*
>
> *— Savanni, solo*

Another common benefit of solohood is a sense of freedom, especially when this can be balanced with connectedness.

> *I love living alone. I love maintaining my independence of spirit, of finances, of Friday nights, of vacations, of all-day pajamas... of the possibility of through-hiking the Pacific Coast Trail without needing anyone's permission or approval.*

> *And I also love having intimate, growing relationships with other people that firmly tether me to relatedness and to the depths of my heart and generosity. I have the best of both worlds, I think.*
> — Jo, solo poly

Some people said that it's very important to feel valued as an individual by their intimate partners. Embracing solohood can be one path to this experience.

> *It's an incredible thing when partners encourage and remind you that autonomy (or, your personal relationship with yourself and your identity) is something to be valued and nurtured — not lost through relationships. I value having a relationship structure that encourages me to constantly explore, and to become more myself.*
> — Stuart, polyamorous

In life-entwined relationships, particularly on the Escalator, it can be easy to drift into enmeshment or codependence. Going solo can help address this concern.

> *In the past, I have completely thrown myself into relationships, to the point where I built my life around a person who was not treating me the way I deserved to be treated.*
> *I have learned from experience that I need to retain my independence and have my own life, regardless of whether I am in a relationship or not.*
> — Megan, single and nonmonogamous

> *Our time together is limited, so we have not become codependently enmeshed. That used to be a pattern of mine.*
> — Amy, polyamorous

Some participants mentioned that they prefer solohood specifically because they desire less emotional intimacy or commitment, or because they can't (or don't wish to) put much energy into intimate relationships.

> *I live with a physical, invisible disability: Lyme disease, a long-term chronic illness. I suspect that my preference for being solo may be partly influenced by my disability since my energy is limited.*
> — Jody, solo poly

> *I have always been a bit cat-like in relationships. I don't particularly like being in a committed relationship.*

> *Honestly, my ideal relationship would probably be as a mistress to one or more people. I'd enjoy all the benefits of sexual intimacy on a regular, caring basis, free from the banality of a full-time relationship.*
> — *Bunny Blake, poly, queer and kinky*

Solo Stigma and Singlism

If an adult prefers to not be strongly coupled-up, this can trigger suspicion: What's wrong with them?

The flip side of social couple privilege is *singlism:* the stigma and prejudice faced by people who are single or solo. At a minimum, people who are not visibly partnered are often viewed as incomplete, perhaps not fully adult. They may be excluded from "coupled" gatherings or be discriminated against for opportunity or advancement. They may receive well-meant but unsolicited attempts to "fix them up" with potential partners — a phrase which implies that single people are somehow "broken."

It's also common to assume that being single for "too long" indicates a character flaw, such as difficulty with intimacy, commitment or relationships. Singles might be assumed to be sex addicts or asexual — and the social stigma against asexuality is another problem.

Singlism is somewhat weighted by gender, especially as people age. Women who are "spinsters" can be judged more harshly than men who are "confirmed bachelors."

> *I would like to see less pressure on people to partner up, as if we are not complete all on our own.*
> *There seems to be a social stigma around being single, as if it's only a transitory stage in between relationships. Or that single people should always be seeking a partner.*
> — *Megan, single and open*

The intimacy and support that solos offer in relationships sometimes is painfully devalued or dismissed, even by their own partners. It can seem as if people believe that solohood confers emotional invulnerability, or that solos don't care much about their relationships.

> *The hardest part for me is negotiating feelings. I was sleeping with someone for several months, who then told me we weren't dating nor emotionally connected. This happened despite our sharing emotionally intense experiences, and despite them asking me for emotional support.*
> — *Jackson, solo poly*

The social stigma against being single or solo can be internalized, too.

> *It took me a long time to become comfortable with the idea that you don't need to constantly increase the level of life entanglement with a partner for it to be a "real relationship," or for it to remain emotionally fulfilling for everyone involved.*
> — *Sarah, polyamorous*

Unlearning solo stigma can be an intensely liberating experience.

> *Only after reading Bella DePaulo's book "Singled Out"[50] did I realize that I can choose to be solo — a choice that has been tremendously empowering to me, since I can now also design my relationships!*
> — *Rachel, solo poly*

Solo Polyamory

There are many ways to practice polyamory. Most media coverage and public discussion about this style of consensual nonmonogamy focus on how couples and families approach polyamory. However, many solos are poly, too.

Speaking personally, I consider myself *solo poly.* This means I'm polyamorous: I only have nonexclusive intimate relationships with all-around informed consent, and also my relationships can get pretty deep. Sometimes I have more than one partner at a time; sometimes just one, or none. But this doesn't much affect how I live my life, because none of my lovers or partners will ever be moving into my home. I need my autonomy, and my space, in order to be the best person and partner I can be.

It can be tricky for solo poly people to navigate couple privilege. For instance, sometimes solo poly people have partners who are in life-entwined relationships, such as living with their spouse. Couple privilege can easily, and often inadvertently, disempower solos within such relationships.

Considerable effort and attention are needed from everyone in a poly relationship network to minimize the impact of couple privilege. Solo poly people often are keenly aware of these imbalances.

> *As a "single" person, it is often expected that I will do most of the heavy lifting in the relationship — such as who has to travel to whose house more often, and who can be more flexible with the schedule. It is assumed that this is easier for one person than a married couple.*
> — *Janey, solo poly*

Many solo poly people responded to my survey, and they shared how solo polyamory shapes their life and intimate relationships.

> *I am currently in three ongoing, committed relationships with women who all are married to someone else.*
>
> *I do not cohabit with anyone. I do not intend to commingle my finances with another person, ever.*
>
> *Additionally, I have a number of other quasi-sexual relationships with men and women who bring great amounts of joy into my life.*
>
> *— Master So-N-So, solo poly*

> *I live alone and meet all of my own needs. I am absolutely in love with my partner; this is my ideal relationship for where my life is at right now. We see each other once or twice a week and talk nearly every day. We don't do check-ins, but he is well aware of my other relationships.*
>
> *Since he is a single parent and very tied down to his child, and since I value solo polyamory, our agreement is that we are committed to each other, but we don't plan to progress our relationship into anything other than what it is.*
>
> *— Karisa, solo poly*

There is definitely room for deeper commitment in the relationships that solo poly people have.

> *I have very little Escalator-style progression going on in any of my relationships. But they do grow, and shift, deepen, or resurface according to the pace we all need. I love them all dearly.*
>
> *— SM, genderqueer and solo poly*

Being solo can offer distinct advantages in polyamory. Most notably, typically it's less complex or awkward for solos to have overnight guests.

> *I like sharing a household with my girlfriend, but I would also like to have intimate relationships with other people — someone else to sleep with, not just have sex with.*
>
> *That is a bit complicated. There are perhaps not many women who would like to come to my house and spend the night with me while my girlfriend is here. So I usually need to meet my other partners in their homes. This was easier when I had my own apartment.*
>
> *— WKD, in an open live-in relationship*

Solo polyamory is still a rather less common approach to polyamory. Most poly people prefer to have at least one nesting partner.

As a minority within a minority, sometimes solo poly people get accused of being "not really poly." And sometimes they face other stigma or suspicion within this subculture, perhaps even from their partners and metamours.

> *Single people are discriminated against in many areas. I've found this is even more true in the poly community.*
> — *Yohko, nonmonogamous*

There can be other tradeoffs to solo polyamory, as well.

> *I spent seven and five years, respectively, in primary relationships. So I strongly feel how hard it is not to have a default relationship. Without that, prioritizing is tricky. It's also harder to deepen a relationship when it doesn't fit on the Relationship Escalator.*
> — *SM, solo poly*

> *I do sometimes feel a void when I have some serious life event to go to, like a funeral, and none of my partners can be with me. When this happens, I remind myself that this situation might happen no matter what relationship approach I choose.*
> — *CB, solo poly*

Solo Monogamy

People who prefer to be monogamous can be solo, too. Sometimes monogamous people do this while in a relationship. However, solohood can also be an option for monogamous people who have a nonmonogamous partner.

> *I am monogamous and my partner is polyamorous. For the time being, I have no need, desire or time for another relationship. Maybe someday, maybe not.*
> *He has another partner who is poly and who lives much closer to him. We all live separately. I have no problem with our current arrangement.*
> — *Jean, monogamous, in a poly relationship*

Typically, monogamous-leaning people who choose to live solo do this just for part of life, while focusing on priorities such as a demanding education, recovering from a major breakup, executing a career change, regaining health or sobriety, or being a single parent or elder caregiver.

According to a 2006 study by Pew Research, 26% of unmarried U.S. adults were in "committed" (presumably monogamous) relationships. Meanwhile, a whopping 55% of unmarried adults were not seeking a committed relationship — especially women, elders and individuals who were widowed or divorced. Only 16% were seeking a committed romantic relationship. [51]

A 2012 feature article in *Boston Magazine*[52] explored the lives and experiences of several people who remain single by choice:

> At 51, Eva has never been married, has never craved children, and has no interest in settling down with anyone in the foreseeable future. The one thing she would like is for everyone else to just accept that she's happy that way.

Still, there is pervasive stigma and prejudice against people who choose to remain single, even when they are do not significantly diverge from other social norms. The *Boston Magazine* article continued:

> Amy, 38, says that between the tabloids and television, she can't escape it. She sometimes wishes she'd gotten hitched — even if it were just for 72 days like Kim Kardashian — if only to get people off her back.
> "People want you to have reached these major life goals that they've reached, and they want you to be like them," she says. "But I don't need a man in my life to make me happy."
> Steve, 43, hails from Lexington but now works in L.A. Remaining single has put distance between him and his married friends, he says. When he returns home, he finds them too focused on their kids to have a conversation. All right, he tells himself, I'll give them a call in 10 years.
> Tara, who's 38 and doesn't want to get married, ended up in an argument with her brother-in-law over Thanksgiving about whether having kids meant your life was automatically busier than a single person's could ever be. "Your whole life is you!" he shouted. That was the end of the conversation.

Solo While Nesting?

Some people who feel solo by nature may be circumstantially nested. They might live with one or more intimate partners, perhaps also sharing finances or other significant resources. They may even be legally married and raising a family together.

Within such nesting relationships, these individuals may consciously strive to maintain autonomy in many aspects of life — for instance, whether or how to conduct other intimate relationships, not automatically putting a live-in partner's feelings or wishes ahead of those of other partners, or not assuming that each other's free time is "we" time. These and other practices can help mitigate the effects of couple privilege within their relationship network.

However, nesting is such a strong social signal of the Relationship Escalator that other people usually treat nesting partners with couple privilege, regardless of how those partners view their own relationship and identity. This can influence their relationship, as well as any other intimate connections they might make. This means that, despite their efforts, they probably will face a social and relationship landscape that is quite different from that of solos who do not nest with any intimate partners. Consequently, it's debatable whether someone can be simultaneously in a nesting relationship and solo. However, anyone's life and relationships can benefit from adopting some aspects of the solo perspective.

Ety's long-term live-in relationship offers an example of maintaining a solo mindset while in a nesting relationship:

> *My live-in partner and I have always self-identified as being more very-close-friends-with-lots-of-benefits over any romantic definition. We've lived together in various capacities for about eight years — sharing finances, partners, and our lives — but they still are not someone I would introduce as my partner, significant other, or any other term like that. I've long held that we are two completely independent people who just happened to get tangled up.*
>
> *So I have a close friend, life partner, someone I know will always be there — whether we're seeing other people, having sex with each other, living together or not. I value friendship over all else. Having that closeness, bond, and history is important.*
>
> *We've had other sexual partners, often without really discussing it with each other. We've run over the sexual safety rules so many times that so long as nobody's being unsafe or unhealthy we don't much care about who might be having sex with whom.*

> *A huge piece of our relationship is the lack of labels and definitions. I tend toward the silence riddle with my relationships: "no sooner spoken than broken." I believe labels like "boyfriend/girlfriend," "husband/wife," "primary," etc. just tend to pigeonhole things in a way that makes me uncomfortable.*
>
> *We're friends, that's enough.*

Comparing Solohood to the Relationship Escalator

Choosing to avoid entwining the infrastructure of one's life with intimate partners departs from Relationship Escalator hallmark #2: merging.

Merging is probably the characteristic of Escalator relationships that affects partners' lives most profoundly. It shapes not just how they live and love, but their very identity and ways of connecting with others.

The example Escalator relationship story of Chris & Dana (see the preface) includes several common indicators and impacts of merging with intimate partners:

> *... At this point, Chris and Dana start considering themselves a couple. They start saying "we" quite often. When speaking to others, they usually refer to each other as "my boyfriend" or "my girlfriend."*

> *...Chris and Dana now spend almost all their free time together. Other people start referring to them as a unit: "Chris & Dana." They become each other's default companion for almost any occasion, especially high-profile events like holiday parties, where invitations ask for a +1. Now they socialize primarily with other committed couples.*

> *...After a few months of serious dating, Chris & Dana do what they've always assumed must happen next: they settle down and move in together. They share a bed and start to merge their finances.*

> *...They start making all major decisions together, and many minor ones too. They discuss (or at least assume) a long-term shared future. They become mutually accountable about their behavior and how they spend their time.*

> *...When Chris gets accepted into a prestigious graduate program in another state, Dana makes a career sacrifice so they can move and stay together. They support each other's goals, interests and dreams, which mostly align well; the ones that don't align so well mostly fade away.*

The social stigma against being single (or at least, being perceived as single) often plays a powerful role in keeping Escalator relationships together.

> *...Sometimes Chris or Dana yearns for something different — usually silently, since they fear growing apart. They believe that the only way to significantly change their relationship would be to break up, which would entail divorce, major life disruption, and stigma for them and their kids. That would be a failure. The thought of being alone (without their other half) and having to start over fills them with dread.*

Although interestingly, as Escalator partners reach middle age, the social aspect of their merging can relax considerably.

> *...Their kids grow up and move out, and the empty nesters peaceably share middle and old age. They develop some separate hobbies, and renew and deepen ties with friends and community.*

Part 3 Questions to Consider and Discuss

- Do you believe living together is an eventual necessity for a healthy, committed, long-term intimate relationship? Why or why not?

- How much personal autonomy do you prefer to retain within your intimate relationships? What does autonomy look like for you and your partner(s)?

- Do you agree with how this book explains the difference between *solo* and *single*? Why or why not?

- What might commitment look like in relationships where partners do not live together or otherwise entwine their life infrastructure?

- Which topics in Chapters 11-13 would you like to read more about, and why? What are your questions about personal autonomy within intimate relationships?

Share your answers or your own story online*
OffEscalator.com/resources/book1questions

* By answering any of these questions or sharing other personal information via the Off the Escalator website, you agree that the Off the Escalator project may quote your responses in our books, web content and in other material. You can answer anonymously if you like.

PART 4

LOVE, RANK AND FAIRNESS

14

UNDERSTANDING
RELATIONSHIP HIERARCHY

Hierarchy is the Escalator hallmark that hides in plain sight. For instance, the social norm of monogamy represents a rather extreme relationship hierarchy: *"There can be only one!"*

However, relationship hierarchy is not limited to romantic, sexual or emotionally intimate connections. It can affect how people handle any type of adult relationship.

It's common for people to mostly follow the traditional default hierarchy in terms of how they prioritize the time, attention, effort, resources and emotional intensity that they bring to their relationships with other adults:

- Spouse above adult family members.
- Immediate family above extended family.
- Lovers above friends, as reflected in the common language of friendship.
- Close or established friends above more casual or newer friends.
- Friends above community.

> *I am currently in two quasi-romantic relationships which are important to me. I don't consider either of these relationships secondary to the other. However, I do consider my other friendships secondary to these two relationships.*
> — *Kris, nonmonogamous*

Tellingly, it's very common for people to not count their platonic friendships as "relationships." When I ask people about their most important relationships, usually they don't mention friendships, without prompting — even though friendships often are the most enduring or strongest connections that human beings share.

On a related note, the social norm of relationship hierarchy can yield a special, bitter twist for people who are asexual or aromantic. When one's most intimate and treasured relationships involve little or no sex or romance, this way of loving can easily be dismissed as "just" friendship.

> *Sometimes people invalidate our relationship because they don't comprehend asexuality or celibacy.*
> — *Joann, celibate by choice*

There is one widely acceptable exception to the traditional ranking of relationship types: commitments to care for people who cannot fully care for themselves. Responsibilities toward children, elders, or the ill or disabled usually are permitted to trump any relationship or priority — including one's Escalator relationship.

Care-based relationship commitments also are widely recognized and honored by employers and institutions. But to merit this privilege, a commitment usually must involve family (by blood or marriage), or equivalent legally recognized relationships such as foster care.

> *My best friend (the most intimate, longest lasting nonsexual relationship in my life) had a terminally ill brother. My company did not understand why I wanted to take so much time off of work to be with her while he was dying. I had to take unpaid leave. They were not willing to call it bereavement leave since he was not a relative of mine.*
> — *Kiana, nonmonogamous*

Telltale Signs of Everyday Hierarchy

Hierarchy is so broadly assumed in mainstream culture that people often don't consciously acknowledge how they rank the people in their life. However, there are clues to this tendency, such as when people feel obliged to justify it when they prioritize a relationship in an unconventional way.

For instance, when a person has an Escalator partner, yet opts to bring a friend as their +1 guest to an important event, they'd probably volunteer an explanation for this deviation from expected behavior: *"My spouse is away on business, but my friend wanted to come."* In contrast, few people might feel similarly obliged to justify bringing their spouse, rather than a friend, as a +1 guest.

If being out as poly was safe, we would be free to be openly affectionate with each other, attend events together, and have others automatically consider all three of us when making invitations to family or couple's events.
— *Lisa, polyamorous*

In practice, relationship hierarchy means establishing a pattern of prioritizing certain relationships above others, perhaps even at the expense of others. Thus, a relationship hierarchy may be unconventional, even if the relationships that are being ranked are traditional. For instance, a monogamous person who habitually prioritizes a close platonic friend above their spouse is practicing relationship hierarchy — just with an unconventional ranking.

The traditional prioritization of romantic relationships often yields unfortunate side effects on friendships. Specifically, when embarking upon a new romantic connection, it's common to hyperfocus on romance while neglecting friendships. This can alienate friends, who may resent both feeling ditched as well as the social pressure to gracefully tolerate this behavior. Eventually, when a romance calms down or ends, people often are surprised and dismayed to learn that some of their friendships have fizzled, as well. That can make recovering from heartbreak or re-establishing social ties even more challenging.

Intriguingly, assumptions about relationship hierarchy and friendship sometimes work both ways.

When I got married, an old friend assumed that this meant that I'd be spending all of my time with my wife. As if being married completely defines me! I told this friend, "Yeah, I'm married and a family guy, but that just adds to who I already was."
— *Anthony, monogamish*

Hierarchy in Consensual Nonmonogamy

Off the Relationship Escalator (and especially in consensual nonmonogamy, where people might have more than one intimate relationship at a time) hierarchy takes on special significance. That's why, when people first hear of consensual nonmonogamy, they commonly ask:

- "Don't you have to choose between your partners sometimes?"
- "Who comes first?"
- "How can you be fair to everyone, especially when different relationships have different levels of commitment?"

These questions are complex and loaded. Many consensually nonmonogamous people addressed such matters at length in my survey. Hierarchy often is especially controversial in polyamory, where more than one intimate relationship at a time might develop deep emotional bonds, a sense of commitment or life entanglement.

That said, hierarchy may occur in any type of consensual nonmonogamy. Notably, swinging, monogamish relationships, and don't ask don't tell relationships nearly always embrace a very strong, clear sense of hierarchy — so much so that hierarchy might be considered a defining trait of these styles. In my survey, people who engage in these forms of nonmonogamy typically had little to say about hierarchy beyond indicating that they practice it. This could indicate that they believe hierarchy is beyond question.

In contrast, people who consider themselves nonmonogamous or open may or may not embrace hierarchy.

> *Ideally, I'd like to live with a primary partner and also be able to have feelings for other people. And sex, if we both considered that okay.*
> *Regarding other partners: It would be nice (and simpler) if one primary partner would be enough. Otherwise, it can get too complicated.*
> *— Rylee, in an open relationship*

> *In my relationships, especially with people who are new to unconventional setups, my partners often cast doubt on my capacity to avoid making hierarchical distinctions between them. Some assume that they always come first with me, or that they must be my Plan B.*
> *— Emily, nonmonogamous*

In polyamory, discussions between people who prefer hierarchy and those who prefer more egalitarian relationships can get quite heated — especially when they all end up together in a relationship network.

Also, the same individual might simultaneously hold different ranks in a poly relationship network. This can get confusing.

> *I'm married to my primary partner. The most difficult part has been understanding the roles, rights and responsibilities of secondary relationships — while also knowing that I'm a secondary partner to my two secondary partners.*
> *— Kitty, married and poly*

Thus, when discussing relationship hierarchy, usually it's helpful to clarify up front what people really mean by "hierarchy." Disagreement and disparities are fine, and perhaps inevitable. However, when people understand why they disagree about relationship hierarchy, this can help clarify compatibility. Or at least, they may find enough common ground to hold a constructive conversation on this subject.

In that spirit, for the purposes of this book, here's how I'm defining relationship hierarchy — recognizing that other people may use this term differently.

> *Relationship hierarchy: In consensual nonmonogamy, this is a framework for making decisions involving overlapping adult intimate relationships. Hierarchy describes how people functionally rank their intimate relationships relative to each other, at least in certain contexts. It also determines how and when this ranking gets exercised.*
>
> *In a relationship hierarchy, some or all choices that might affect more than one relationship are foregone conclusions. They are effectively decided in advance, by default, in favor of the relationship or partners deemed "primary."*

A decade or more ago, it was widely assumed that hierarchy was necessary for polyamorous relationships to function at all, let alone thrive. But today, many poly people question the ethics and efficacy of hierarchy.

Despite the rising trend toward more egalitarian polyamory, there is nothing intrinsically nefarious or unethical about hierarchical polyamory. It remains a valid option that can be practiced ethically, depending on the ethics and informed consent of all people involved.

Many poly people do find that hierarchy helps promote clarity and harmony in their relationship networks. That said, in my survey, primary partners were far more likely than secondary partners to say that hierarchy is mostly beneficial.

Typically, hierarchical polyamory works best where everyone involved clearly understands that they are practicing or participating in hierarchy, how that hierarchy works, its purpose, and how it might affect each person involved.

It also helps if there is clear and forthright communication about hierarchy (not just initially but periodically over the life of a relationship), as well as awareness and consideration of alternatives to hierarchy.

Primary Relationships

Generally, primary relationships and partners take precedence by default in some, most or all choices that might affect more than one relationship in a network.

In hierarchical polyamory, ranking labels such as "primary" and "secondary" are common but not universal. Some people use alternate labels that might imply rank, such as anchor/satellite. Also, some people rigorously eschew hierarchical labels, but still effectively practice hierarchy. Usually, behavior patterns over time are better indicators than labels about the presence or strength of relationship hierarchy.

Also, many people who are poly or otherwise consensually nonmonogamous habitually use hierarchical language, even though they might not practice hierarchy. For instance, people sometimes default to referring to their sole or longest-lasting intimate relationship as "primary," even if their feelings and behavior do not match this label. This can be confusing, especially when new partners enter a network.

What makes a relationship primary? In practice, primary relationships typically are heavily life-entwined, or they are clearly on track toward that Escalator-like goal. Social validation (such as legal marriage), living together (especially buying a home together) and co-parenting also correlate strongly with primary status.

Usually, only two partners in a network consider each other primaries. All of their other partners would be secondary, or at least not primary.

> *My girlfriend and I are each other's only primary partner — which for us means the only one we call "girlfriend," the only one we live with, the only one we are in love with, even the only one we go on dinner dates with. Neither of us has plans to acquire any other primary partners in the near future.*
> *— Liddy, nonmonogamous*

> *We definitely feel the idea of "primary" and "secondary" relationships is important. We share a very deep bond that we believe is impossible (in the near future) to duplicate due to the restraints of space and time.*
> *We would want other partners to respect our limited time for them, due to the importance of nurturing our primary relationship. And especially, our son's needs come first!*
> *— GMA, polyamorous*

However, some poly relationships allow for three or more people to be primary partners to each other.

> *I am married to my husband, and we share a female partner. The three of us live together. We're a poly triad, with all of us open to more relationships.*

> *We share homeownership, finances, and our lives. However, we preserve autonomous individual space — everyone has their own personal suite.*
> *— E.H., polyamorous*

Life entwinement and relationship longevity do commonly lead partners to consider each other primary and to practice hierarchy. This outcome is not inevitable, but it can be a struggle to fight that tide, thanks to common assumptions rooted in social couple privilege.

> *In my longest-lasting relationship (13 years), we have chosen to treat marriage as nothing more than a choice of tax status and a shared bank account. We have lived apart more than together, putting our careers first. Currently, we live together — but until nine months ago, my other partner (of seven years) had been living with us us well.*
> *Not having scripts for what an off-the-Escalator relationship looks like, we do sometimes find ourselves defaulting back to those scripts. When we're unconsciously operating from Escalator assumptions, there can be dissonance between what we each think we want for ourselves, or what we assume the others want, vs. what actually makes us all happy.*
> *— Bitsy, polyamorous*

In most hierarchical relationships, primary partners do value and consider the feelings, needs and wishes of their secondary partners. Primary partners are rarely oblivious or callous to the disproportionate power they wield over their secondary relationships. In my survey, primary partners often voiced their desire to be as considerate, or at least as transparent, as possible in exercising hierarchy.

> *How do I make sure I keep my husband as my top priority, while also taking care of my secondary partners' needs and wants, and not making them feel like they are expendable?*
> *— Rose, polyamorous*

Even so, secondary partners usually can be overridden by primary partners. Thus, hierarchy dictates the balance of power across a relationship network.

> *Our secondary partner (she wished only to be a secondary) decided after two months of dating us as a couple that she didn't want to date a couple. However, she still wished to date me.*

> *This would have been completely acceptable had it occurred initially. But after dating both of us, I felt it was completely unfair and wrong to continue to date her. The pressure on my primary partner would have been tremendous.*
> — *Roger, polyamorous*

Secondary Relationships

In hierarchical polyamory, *secondary* relationships are usually, though not always, less life-entwined. This means that they typically have fewer logistical and financial interdependencies. From this perspective, secondary relationships might seem intrinsically lighter, or more flexible, recreational or expendable.

But secondary relationships often grow quite substantial, with deep mutual emotional investment and commitment. Many endure for years or decades. It's even possible (though rare) for someone's secondary relationship to predate their primary relationship; the primary relationship doesn't always come first, chronologically.

In some cases, secondary relationships do entail significant financial or logistical entanglement, especially if a secondary partner moves into a household established by primary partners.

Partners in secondary relationships often adapt their lives to accommodate each other. They may even celebrate their commitment with a ceremony, similar to the Relationship Escalator. This can happen even when either of the secondary partners is also in a primary relationship. However, in a hierarchy, secondary partners usually adapt to each other only as much as the terms of the primary relationship allow.

Many secondary partners report being happy with this status.

> *One of my favorite relationship models is when I'm dating an already established couple. It is very important to me that their relationship is in good shape and happy.*
> *I never aim to "take one away" from the other. If they're experiencing hardship, it's time to give them space unless I am part of the healing.*
> — *Comet, nonmonogamous, genderqueer, pansexual*

> *In the past, I was a secondary partner to someone in a committed primary poly relationship. That allowed involvement under very clear terms. The need to clarify those terms meant that we talked about everything very explicitly, right away. I think any relationship would benefit from this.*
> — *Robin, currently monogamous*

Also, some secondary partners willingly defer to a partner's primary relationship.

As a secondary partner, sometimes I really want attention, but I have other people to consider. So my wishes may have to take a backseat to something else that is equally (or sometimes even less) important in my eyes, in order to be fair to the other people involved.
— Jennifer, secondary partner in a hierarchical triad

But it's sadly common for secondary partners to express profound dissatisfaction or frustration with their status, or with how they get treated by their partners and metamours in primary relationships.

Being a single secondary partner is not all roses and happy days. Sure, I value my personal space and time alone. But there also are deeply lonely times, and these are often painful.
Even worse, when I talk to my partners or metamours about these painful feelings, often that is not well received. Their common response is to "find someone else," or "leave the relationship." Those options are not always workable, or what I want to do.
So I learn to suck it up.
— Krissy, polyamorous

I've dated polyamorous people who have primary partners. Often, they assume that I will be interested in continuing our relationship regardless of how I am treated.
— Yohko, nonmonogamous

Good Intentions and Hierarchy

Relationship hierarchy typically springs from good intentions. Partners wish to ensure that their existing shared commitments, investments and goals are honored. They also wish to ensure that additional relationships complement their life and their primary relationship — or at least, that they do not derail it.

Also, relationship hierarchy can be viewed as a way to promote stability and minimize disruption in an established relationship — often to benefit children as well as partners. And it can be a tool to manage jealousy or other uncomfortable emotions, as well as disruptive change.

Hierarchy is often intended as a gesture of love, kindness, reassurance and mutual support between primary partners. They usually wish to help each other feel secure and happy, especially during the notoriously uncomfortable initial stages of learning to let go of exclusivity. Hierarchy can also support partners in coping with the stress of facing social stigma when they step off the Relationship Escalator.

Hierarchy can also be intended as consideration toward secondary partners — a way to manage expectations, to prevent secondary partners from being disappointed, or to discourage primary partners from making additional commitments that they cannot really support.

Sometimes hierarchy does help primary partners achieve these goals. However, it can undermine these goals, too. Good intentions often yield mixed effects.

For instance, it can be disheartening to realize that one's choices might disempower or hurt a loved one.

> *Our hierarchy tends to hurt our secondary partners' feelings more than ours. My primary partner and I have each other to lean on — but our secondary partners tend to get short shrift. Especially when I don't check in with my primary partner as often as I should when forming deeper emotional bonds with secondary partners.*
> *— Andrew, nonmonogamous*

This is why, when nonmonogamous people say *"Relationship hierarchy works for us,"* it's important to consider who, exactly, is included in that "us." Seeking all involved perspectives can yield a more complete picture.

Descriptive vs. Prescriptive Hierarchy

In polyamory, some people like to distinguish between *descriptive* hierarchy (which reflects how people's existing responsibilities steer their decisions in intimate relationships) vs. *prescriptive* hierarchy (which is usually intended to ensure that certain relationships retain top ranking perpetually).

Some people believe that their use of ranking labels such as "primary" and "secondary" merely reflects the level of accumulated investment in a relationship.

Theoretically, descriptive hierarchy leaves room for change as circumstances and responsibilities evolve. Thus, it may lessen as commitments wane. (For instance, as kids grow up, reducing parenting responsibilities. Or, as newer relationships persist and deepen, and thus begin to accumulate comparable investments.) For this reason, some people will only agree to participate in hierarchy which is descriptive in nature.

> *Except for relationships that involve children (and I am past child-bearing age), I don't like relationships that are hierarchical.*
> *— Querkee, nonmonogamous*

In contrast, prescriptive hierarchy typically seeks to preserve the relative ranking of relationships, despite changes in circumstances or responsibilities.

> *I would love to be in an off-the-Escalator relationship with one or more people. We would not feel the need to constantly give each other attention since we'd already know that no matter what when push comes to shove we're the primary couple. Any other relationships would not be serious — or at least not primary.*
> *— Vyanni, asexual*

Some people find that distinguishing between descriptive and prescriptive hierarchy helps them remain conscious of when their hierarchy might need to change. However, the practical impact of this distinction might otherwise be minimal. That is, a secondary partner or relationship might experience roughly the same limitations via either descriptive or prescriptive hierarchy.

Power Imbalances Inside vs. Between Relationships

In consensual nonmonogamy, relationship hierarchy concerns power imbalances that occur between overlapping intimate relationships — specifically, when an effectively primary relationship has the power to control or constrain relationships in the network that are effectively secondary.

This is different from power imbalances that might exist inside a given relationship: that is, between the partners in that relationship.

Historic and cultural sexism often give rise to a gender-based power disparity between partners in traditional opposite-sex relationships. For instance, the conservative religious belief that a husband should be the head of the household, and that a wife should be subservient to her husband, has substantially skewed the balance of power in many marriages. However, this overt practice has significantly waned in mainstream culture, to the point that in many places it's widely considered outdated and even potentially abusive.

For this reason, *polygamy* (plural marriage) motivated by patriarchal religious tenets is widely held to be abusive,[53] not because it's nonmonogamous, but because it can be sexist. Indeed, patriarchal polygamy is often practiced in ways that actively disempower and disadvantage women, violate their consent and pit them against each other. However, there are exceptions to this.[54]

Similarly, relationship hierarchy is not about which partner tends to dominate key decisions within the relationship, either through assertiveness or passive aggression.

Nor is it about which partner earns more money, has a more prestigious career, might be more conventionally attractive, or might be more emotionally or logistically independent. Such things often do create power imbalances within a relationship, but they don't necessarily impact other relationships that those partners might have.

BDSM and Relationship Hierarchy

Kink is not the same thing as relationship hierarchy. However, the interplay between them can be interesting.

One of the most popular realms of kink is *BDSM: bondage, domination/submission,* and *sadism/masochism.*

BDSM often involves *power exchange.* This is when consenting adults deliberately manipulate roles or power dynamics to heighten their erotic tension or emotional intensity. However, even though BDSM is often about who's "on top," when it's rooted in consent, it's really a collaboration among equals. This applies to how the power exchange works, as well as how the relationship works.

> *My Mistress owns me but prefers that I maintain a high level of independence when we're apart. Also, we're polyamorous; open to other significant erotic relationships in either of our lives.*
>
> *My Mistress is very careful to give the nonsexual relationships in her life the same level of care and commitment as her sexual relationships. That's been very inspiring for me to witness.*
>
> *I like feeling free, and owned, and valued.*
> *— NCN, solo poly and kinky*

Ideally, partners or playmates collaboratively design a power dynamic that suits, and benefits, them all. Submissives are as integral to this process as dominants. In mutually consensual dom/sub (D/S) relationships, submissive partners sometimes voluntarily yield to their dominant partners some deciding power over personal choices, perhaps involving other relationships.

Also, in mutually consensual BDSM, any partner or playmate can decide at any time to renegotiate or end their relationship, or how they will practice their kink — regardless of their status within the power dynamic. For instance, if a submissive partner decides that they no longer wish to ask permission to go out in the evening, they can renegotiate that agreement with their dominant.

Thus, in BDSM, relationship hierarchy (or the lack of it) might deliberately run counter to the negotiated power exchange.

There are many ways that I like to play, and some things I would not want my primary partner to be part of. I like being flogged and slapped around, but I don't feel that it is my primary partner's place to be inflicting that upon me. He loves me, therefore should not be subjecting me to pain.

I get to explore sexuality through play with my other partners — which is good for me, but also good for my primary partner. As a submissive, I feel protected, loved and cherished by my tops. They teach me, and I learn.

— Nora, poly and kinky

I would like to be involved in decisions about relationship issues and day-to-day issues. However, I also desire a power exchange dynamic where I take the bottom role. It's kind of hard to explain. I want more involvement than I do now, but I also want to be submissive. I'm not really sure how to make that possible.

— Jennifer, secondary partner in a hierarchical triad

That said, sometimes kinky people do prefer to implement a relationship hierarchy that mirrors their power exchange dynamic.

I enjoy maintaining a separate household from my Master but would live with Him if He desired. (There are pros and cons either way.) I would want to maintain significant emotional and sexual relationships outside our relationship — with the acknowledgment that He takes precedence.

— Chrisstopher, poly and kinky

Since BDSM culture generally has a strong focus on negotiation and informed consent (*"Safe, sane and consensual"* is a popular BDSM mantra), people experienced in kink may be especially likely to ponder the ethics of relationship hierarchy.

As my wife's Owner, I technically have veto power over her romantic relationships. But I consistently return to the conclusion that actually exercising that veto would be an abuse of power, as well as "doing it for the wrong reasons."

— Amazon Syren, married, poly, queer and kinky

In contrast, in hierarchical nonmonogamy, secondary partners may not have the power to negotiate for, say, more frequent dates, or for social recognition of their relationship. It can be true that the only real power a secondary partner holds within their own relationship is the power to leave. This might feel like no choice at all.

Therefore, a submissive in consensual BDSM might be relatively more empowered within their relationship, compared to a secondary partner in hierarchical polyamory. However, that all depends on how much active negotiation and consent is present in each of those relationships.

Story: Hierarchy Can Be a Phase

Relationship hierarchy is most commonly practiced by people who are new to polyamory, as well as in blended relationships where not everyone is polyamorous. This may be because hierarchy can make polyamory function somewhat like a traditional relationship, since hierarchy is an Escalator hallmark. Thus hierarchy can feel more familiar and secure to people who are accustomed to, or who might even prefer, monogamy.

Hierarchy can be a permanent feature of poly relationships. But often, as people gain experience with polyamory, they relax their hierarchy and move toward egalitarian relationships. Typically this shift starts when they begin to encounter firsthand how hierarchy can have mixed and unexpected effects on any relationship, including primary ones.

Sadly, this evolution often happens only after hierarchy has played a strong role in destroying important relationships. Chardsmure, who is currently single and poly, recounted the experiences that turned her off from practicing hierarchy.

> When I was in a primary poly relationship, our longest relationship was with another couple. They were swingers, and my primary partner had a hard time handling that, so he broke up with the wife in the other couple. For a brief time afterward, I continued my relationship with the husband in the other couple. But my primary partner felt this was unfair, since he no longer liked my secondary partner's wife.
>
> Meanwhile, my secondary partner's wife didn't like the fact that her husband loved me as much as he loved her — so she pulled the veto card.
>
> My secondary partner and I both tried to make compromises to allow our primary partners to be comfortable, thus allowing us to continue our relationship. But eventually, my primary partner demanded that I have no other romantic relationships that did not include him. He insisted that I accompany him on his search for another couple who we'd both like equally. But then he ended up falling for a woman in a poly couple who I had no interest in.

I remember how it felt to be told I could not have a relationship I so wanted, while I assured my primary partner that he was welcome to date the new woman separately. That blew up spectacularly when my primary partner began to completely ignore our relationship and focus every bit of his attention on his new partner.

After trying for months to talk and communicate with both of them, with no progress, I quit. I was then told that I was the one who was causing problems, by stifling his new relationship.

I held a lot of resentment over the fact that I had to end my happy secondary relationship, only to be ignored when he found love with another — and then being told that I wouldn't miss the intimacy of my relationship so much if I could "find someone." Sigh.

15

RULES, POWER AND HIERARCHY

Every intimate relationship operates on terms that are determined by its partners. How these terms get set varies by relationship style, and relationship hierarchy can play a big role here.

Rules and agreements are two common ways to explicitly set relationship terms. They can also be set implicitly, by making assumptions about what the relationship is and how it should function. That is common practice on the Relationship Escalator, but assumptions are notoriously prone to misunderstandings.

A *rule* is a requirement or restriction that must be met in order to enter, continue or change a relationship. Breaking a rule always entails negative consequences on the perceived offender: from blame, to curtailed options or withheld connection, to severing a relationship.

Hierarchical nonmonogamy generally allows relationship rules to be imposed upon third parties, impacting people who had no say in making those rules. Usually, the rationale for this is to "protect" the primary relationship. This is interesting, since the balance of power in relationship networks usually favors established or life-entwined relationships over newer or noncohabiting ones.

For example, the rule *"Secondary partners are not allowed to call primary partners at home"* is a non-negotiable rule sometimes imposed by primary partners.

> *My boyfriend is poly and married. I've had problems with not being able to call him at any time. Also, there are scheduling problems since his wife and kids come first. They have rules in place to protect their primary relationship.*
> — *Kara, solo poly*

Rulemaking power is asymmetrical. Typically, only primary partners get to make the rules. Secondary partners usually lack the power to renegotiate rules imposed upon their relationship or to impose rules upon a primary relationship, unless the primary partners decide to allow this.

> *Our relationship is open to additional partners, as long as everyone behaves according to rules established by me and my primary partner.*
> — *Josie, In an open relationship*

In my survey, several secondary partners mentioned feeling disempowered and discouraged by this power imbalance.

> *My boyfriend and his wife decide together how much he can spend with me; I am not part of that decision process. All I can do is make requests, hope that they will respond to it, and accept their decisions — or leave. They don't always respond to my requests, or sometimes ask me to wait for an undefined time.*
>
> *This relationship is not fulfilling for me. My boyfriend and I are deeply in love, and I would like our relationship to be more co-primary than secondary — but they are not open to that. He and I have one date a week, including sleeping over only once a month.*
>
> *He and his wife always want to make their relationship a higher priority than my relationship with him. This, I think, unfairly limits how much my relationship can grow.*
> — *Karen, polyamorous*

Examples of Rules, Agreements and Boundaries

Sex is a common and obvious area where rules arise in hierarchical polyamory. For instance, many primary partners agree to not use condoms during certain kinds of sex with each other (sometimes called *fluid bonding*). It's also common for primary partners to set a rule that no fluid bonding is allowed with any other partners. Typically, secondary partners are not permitted to advocate for relaxation of this rule, regardless of circumstances. Also, typically a secondary partner cannot require primary partners to start using condoms with each other.

Taken further, the one-way approach to sexual rule making can yield stunning examples of probable violations of the consent and privacy of third parties.

There are certain rules that go along with our relationship, and compromises that were made to satisfy both of us. Our rules are: wear condoms, no romantic shit, and take pictures.

My partner has a cuckold fetish that he was never able to explore, so when I set up a sex date with another person I am required to take pictures and/or videos.

We go online together and find people for me to set up dates with, both of us logged into the same account and responding to messages simultaneously. We laugh about the silly messages and he gets sexually excited when he sees me flirt with other people.
— *Amy, nonmonogamous*

In contrast, an *agreement* is made when all directly involved or affected parties negotiate together how their relationship, or set of overlapping relationships, will work. Unlike rules, agreements apply only to the people who participate in these negotiations. Agreements are never presented to third parties as take-it-or-leave-it choices. All parties are empowered to renegotiate existing agreements that may no longer fit well.

For example, a polyamorous couple might make agreements about how they will share responsibilities for, and space in, their shared home. When another partner moves in with them, all three partners renegotiate these agreements together. Everyone involved has a voice that counts in the process.

While rules are not unethical (as long as they are clearly presented up front as such to potentially affected parties), they are almost never necessary. It's usually possible to make agreements, rather than rules — even about sex.

My partner and I have an open relationship. We both have sexual and emotional connections with other people. Our agreement is that we don't need each other's permission, but we do disclose to each other that sex with someone else has happened.
— *Suzanne, in an open relationship*

Personal boundaries also can affect relationships. However, boundaries are individual choices, not terms of a relationship per se.

A personal *boundary* is an individual opt-out decision. Any individual may set their own boundaries, regardless of relationship style or status. A boundary is set when someone clarifies which situations or activities they personally plan to avoid.

Many people prefer solohood because this can make it easier to set boundaries in order to honor one's own needs and goals.

> *Not living together (nor planning to) reduces the role that everyday life plays in my relationships to a level I can manage. It also enables me to look forward to my partners having children one day. I don't wish to parent, but I could enjoy helping to care for a partners' kids.*
> — *Chris, solo poly*

If a boundary is transgressed, the consequence may be that the person who set the boundary might decide to exit that situation, or perhaps even leave the relationship. Thus, boundaries are about personal decisions, not controlling others — even though others might feel hurt or otherwise affected by the decision to enforce a boundary.

For instance, someone who prefers don't ask don't tell nonmonogamy might set a boundary that they do not wish to hear about their partner's other relationships. If, despite knowing this boundary, their partner insists on sharing unwanted information about other relationships, then the person who set that boundary might choose to leave those conversations, or exit that relationship.

Is It Really a Rule?

It's common for partners in consensually nonmonogamy to attempt to impose requirements or limits upon each other, or upon their other partners. However, they avoid calling these efforts "rules." Rather, they may label them "agreements" or "boundaries;" words that tend to sound fairer, or at least less harsh.

> *Even changing the words away from terms like "rules" didn't help. The rules-based behaviors and mindsets are buried deep and came out in many subtle ways — even from people who insisted that they don't "do rules" or who used other terms like "agreements."*
> — *Janey, solo poly*

Calling rules "agreements" can become a way to skirt accountability for how one's limits or requirements might impact other people. For example:

> *My spouse and I don't invest much emotion in our other sexual partners (although I tend to fall in love a bit in the beginning). Our agreement is that we can do anything we want as long as we check in with each other to make sure we're both okay with it. We don't yet feel secure in letting each other run loose.*
> — *Tove, in a sexually open marriage*

This "agreement" between primary partners effectively would impose two rules that would direct impact their secondary relationships and partners:

- "Our secondary partners will not receive significant emotional connection or support from us."

- "We reserve the right to limit the pace and scope of each other's secondary relationships."

The book *More Than Two* suggests the following test to see whether something presented as an agreement might really be a rule:

> *The absence or presence of empowerment is a litmus test for whether something is a rule or an agreement.*
>
> *Are all the people affected empowered to make their objections heard? Will the others consider the objections seriously, or can some people's objections always be overruled? What happens if someone wants a structure that doesn't work for someone else? Are negotiation and compromise possible, or is leaving the only alternative?*
>
> *Agreements empower people; rules enforce power imbalances.*
> — *Franklin Veaux and Eve Rickert, "More than Two"*[55]

Similarly, effective rules are sometimes described as boundaries. This can be quite confusing on the receiving end — especially for partners who desire reciprocity but who are effectively secondary.

> *I dislike having to consider my metamours' boundaries and needs. It can be very difficult to have such a big part of my life being determined by someone else.*
>
> *That's to be expected; I don't resent them for it. However, I'd also hope that they'd consider my needs, too, if the situation were reversed.*
> — *Annie, polyamorous*

Story: Consideration vs. Control

Hierarchical rules usually are not implemented heartlessly. Most primary partners want to hear their secondary partners speak up about wants, needs and feelings. Many primary partners also are willing to negotiate directly with secondary partners, or to accommodate their needs and requests to some extent.

> *Our outside relationships should not harm our primary relationship, but we try to be conscious and mindful of the needs of our secondary partners and metamours.*
> — *Eileen, polyamorous*

But sometimes, hierarchical rules amount to micromanagement, even toward relationships that don't yet exist. Jessica shared the rules of her open marriage.

> *My husband and I have been together for 13 years, the last two of which have been an open marriage.*
>
> *Our relationship structure is based on a set of stages which represents a set of allowable permissions that let each of us know where the other is in our extramarital relationships.*
>
> *Here are the stages we have defined, our rules for what is allowed with other partners. An outside relationship can only progress to the next stage if my husband and I both agree:*
>
> - *Stage 1. Kissing, hugging, snuggling.*
>
> - *Stage 2. Kissing like you mean it. Groping over clothing above the waist. Necking. Before this is approved, we'd both need to meet this new partner. Also, everyone must understand our stages: what is and isn't acceptable, and what stage they are authorized for.*
>
> - *Stage 3. Above-the-waist nudity, touching under "top" clothing, oral/breast contact, groping over clothing below the waist (including digital manipulation over clothes).*
>
> - *Stage 4. Masturbation, digital/genital manipulation/penetration. Full nudity and/or touching under "bottom" clothing level. Oral sex requires STI paperwork from all parties plus anyone else who they are sleeping with.*
>
> - *Stage 5: Vaginal/genital sex, anal/genital sex. Requires relationship status (defined as someone who, if we weren't married, you would take home to your parents to meet as your boyfriend/girlfriend). We both have to agree that this is what is happening. Also, STI testing paperwork is required, as well as much discussion and agreement of all parties.*

- *Veto (red card) can be exercised at any point. No discussion or explanation is necessary at the time, but must be done later when alone. Veto can be reconsidered; discussion may change things. Veto can happen at any point for any reason. All parties need to at all times know the situation.*

The hard part is explaining that there are rules to our relationship and that I'm going to stick to them.

16

ETHICAL ISSUES WITH
RELATIONSHIP HIERARCHY

Knowing right from wrong is important in any type of relationship. Ethics can signal whether a relationship is helpful or harmful to the people in it, or to others who might be affected by it. This can steer people's choices about who they wish to become intimate with, and how.

In my survey, many people discussed how ethics affect their unconventional intimate relationships. Typically this came up when they explained why they prefer or avoid a particular style of relationship, or when sharing their relationship problems, solutions or quandaries.

The significance of ethics was particularly striking when nonmonogamous people shared their experiences with, and views on, relationship hierarchy. This chapter attempts to scratch the surface of ethics off the Relationship Escalator by exploring the ethics of hierarchy in consensual nonmonogamy.

I read a lot about how prescriptive rules can be unfair to nonprimary partners. What about similar restrictions which are there because you want them there? Or because you are busy with job, hobby or children and thus have limited space in your life? Is it okay to prescribe relationships because you don't have the flexibility to offer anything else?
— Clare, poly

I'd like to learn more about the day-to-day work of maintaining relationships that are not primary. How do you give yourself to someone in an honest way, and also reserve the power for certain types of decisions to yourself or other partners?
— J, married and nonmonogamous

Relationship Ethics: It's Complicated

Confusion and disagreements abound concerning *ethics* and *morals,* especially regarding personal relationships, rather than professional or organizational codes of conduct. That's understandable. These terms have been defined and differentiated in many ways over centuries. Scholars and philosophers routinely contradict each other (and even themselves) about this distinction.

For clarity, here's how I'm using use these terms in this book:

- **Ethics** are personal and unique. They're how individuals prefer to walk their talk on their personal values. For instance, someone who values honesty might make an ethical choice to avoid saying untrue things. However, if that person values interpersonal harmony even more strongly, then they might make the ethical choice to avoid proactively volunteering honest, relevant information that might significantly disappoint or upset others — such as, *"I had sex with your spouse last week."* (Of course, someone else with different ethical priorities differ might view that as a lie of omission.)

- **Morals** are social, or at least group- or authority-based. They're the sense of right and wrong that people might adopt from society at large *(murder is wrong),* from a philosophy or religion *(suicide is a grave sin),* from family *(Father knows best, so it's wrong to defy him),* or from another group or community. This is how morals are context-dependent. For instance, consensual nonmonogamy may be considered gravely immoral in a conservative suburb, but not at a nearby swinger club.

The Conversation (an Australian website that publishes news and analysis from the academic and research communities) offered a similar take on ethics vs. morals:

"Ethics" leans towards decisions based upon individual character, and the more subjective understanding of right and wrong by individuals. Whereas "morals" emphasizes the widely-shared communal or societal norms about right and wrong.

> *Put another way, ethics is a more individual assessment of values as relatively good or bad. Meanwhile, morality is a more intersubjective community assessment of what is good, right or just for all.*
> — *Paul Walker and Terry Lovat, Newcastle University*[56]

The polyamory guidebook *More Than Two* sought to distill ethics in polyamory. The authors suggested two key axioms to support ethical decisions in relationships, rooted in considerations of basic human rights. [57]

> 1. *The people in the relationship are more important than the relationship.*
> 2. *Don't treat people as things.*

These axioms can help simplify decisions in any kind of relationship, not just poly relationships. For instance: is it ever acceptable to use people? To treat a person as a kind of prop to "spice up" a relationship? (Or, as *More Than Two* described it, as a "need fulfillment machine.")

For example, some people approach consensual nonmonogamy as a solution to the dilemma presented by the Relationship Escalator notion that there is one perfect partner who will meet every need. In real life, humans tend to fall short of this ideal.

> *No one person is required to meet all your needs. This was a huge revelation for me! I learned that I could get some needs met by one or more people, and other needs met by other people.*
> — *Andy, poly*

However, is it ethical to approach consensual nonmonogamy primarily as a way to fill in missing pieces? Assembling a Franken-partner may be more realistic than finding Mr./Ms. Right. But is it ethical to allow this motive to limit relationships?

> *In one relationship I wound up feeling like a marital aid.*
> — *Deanna, poly*

Why Power is Hard to Discuss

Ethical nonmonogamy is a popular phrase in poly circles. Still, conversations about the ethics of hierarchical polyamory commonly derail when people disagree about which ethics are most important in specific circumstances. And also, because people commonly have a hard time talking about power in relationships.

> *In polyamory, it can be painful that the prioritizing between different people and activities (which, to be honest, everyone does) has to be done in the open. It's a lot easier to pretend you're not making those choices.*
> — *Anders, poly*

Frank discussions about who holds how much power in an intimate relationship or network — and especially, who lacks this power, and whether that disparity is ethical — can feel divisive, unloving or even vaguely threatening or accusatory. It is frustrating to feel disempowered by relationship hierarchy, and uncomfortable to acknowledge one's potential complicity in disempowering a loved one.

> *I was a secondary partner to someone in a primary relationship. I felt a lot of frustration around their rules, which had been imposed on me by someone I hadn't met.*
> — *Morgan, polyamorous*

> *In the past, I've been badly hurt by a partner's other relationships. I'd like to someday have a primary partner. Consequently, I am tempted to limit my future significant relationships to us being the only primaries. But intellectually, I don't like such a limitation.*
> — *David, in an undefined relationship*

A common ethical complication in consensual nonmonogamy is that relationship hierarchy is nearly always a manifestation of couple privilege. This controversial topic tends to stir strong emotions, which can complicate discussion and negotiation. Also, some people deny that couple privilege exists, or that it is a problem — which tends to stonewall conversation about it.

Many people recognize that couple privilege exists, and understand that it can compromise fairness — a value that many poly people, in particular, hold dear. This can trigger questions about whether couple privilege might be ethical or avoidable. Usually, the descriptive vs. prescriptive hierarchy distinction is an attempt to address such concerns. Beliefs and feelings about couple privilege can color how secondary partners perceive good-faith efforts by primary partners to be considerate.

> *I constantly face couple privilege. When you're a nonprimary partner to someone who has a primary relationship, important decisions that affect your life are often made without you. Even when great effort has been made to consider your feelings, that is not the same as being part of the decision.*
> — *Master So-n-So, solo poly*

Third-Party Control in Relationships

Relationship hierarchy often fosters at least the appearance of third-party control over intimate relationships, which can conflict with ethics around autonomy. Usually, this involves limits on how much room a secondary relationship has to grow.

> *We limit our time with our other partners. This helps to keep things from getting too heavy while also allowing for a level of intimacy deeper than casual sex.*
> *— Andrew, in a hierarchical open relationship*

Sometimes third-party control involves requirements, instead of (or in addition to) limits. For instance, some primary couples require their secondary partners to be sexually and emotionally intimate with both members of that primary couple.

Requirements or rules concerning feelings, not just behavior, commonly prove impractical as well as ethically dicey. Notably, emotional requirements that attempt to make one person responsible for maintaining another person's sense of happiness or security tend to yield no-win situations.

> *Over a year ago, my husband became involved with a coworker, and I chose to let that develop into something. We basically tried to make a workable triad, but that recently failed.*
>
> *I don't know if it is couple privilege, but as things turned out, she and I didn't really get along. I felt that she didn't like me — at least, not the way I needed to be liked. I don't like my husband being involved with someone who doesn't like me. She never did become my girlfriend, emotionally. She was in love with him, and I was tolerated because I was his wife. That colored all interactions the three of us had together, and I felt very bad (insulted, negative, rejected) about it. Their relationship also had a significant time involvement, at least six hours a week.*
>
> *There was the sense that I should have been able or willing to let the relationship exist as a V, rather than a triad. That wasn't okay with me.*
>
> *My main goal (which may be why the triad failed), is that I wanted to maintain my marriage as the primary relationship. Not just because of the two young kids (although that's pretty important), but because my relationship with my husband is vitally important to me.*
>
> *I feel grief about everything failing, but I doubt that my husband's former girlfriend knows that.*
> *— Louise, married and nonmonogamous*

Consent, Hierarchy and Sneakyarchy

Most poly people strongly value all-around active consent in their relationships. For instance, many people choose to consent to playing an explicitly secondary role in polyamory — an arrangement that may prove satisfying for everyone involved, even for long-lasting relationships.

However, consent is an ongoing process, not a one-time choice. As circumstances and feelings evolve, people may change their minds about what they want in their relationships, and what they are willing or able to consent to. *"You signed up for this"* is often used to silence partners who attempt to renegotiate rules — by implying that consent, once given, is immutable.

Whether a relationship has rules, why those rules exist, whether they can change, and who has the power to initiate renegotiation are key ethical and emotional issues in relationship hierarchy.

> *Our culture defines a "good person" as someone who follows rules. I think this leads to rule-based polyamory, in which people attempt to demonstrate that they're still Good People by armoring themselves in new rules, despite breaking The Big Relationship Rule.*
>
> *I wish that being a Good Person commonly meant treating other people with empathy.*
>
> *— Chaos, polyamorous*

Generally, consent is considered valid only when it is informed. As with cheating, people cannot consent to an aspect of a relationship that they don't know exists. Still, hierarchy isn't always obvious — and that can complicate informed consent.

Sometimes, people who practice hierarchy (or who might do so, under certain circumstances) don't necessarily volunteer this information up front. However, many people prefer to avoid hierarchical nonmonogamy; they will not consent to hierarchy if they are aware that it's a price of entry. When people gloss over this disclosure, it can compromise informed consent.

Often, this omission is not intentional. Social assumptions of couple privilege make it relatively easy for established, nonexclusive couples to unthinkingly adopt the habit of favoring their existing relationship, even at others' expense. Similarly, they might not realize that this habit warrants disclosure and consent, because of how it can impact other people. And if they've never learned how relationship hierarchy can feel on the receiving end, they might unintentionally discount the perspective, needs or feelings of their other partners.

186

In contrast, some people avoid mentioning their hierarchy, more or less. That is, they know at some level that they practice relationship hierarchy, or that they would probably resort to it under certain stresses (jealousy, insecurity, illness, pregnancy, etc.). Yet they don't consistently volunteer this information to prospective partners. They may even deny being hierarchical, if it contradicts their optimism, excitement, self-image or professed values. Or if hierarchy might alienate a potential partner.

Consequently, hierarchy often appears by surprise, well after a nonprimary relationship has become established.

> *Recently my partner's wife has begun to believe in hierarchy. She consistently trumps my time with our shared partner. She's asked him on multiple occasions to prove his love to her by leaving me without the time that had been committed to me, or in my hour of need. She didn't use to interfere with our time together.*
> *— Ina, polyamorous*

Sneakyarchy happens when previously undisclosed or denied hierarchy impacts a relationship network.[58] This can be a rude awakening, especially when some partners are surprised to discover just how secondary they really are.

> *I totally ran into sneakyarchy in my last relationship. My partner kept saying, "We don't do hierarchy. What works for me in my relationships is what works for me in my relationships." However, we never could plan trips for occasions like my birthday since he couldn't commit in advance to go away; something might come up with his family. Yet he would often commit to taking trips with his wife, even without their children.*
> *He was definitely kidding himself about not being hierarchical. That became evident as our relationship continued. I honestly think that he just couldn't see his own hierarchy and couple privilege.*
> *— Emily, solo poly*

That said, sneakyarchy is an equal-opportunity pitfall. It can sneak up on anyone in consensual nonmonogamy, including primary partners.

> *It sort of evolved that none of our other relationships were viewed as potentially approaching the level of involvement of our marriage. We weren't doing this to protect our couplehood. Rather, it just didn't occur to us that other relationships might become more significant or entwined in our lives.*

> *A couple years ago he had a serious girlfriend of about a year. She broke up with him because she could not handle being "secondary" (her term, but I guess that was pretty accurate in terms of life entanglement) without having a primary partner of her own. His devastation made us look at and fix a bunch of things about our marriage.*
> — *Jen, married and poly*

Sneakyarchy often wreaks considerable emotional turmoil; it often leaves people feeling blindsided and betrayed. But from an ethical perspective, the key problem is that sneakyarchy deprives people of the opportunity to consider, and consent to, participating in a hierarchy.

How can people tell whether sneakyarchy is afoot? This can be murky. Patterns of relationship choices over time tend to be more telling than individual incidents. For instance, does someone usually seek permission or approval from a certain intimate partner before, say, scheduling dates or starting to have sex with others? Or, do they usually comply when a certain partner asks them to cancel or postpone plans with other partners, or to refrain from exploring or deepening other relationships?

When people engage in such behaviors while also believing, and contending, that third-party control over relationships is unethical, mixed messages can result.

> *I started dating a guy who explicitly rejected hierarchy, but would "check in" with his (functional) primary partner about any milestone we might have. That's fine, I do this sometimes with partners if my decisions will impact them.*
>
> *Except that when she vetoed something, which happened more than once, it wasn't actually called a veto. Rather, he said he was "just being considerate of her feelings."*
>
> *This came with no conversation with me; just "I'm not doing [X activity] because [primary] said it would upset her." Or, once, "I asked [primary] and she said it would be a bad idea, so I'm not going to do it."*
> — *Zan, polyamorous*

Veto Power

Veto power is when primary partners agree that they can require each other to curtail or end a secondary relationship. It's an extreme, controversial manifestation of relationship hierarchy.

Romantically we have agreed not to allow any other relationship to threaten the integrity of ours, and to end any that does.
  — *Sentou, poly and swinger*

My boyfriend and I have veto power over each other's relationships. For instance, if I were interested in a new guy, but my boyfriend felt he was getting bad vibes for whatever reason, he could say "no." Then I wouldn't pursue that relationship.
  — *Sarah, in an open relationship*

A kill switch is the ultimate form of third-party relationship control. Furthermore, it represents the power to summarily negate all investment of time, energy, emotion and commitment that people might make in secondary relationships, even over the course of years. Such a substantial risk can discourage people from investing much into secondary relationships, which can undermine them from the start.

Another ethical concern is the way that veto power can obscure personal agency and accountability. Someone who says, *"I must break up with you. I have no choice, my primary partner demands it,"* has, in fact, personally decided to end that relationship. Semantically shifting responsibility for this choice onto a third party (or phrasing a breakup decision in terms of "we," when only primary partners comprise that "we") can deflect or downplay personal accountability while hurting someone.

Veto power is almost always intended to protect established relationships. However, its existence casts newer or less-entwined relationships as intrinsic threats, an assumption with ethical implications. Is it fair to get intimately involved with someone while treating them as a threat? The mere possibility of a veto lingering silently in the air can lead people to feel wary and insecure in their relationships; to not fully trust their partners and metamours.

Also, primary partners sometimes use veto power to manipulate each other in potentially unethical ways.

When I was married, my husband was initially excited by the idea of polyamory. It turns out that his conception was more like swinging. He became very interested in using guilt-trips and veto power whenever it looked like I was becoming emotionally attached to a partner.
  — *Clothilde, solo poly*

Addressing Relationship Risk

When people practice polyamory and also value fairness and consent, walking that talk can feel profoundly scary. They might fear, for instance, that prioritizing those values could jeopardize the considerable time, money and effort they have invested in a home, a family, a lifestyle or future plans. This perception of risk fuels many strategies, including relationship hierarchy, to control or prevent change.

Desiring safety, security and stability in one's intimate relationships, and in life, is not wrong. Still, it helps to realize that people usually have many options to support feeling secure, to protect shared investments, and to improve the chances that partners will continue to meet existing commitments. These goals need not rely on limiting or controlling other people or relationships. Indeed, often other people and relationships can actively support these goals.

It's important to consider the big picture of risk. Love and relationships, of any kind, are never, ever safe. Even on the Relationship Escalator, risk is omnipresent. Monogamous partners abandon and betray each other all the time. And eventually, everyone dies. Any type of relationship might end at any time, for any number of reasons. How people perceive and manage relationship risk largely comes down to how they see their options.

Considering personal levels of relationship risk tolerance is precisely why many people make the ethical choice to engage only in forms of consensual nonmonogamy that tightly regulate intimacy beyond an established relationship.

> *To me, if the intent is to stay with a certain primary partner "no matter what," that's partnered nonmonogamy, not polyamory. The extra level of "whatever goes" in polyamory is probably not what I want. This is partly a desire for stability on my part, and to avoid hurting people.*
> *— Ace, gay man in a hierarchical open relationship*

Story: Be Excellent to Each Other

Relationship ethics don't need to be complicated. Some of the best advice on how people can treat each other in any kind of relationship is stunningly simple.

> *Be excellent to each other.*
> *— Bill & Ted[59]*

> *Don't be a dick.*
> *— Will Wheaton[60]*

Many survey participants noted how considering one's personal values and ethics, and being able to discuss them clearly with partners and metamours, typically yields better relationships while also supporting the greater good. This takes practice. However, in consensual nonmonogamy, such introspection and conversations often become remarkably valuable when navigating relationship hierarchy or seeking alternatives to it.

While sharing her experience of a live-in poly relationship in which hierarchy contributed to emotional abuse, Dragon Fox offered this insight.

> *There are never going to be rules that suit to everyone, to govern how we should behave or what we should do. But there are things we should all value. For instance: We should all have the utmost respect for others as the incredible human beings they are, as well as the utmost respect for yourself as the unique and valuable being you are.*
>
> *Also, honesty — especially regarding our perceived weaknesses and failings. And compassion for ourselves as well as others. And the realities of creating love; it can be easy, it can be hard, and it will almost always be both in turns.*
>
> *Not everyone is going to fit a formula. Still, as long as we treat each other with honor and try not take others for granted or treat them as less important, then we should at least be on the right track for living in a better world, not to mention having better relationships.*

17

EGALITARIAN RELATIONSHIPS

In mainstream culture, the default pecking order of relationships isn't nearly as rigid as it used to be.

For instance, in recent decades, mainstream culture has become more accepting that people may wish to spend a fair amount of time with friends, community or alone   rather than be socially joined at the hip to their Escalator partner whenever they're not occupied by commitments to work, parenting and caregiving.

Similarly, platonic friendships with potentially attractive or available people have become commonplace and accepted. They are now less likely to be reflexively cast as distractions from, or as obstacles or threats to, existing or potential relationships.

> *In my experience, there's no longer any need to worry if your spouse*
> *has friends of the opposite gender. But my grandmother was worried*
> *that my husband would be unhappy that I had male friends who I spent*
> *time with and who seemed too "huggy."*
> — *Winona, married*

However, relationship hierarchy still appears to reign over some common choices that people make between conventional relationships.

For instance, when people cheat in an ostensibly monogamous relationship, the "illegitimate" partner typically is assumed to be unimportant and disposable (unless they're being readied as a replacement Escalator partner). Also, when cheating is discovered, veto power is assumed. That is, the partner who was "cheated on" is presumed to have the right or duty to demand an immediate end to the clandestine relationship, and to insist that all contact with the other partner cease.

Meanwhile, off the Escalator, relationship hierarchy is not dying off anytime soon. For instance, hierarchy remains a defining feature of several popular approaches to consensual nonmonogamy: swinging, don't ask don't tell, and being monogamish.

But in polyamory, at least, hierarchy appears to be on the wane.

As the culture of modern polyamory emerged in the 80s and 90s, hierarchy was generally presumed necessary. But today, it's becoming less common for people in poly relationships to use hierarchical terms like "primary" and "secondary." Or to claim veto power or unilateral rule-making power. Or to expect that newer or less life-entwined relationships should always defer to more established ones.

It's still common for people who are new to polyamory to initially practice a strong primary/secondary hierarchy, since this may feel more familiar and thus secure. But often, experience fosters a preference for more egalitarian polyamory. Sometimes this transition is difficult for their partners to accept.

> *Since my divorce, I've been on what I've been calling my "no-primary-partners" kick. When I left my hierarchical polyamorous marriage, my then-secondary partner was somewhat offended that he didn't rise up the Escalator upon my divorce.*
> *— Mitsuko, solo poly*

While the trend away from hierarchical polyamory is sometimes just semantics, for many people, egalitarian polyamory has proven to be a valid, feasible and more fulfilling approach.

> *My partner and I are both polyamorous. I have one other partner, and she has no other major partner — but both of us can, and sometimes do, have other lovers.*
> *We aren't "primary" with each other. Any of these relationships might become equal to, or more than, our relationship to each other.*
> *— Greg, polyamorous*

In open or poly relationships that are more *egalitarian*, hierarchy plays little or no role in decision making. Each partner and relationship in the network holds unique value. Someone's level of empowerment within their relationship, or a relationship's capacity to develop or deepen, is not predetermined explicitly by rank, nor implicitly by longevity or level of life entwinement.

Egalitarian relationships are about partners having an equal ability to effectively advocate for themselves in their own relationships. Also, partners have a reasonable expectation that their self-advocacy will be met with consideration and negotiation, not *"my way or the highway."* Empowerment means more than the Hobson's choice to stay or go.[61]

Of course, egalitarianism doesn't mean that every partner always gets everything they want, or that every conflict must be resolved through compromise, or that no one is allowed to have priorities or hard limits. Rather it means that all partners are equally empowered to speak up. They can expect to be heard and considered. Third parties cannot override the decisions partners make about their relationship.

Much like making a new friend or having a new child, in egalitarian relationship networks, newer or less-entwined relationships are honored as having intrinsic value and a right to exist and grow. No person or relationship trumps or precludes others by default. Each relationship gets to discover its own natural level and rhythm. Networks adapt to accommodate evolving, emerging and waning relationships.

> *I can commit to people and relationships without needing to exclude other relationships. Each relationship can be looked at independently of how the other relationships are doing.*
> *— Fruitnymph, polyamorous*

Some nonmonogamous people prefer more egalitarian relationships as a way to stay true to their personal values. They believe strongly that every individual within a relationship network counts as a complete human being whose feelings, needs, goals and priorities matter as much as those of anyone else in the network.

> *I don't do primary vs. secondary relationships. That feels like I'm saying my relationship with the "secondary" partner is less important.*
> *Even when I've been in both casual and serious relationships at the same time, I would not have sacrificed the casual relationship for the serious one, because I cared about my casual partner quite a lot. I just didn't want to spend the rest of my life with him.*
> *— Skyler, in an open relationship*

Today, many poly people avoid labeling relationships as "primary" or "secondary." Usually they simply refer to partners or lovers without explicit or implicit rank. Some may call a relationship *nonprimary* to clarify that it is not nesting or otherwise life-entwined, but this flexible label still leaves room for an intimate relationship to be as emotionally deep, committed or long-lasting as those partners desire.

Egalitarian relationships tend to rely on trust and accountability, rather than rules and roles, to keep relationships strong and healthy.

> *There are no limitations or restrictions placed on any of us. I trust my partners to be mature adults and to make choices in line with their desires and needs. If I didn't, I wouldn't be with them.*
> — *Jon, polyamorous*

Mutual goodwill is essential in egalitarian relationships. This is when everyone involved offers and assumes goodwill, and tries to be considerate, and is willing to communicate directly as needed. With these practices, it's more likely that partners and metamours will treat each other as complements, allies or resources, rather than as threats or rivals.

> *We tend to look outside the box for solutions that will work for everyone involved, and that will promote a feeling of goodwill instead of competition between metamours.*
> *I believe that, regardless of jealousy, insecurity, etc., if we focus on treating everyone involved with respect and compassion, we can come up with solutions where everyone wins.*
> — *Tracy, poly and kinky*

Many people strongly value fairness. Consequently, they are unwilling to expect some partners or metamours to shoulder disproportionate risk, simply because their relationships are newer or less life-entwined.

> *I would definitely love to live with and share my life with my partner. However, "primary" status is not an issue for me.*
> *I am monogamous; my partner is polyamorous. I feel it's important that his relationships be fair. As long as I feel important, valued and desired, I am happy.*
> — *Jean, in a poly relationship*

Fair and Equitable, Not Identical

Fairness and equity are key values in egalitarian relationships, but not necessarily in the way people often assume.

Fairness is about making choices that support equitable outcomes, taking into consideration factors which might place some people or relationships at an initial disadvantage. Fairness creates room for people to treat each other well, regardless of differences in goals, needs or circumstances. In relationships and networks that are egalitarian, people tend to prioritize fairness in their ethical choices.

> *I asked [my mother] how she could do it, love them both, and how they could stand it. And she said, "Love is not a pie, honey. I love you and [your sister] Ellen differently because you are different people, wonderful people, but not at all the same. And so who I am with each of you is different, unique to us. I didn't choose between you. And it's the same way with Daddy and Bolivar. People think it can't be that way, but it can. You just have to find the right people."*
> — *Dialogue from "Love Is Not a Pie," short story by Amy Bloom*[62]

Equity often is confused with equality. The key difference is that *equality* is about sameness (treating all people or relationships identically), while *equity* is about being invested and having a voice that counts.[63]

Egalitarian polyamory strives to be fair, but not necessarily equal. It's not about every partner getting precisely the same amount of time, sex, love or resources. It's not about putting every partner on the mortgage or spending precisely 2.33333 nights per week with each of your three partners.

Rather, egalitarian polyamory supports equitable empowerment and opportunity, not equal portions in a measurable sense.

More Than Two includes a chapter on "empowered" relationships. Basically, this is an egalitarian approach to polyamory. The authors of that book acknowledge that relationships in any network usually aren't all starting from the same point; some may have accumulated more investment and obligations than others. Nor is it a common goal that all relationships should become identical to each other. But if the network is egalitarian, new relationships are not stunted by design.

> *People who have been together for a long time often have a vested "sweat equity" in the relationship. They've made sacrifices and incurred obligations together.*
> *...In an empowered relationship, a person is not told, "You have the same standing and the same voice in these existing obligations and responsibilities."*
> *Rather, that person is told, "As you invest in this relationship, you, too will build sweat equity. You will not be denied the opportunity to do this."*
> — *Franklin Veaux and Eve Rickert, "More Than Two"*[64]

In egalitarian polyamory, the quest for fairness generally precludes third-party power. That is, only the people who are partners in a relationship have the power to make decisions about their relationship; third parties (such as metamours) cannot override partners' choices. That said, the quest for fairness usually includes active consideration of people who might be affected by a relationship decision: asking about their feelings and listening to their suggestions.

When partners manage to treat each other as equals, when each relationship in a network has room to deepen and evolve, and when there is mutual goodwill and direct communication, it is generally easier to make relationships and networks feel more fair.

For a relationship network to be fair, everyone must be flexible. In particular, it helps if established partners are willing to adapt to, accommodate and respect newer partners and relationships. This is relatively uncommon in hierarchical polyamory.

> *When my husband and I have other partners, all of us work together to negotiate time. With his last girlfriend, I would encourage him to take as much time as he felt he needed with her — and of course, I offered more time and patience for his new relationship energy (NRE).*
>
> *He's also fine with me taking the time I need when NRE takes hold of me, too. Once the NRE settles, it usually works out to two nights a week with our other partners.*
>
> *We don't have rules, just safer sex boundaries. I request that if he ever chooses to stop using condoms with another partner, I'd prefer to be kept in the loop if they are discussing it — or let me know if they make that decision without me, so I can take proper precautions.*
>
> *We have had some awesome partners, and we are so grateful to have had confident metamours. We've never had any issues. He has great taste, and he's never disrespected me or my time.*
>
> *— Abbey, poly and married*

Increasingly, established partners who cohabit or are otherwise life-entwined are choosing to organize key aspects of their lives so that they can offer their other relationships more consideration, respect and room to grow.

> *My nesting partner and I recently secured a new home to live in. To make things work well, we sourced a house that had two separate living quarters. We have created a space where we can host others without significantly disturbing each other. We schedule our time with others, as well as ourselves; we don't presume each other's time is necessarily ours.*
>
> *We've consciously decided to conduct our relationship with others in mind. We actively practice communication that can be uncomfortable, to support this goal.*
>
> *— Leland, ethically nonmonogamous*

However, some people feel an emotional pull to divide relationship resources into equal portions. Sometimes this practice can ease tensions or support goals of fairness or mutual satisfaction.

> *When I had three partners, I tried to spend two days each week with each partner. I let them choose which days, and the one with the most restrictive schedule got to choose first. The extra day was meant to be for myself. My goal really was to be on equal footing with all my partners.*
>
> *I suppose I could have spent different amounts of time with different partners and still achieved that — but that didn't feel quite fair to me.*
> — *Bianca, polyamorous*

In rare cases, people feel so strongly that hierarchy is wrong for them that they actively dismantle manifestations of hierarchy in an existing relationship.

> *My former primary partner and I decided to be nonhierarchical instead. Now we treat all of our partners as equal and unique. We are currently dissolving our shared household to live separately while continuing to co-parent our children.*
>
> *Rather than considering this a failure (as it would be in the Escalator model), we consider this a healthy transition to a more sustainable relationship — while meeting more of our individual needs.*
> — *Andy, polyamorous*

Situational, Inclusive Negotiation

In egalitarian networks, partners and metamours handle relationship quandaries collaboratively as they arise. Decisions are based on current needs, feelings, priorities and circumstances. Everyone is empowered to negotiate in their own relationship, and to consult on matters that affect them. Everyone can suggest solutions. A big potential advantage of this approach is that it can yield more options and resources across a network. When challenging circumstances hit, egalitarianism can make it easier for everyone in a network to pitch in.

In my own life, while I was married, for several years my spouse and I were in a quad relationship with another couple. Early in that relationship, my boyfriend and his wife had their second child. The support, care and love that my spouse and I were able to offer our partners, and their kids, helped ease the logistics of pregnancy and parenting. This egalitarian approach generally strengthened all of the relationships, including between metamours and between all of the adults and both kids.

In contrast, in hierarchical polyamory, secondary relationships often get curtailed or ended when primary partners are expecting a new child. Typically this is based on the assumption that secondary partners are a drain or luxury, not a resource.

> *What's radical about polyamory is not that you have more than one partner. It's that you don't just jettison some partners if things get hard.*
> — *Robyn Trask, executive director of Loving More* [65]

In more egalitarian relationships, decisions are not presented as a done deal to the people who are affected. Rather, when challenges, conflicts and opportunities occur, everyone involved can propose options and raise considerations.

> *My partner and I had been in in a romantic relationship for two years when he began dating an old friend in an emotionally serious way He and I did not live together.*
>
> *I am estranged from my family of origin, making the holidays difficult. The first holiday season after he started dating my friend, I still wanted to spend Thanksgiving and Christmas with my partner, like we had in years past. But my new metamour wanted to take him with her to spend Thanksgiving and Christmas with her family, instead.*
>
> *I decided that of the two holidays, Christmas was the most potentially triggering for me to spend alone if I could not secure other local plans. We all discussed it together and came up with a plan.*
>
> *We agreed that he and I would host a pre-Thanksgiving potluck for friends at my house. Then he would spend Thanksgiving day with her family, and call me that afternoon. Later, he and I would spend Christmas Eve and Day together, and he would spend New Year's Eve with her.*
> — *Nicole, solo poly*

This process isn't always fun or smooth. Situational, inclusive negotiation usually does take more time. And it can feel like more work, especially when people are first learning how to do it.

> *In a poly relationship network, it can be a struggle to take everyone's needs, comfort levels and boundaries into consideration. It's like taking a vacation with five people and trying to please everyone.*
> — *Julia, polyamorous*

That said, people who handle relationship decisions and challenges this way often say it feels fairer and creates less stress. These benefits can help them feel more certain and satisfied about their decisions, even hard ones.

> *For me, the most difficult part of my nontraditional relationship has been negotiating. Since there are no pre-set guidelines, everything needs to be talked about!*
>
> *In a couple of my relationships, the nonmonogamy guidelines were negotiated at the baseline for at least four or five days. And then, they've been the subject of discussion later. That can be a little exhausting, but it needs to be done.*
>
> *— Jackie, genderqueer, poly and kinky*

Fortunately, inclusive negotiation does get easier with practice, and it can be better than dealing with the fallout from default or unilateral decisions.

> *I've learned about how to have difficult conversations. I used to fear that so much, not wanting to rock the boat. I would get so anxious. Now I bring things up when they bother me, and the results have been fantastic. It dulls my fear of the worst happening.*
>
> *— Ruy, solo poly*

Some egalitarian poly networks are methodical about having regular, inclusive check-ins for scheduling and other purposes:

> *The five of us (my partners and metamours) hold a monthly meeting, usually over Whatsapp or Skype. We methodically make plans for the next month or two, taking each week in turn.*
>
> *Each of us gets to propose possible events or activities. This process allows us to plan who gets to see who when. It works really well so far.*
>
> *This is not about making sure everyone gets equal time with their partner(s), but rather about us all getting an equal platform to voice ideas and concerns.*
>
> *— Sam, solo poly*

Other networks are less formal; negotiation and accommodation happen more via habit and style. EJ, who is solo poly, has adopted this approach with her partner and his wife:

> *I can only spend limited time with my partner because of our work schedules and other commitments. So when I'm with him at the home he shares with his wife, and she's heading to bed, she always asks if we want her to take the guest room. We always tell her no, but she always offers.*
>
> *When we all go somewhere together, who sits where depends on who wants to sit where — not on some choreographed seating arrangement.*

When my partner stays at my house, his wife texts and/or calls just as she would any other time. Similarly, I feel free to contact him when he's at home with his wife. Neither my metamour nor I have a goal of disrupting each other's evening, and we both know it. It's totally cool, and it actually makes both of us happy.

My priorities are very different from my metamour's, along with life experiences, personalities, skills, etc. I get moral support in the ways I need it. And I support him, her and them in the ways they need it.

Example: In the past couple years, we have all moved house at some time. I supported them by helping her pack and stay focused. They helped me by getting the hell out of my way and arranging for a trailer.

Comparing Nonhierarchical Relationships to the Escalator

In traditional intimate relationships, there are few easily visible indicators of Relationship Escalator hallmark #3, *hierarchy,* aside from the way that monogamy accords special rights and status to only two people. This is because, on the Escalator, monogamy represents more than a preference for sexual conduct. It is also an emblem of how an Escalator relationship takes precedence over nearly every other adult connection, especially friendships. The Escalator relationship story of Chris & Dana *(see the preface)* indicates a few ways that relationship hierarchy commonly affects the friendships that Escalator partners may have with others.

...Chris & Dana now spend almost all their free time together. This means they see their friends far less often, but they assume their friends understand and support this.

...Several of their single friends lament how little they see of Chris or Dana these days.

...They still each maintain connections with friends, although their friendships mostly don't feel as close or important as they once did.

In contrast, egalitarian relationships (as well as relationship anarchy) tend to put life-entwined relationships on an equal footing with other kinds of relationships.

≈

18

RELATIONSHIP ANARCHY: DO-IT-YOURSELF LOVE

Some people don't find it useful to sort their relationships into categories. Rather, they prefer to focus on the unique, emerging and evolving nature of their connection with each person who matters to them. They treat each relationship as a special case, with its own intrinsic value. And they consciously and explicitly collaborate to design how each relationship works.

There's a relatively new and not-yet-commonplace term for this ultimate do-it-yourself approach to relationships: *relationship anarchy.*

More a philosophy than a specific relationship style, relationship anarchists do not gauge the importance of a relationship based on whether it involves sex, romance, life entwinement, or ties of blood or marriage. Rather, they prize autonomy, accept that people are in constant flux, and believe in negotiating and adapting relationships to suit the people in them.

> *I do not have formal relationships. I do have significant committed*
> *relationships. Some of these are sexual, erotic or romantic; others not.*
> *— Morgan, relationship anarchist*

The *Short Instructional Manifesto for Relationship Anarchy* by Andie Nordgren lists these principles for relationship anarchy: [66]

- Love is abundant, and every relationship is unique.
- Build from love and respect, not entitlement.
- Identify your core relationship values.

- Don't let fear lead you.
- Allow for the lovely unexpected.
- Fake it 'til you make it: relationship anarchy can feel awkward and scary at first.
- Trust is better than relying on control of partners, or validation from them.
- Enact change through communication.
- Customize your commitments.

The cumulative impact of such simple principles can be profound. They have an overall egalitarian effect of placing all of a person's relationships on more equitable footing, and allowing considerable autonomy, flexibility, commitment, responsibility and collaboration.

> *Essentially, I view my relationships as having varying dimensions, including affection, mutual interest, sex, cohabitation, co-parenting, etc. Not all of these will be present with all partners to the same degrees.*
> *Everyone in my network passes the "friends" bar. But beyond that, I have a variety of connections of varying strengths. Some of these I would like to advance on some dimensions, others not — but I don't need to.*
> *I also don't need to govern others' relationships with rules. Everyone is accountable for agreements made, and for their own happiness.*
> *— Chris, relationship anarchist*

The term *anarchy* is widely misunderstood, especially regarding relationships. It's often perceived as implying a lack of structure and accountability. Far too often, people toss the term "anarchy" around as a cool-sounding synonym for chaos or nihilism, or to rationalize shirking responsibility or consideration.

Such unfortunate conflations have led many people to cringe at, or disparage, relationship anarchy — even though they might agree with its tenets, or practice some of its methods. Sure, the term can sound pretentious. But done conscientiously, relationship anarchy (and anarchy in general) strongly encourages taking personal responsibility for consideration, communication, negotiation and collaboration.

Thus, relationship anarchy is far from an excuse to treat people carelessly or to dodge important conversations about relationships — even though some individuals inevitably attempt to misuse it to camouflage such negligence.

Relationship anarchy can be counterintuitive in other ways, too.

For instance, through relationship anarchy, a relationship might take any form. Relationship anarchists might agree to monogamy or nonmonogamy. They might live together or apart, share sex or not, adopt or avoid certain relationship labels, invest in a shared future or be together strictly in the moment, and much more.

Indeed, probably the only structures that relationship anarchy might preclude would be those which attempt to impose conditions on people without negotiation (such as more prescriptive forms of relationship hierarchy). Or relationship styles that tend to discourage renegotiation or change (such as the traditional Escalator).

Consequently, it's theoretically possible that two relationship anarchists might — through conscious, ongoing negotiation — develop a relationship that looks, from the outside, very much like the Relationship Escalator: married, sexual, romantic, monogamous, shared home and finances, and so on. However, they would probably handle some aspects of their relationship far less conventionally. For instance, such partners might put a surprising amount of energy, time and attention toward their friendships. They might not always put each other "first." Or they might consider and discuss options such as living apart, or discontinuing their sexual connection, or sharing sex or romance with others, or divorcing — without assuming that exercising these options would mean that their relationship is broken or over.

Also, relationship anarchists probably wouldn't feel entitled to each other's time, attention or other resources by default. Even after decades of living together, relationship anarchists might still be likely to ask each other, *"Would you like to hang out and watch TV with me tonight?"*

However, in practice, the philosophy of relationship anarchy more typically produces relationships that are structured quite unconventionally. It has a tendency to encourage people to ask unusual questions and to put more options on the table.

> *We are free to explore sexual and romantic connections with others, and we are open to those other connections potentially growing to the same level of depth as ours.*
> — Chris, relationship anarchist

> *Relationship anarchy can lead to mind-blowing questions. What if you got married to your platonic best friend? What if you held your friendships in higher regard than your closest romantic relationships? What if the most important person in your life is your college roommate?*
> *I was thinking about it the other day, thinking about how much love I share with one of my best friends — someone I only see a few times a month and who I've never had sex with.*
> — Seth, relationship anarchist

Relationship anarchy lends considerable room for relationships to evolve, shifting in and out of sexuality, romance, commitments, living arrangements and more.

> *I co-parent a 15-month-old kid with a lovely couple in a monogamous relationship. The mother and I had a romantic relationship five years ago, but now I am her mentor and she is a part of my extended family.*
> — *Morgan, relationship anarchist*

People who call themselves relationship anarchists can sometimes come across as relationship nerds since they're particularly likely to consider, negotiate and explain their relationships in great detail. This nerdiness is useful when it helps people better express themselves and understand each other. This might support significant social benefits if relationship anarchy becomes popular, or at least better known.

> *It would be nice if relationship anarchy was the social standard for how people connect. That way, everyone would have a choice for how their important relationships work. There would be less pandering to fixed rules and categories.*
> — *Guzica, relationship anarchist*

Busting the Friend/Lover Binary

How people categorize their relationships often reflects social norms, especially the distinctions between friends, lovers and partners. Many relationship anarchists resist drawing such common distinctions.

> *I have a lot of friends, but I don't delineate between who is a lover and who is not.*
> — *Lyra, relationship anarchist*

> *My personal flavor of relationship anarchy includes not using the romantic/platonic distinction. I've found that using these adjectives to describe my feelings, attractions, and relationships is no longer useful for me. I choose not to categorize my relationships that way, preferring to instead describe my relationships on a case-by-case basis. In addition, I consider all intimate relationships (possibly "romantic" ones, if you're using that term) to be variations on close friendship. I don't consider the two to be mutually exclusive categories.*
> — *Lynn, relationship anarchist*

A big reason why some people blur or avoid common relationship labels is that these terms are burdened with substantial social baggage.

> *I personally think that using terms like boyfriend/girlfriend (or even partner) hides the complexities of human relationships.*
> *I've seen too many conflicts in relationships due to assumptions made about what "a relationship" means. People often assume that "everyone knows" what it means to be in a relationship with someone.*
>   *— Karl, relationship anarchist*

Similarly, many people assume that "friendship" is a type of relationship that does not include sex or romance. However, sexual friendships are common, as is emotional and sometimes even romantic intimacy within a friendship. Relationship anarchists tend to be comfortable with these blurred lines.

> *I hold the conviction that every healthy relationship I would enter must, at its core, be a friendship. Everything besides that is just some kind of fuzzily defined additional benefit.*
> *The most important part is that I consider my partner my best friend.*
>   *— Ben, asexual and solo poly*

For relationship anarchists, a key problem with common relationship labels is that they tend to give rise to assumptions, especially about which relationships are closest or most important. This tends to bolster hierarchy both on and off the Relationship Escalator. Such labels also might alienate people who approach relationships from an unconventional perspective.

> *I constantly feel "in love" with, and would do nearly anything for, a wide range of people — not necessarily just sexual partners.*
>   *— Yoni Wolf, queer and poly*

Monogamy and Relationship Anarchy

Relationship anarchy is not the same thing as either consensual nonmonogamy or polyamory. Many relationship anarchists practice consensual nonmonogamy. But some opt to agree to sexual exclusivity, either temporarily or permanently. So yes, there can be such a thing as a monogamous relationship anarchist. Tasha explains:

I am a strong believer in relationship anarchy. I am also single/solo by choice, but not poly/open. At the moment, I have a sexual relationship with one man. I am not at all interested in an Escalator relationship. I am a fully independent woman, living on my own, looking after myself, with no pressure to conform to what society says I should want. It's awesome!

Since discovering relationship anarchy, I have been a lot happier. It suits me perfectly. I can just be myself, live as an independent woman, and have whatever interactions with people I meet that we both want, without the need to label anything and make it formal in any way. It is fluid and dynamic.

While there is potential for more than one relationship in my life to have a sexual aspect to it, at this stage only one of my relationships does. Right now, that is good for me. This may not be the case all the time, and may or may be the case for the gentleman in question.

Part 4 Questions to Consider and Discuss

- Do you agree with the description of relationship hierarchy offered in Ch. 14? Why or why not?

- How has hierarchy affected your personal relationships (intimate or otherwise) with other adults? Can you give examples?

- In consensual nonmonogamy, what do you see as the likely pros and cons of allowing one intimate relationship to outweigh others by default? How might these pros and cons vary for primary vs. secondary partners?

- In your intimate relationships, which basic assumptions do you and your partner(s) tend to make without discussion? How might you approach negotiating these issues, instead?

- Which topics in Chapters 14-18 would you like to read more about, and why? What are your questions about relationship hierarchy and relationship anarchy?

Share your answers or your own story online*
OffEscalator.com/resources/book1questions

* By answering any of these questions or sharing other personal information via the Off the Escalator website, you agree that the Off the Escalator project may quote your responses in our books, web content and in other material. You can answer anonymously if you like.

PART 5

LOVE MINUS SEX OR ROMANCE

19

ASEXUAL AND AROMANTIC:
PART OF THE RAINBOW

Not everyone is heterosexual. Similarly, not everyone desires sex. People on the spectrum of *asexuality* experience little or no desire for sexual contact.

> *Both my partner and I are asexual. While currently it's just the two of us, we are open to polyamory.*
>
> *We each have interests (sometimes romantic) in other people, but we do not have sex with each other or anyone else.*
> — *A, asexual*

> *As an asexual person, I'm most comfortable in relationships that don't involve sex. Also, I am someone who experiences love passionately and prizes physical affection more than any other expression of love. My relationships resonate with who I really am. They excite me and make me happy, and they give me the freedom to be myself.*
>
> *It's also gratifying as hell to be involved with a fellow asexual person, to know that I'm making that person feel loved. I'm giving them the same freedom and comfort to be who they are, to live their natural preference for celibacy while still getting love.*
> — *Samantha, asexual*

One of the most unexpected and enlightening parts of my survey was hearing from dozens of people in the *ace* (slang for asexual) community, as well as many more who have been intimately involved with asexual partners.

These were some of the most eloquent and thoughtful responses I received. But in retrospect, that isn't very surprising: if you want to think really, really hard about intimacy and relationships, try taking sex and/or romance out of the picture.

> *It's definitely isolating to have such a unique philosophy of love and to want very unique, unconventional relationships.*
>
> *I feel disconnected from most of the world, since most of the world is sexual Most of the world constructs personal relationship hierarchies based on romance and sex that very rigidly separate "friendship" from "romance." This is the opposite of my own philosophy, and I think that will always be the case.*
> — *Marie, asexual relationship anarchist*

Being Aromantic

Similarly, *aromantic* people experience little or none of the emotional rush often associated with crushes or "falling in love."

> *I identify as aromantic. My partner and I share no gushing romantic feelings, yet we have deep emotional intimacy.*
>
> *I skip the dominant narrative of how intimate relationships begin. Instead, I go straight to this recognition: "This is a person who matters to me, and I want to love them unconditionally. So I have no choice but to invest energy into this relationship since we are already connected on some soul level."*
>
> *The people I love reside in my heart from early in our relationship. I look forward to getting to know them better and deepening over time.*
> — *Trix, aromantic*

People who are aromantic (*aro*) may or may not behave in ways that are typically considered romantic. Some examples of *romantic-coded* behaviors[67] are planning and sharing intimate one-on-one time (*dates*), affectionate pet names, lingering kisses on the mouth, tagging each other as "in a relationship with" on social media, acquiring keepsakes commemorating an affectionate bond, etc.

What's unique about aromantic people is that they usually don't have the patterns of feelings and thoughts commonly associated with romantic attraction. This is a difficult-to-define blend of exhilaration, infatuation, obsession, idealization and a strong desire to spend lots of time with (or communicate frequently with) the object of one's affection. In mainstream culture, romantic attraction is usually what people mean when they say they're "falling in love." And in the polyamorous community, romantic attraction is often called *new relationship energy (NRE)*. Romantic attraction may persist at some level throughout a long-term relationship, but it's usually strongest at the beginning.

Since aromantic people don't experience romantic attraction, they're sometimes perceived as being emotionally aloof, or even "unable to love." This accusation can be quite hurtful, since aromantic people can and do feel love, often quite profoundly. It is possible to love someone in a deeply intimate way, without feeling "in love" with them in a romantic sense.

Asexuality and aromanticism exist along a spectrum. Some individuals never experience any sexual and/or romantic desire or attraction. Others may experience it at some level, or under certain circumstances. For instance, people who consider themselves *gray-ace* experience sexual attraction only on rare occasions. Also, people who are *demisexual* or *demiromantic* may experience sexual or romantic attraction for someone only after forming a close emotional bond.

> *I'm demisexual and my girlfriend is pre-op transgender. Some aspects of our relationship are nonsexual, but others aren't.*
> — *River, demisexual*

A Matter of Orientation

Being asexual or aromantic is a matter of orientation or identity, just like some people consider themselves gay, bisexual, straight or submissive. Consequently, this chapter is a bit of a departure from the rest of this book.

This book focuses mostly on the structure of intimate relationships, rather than the identity or sexual orientation of individuals in relationships. For instance, in many countries, people of any sexual orientation are now free to engage in relationships with a very traditional, conventional structure, even to the point of legal marriage. This means that same-sex couples can have relationships that are as traditional as an opposite-sex marriage, at least as far as structure is concerned. That's also true for asexual and aromantic people, who are free to ride the Relationship Escalator all the way up. But there's a key difference, at least for asexual people.

Under current social norms, sex (rather more than romance) is typically deemed essential for a relationship to be called "intimate" — at least at some level, and at some point, usually at the beginning. Romantic connection is also widely assumed, but "intimate" is most commonly a code word for "sex." Consequently, relationships which do include sex generally are presumed to be more important, or at least more intimate, than those which do not.

Relationships where sex either does not happen or is not an important part of the partners' bond often get discounted being neither real nor important.

> *Two people who are quite tactile with one another aren't necessarily heading for a sexual relationship, any more than two who don't actively hate one another.*
> — *Melissa, single*

> *Most people would not think that we are in a relationship, looking at how we act to each other. I am cuddly with everyone I'm close too, and my partner and I don't kiss (kissing is way gross to me). Still, this is a very significant relationship to both of us.*
> — *Chamomile, asexual and polyamorous*

Thus, simply by having intimate relationships at all, on their own terms, asexual people are taking a big step off the Relationship Escalator.

This is true even when relationships that include asexual people bear other hallmarks of Escalator relationships — such as including no more than two partners, not sharing sex or romance with anyone else, presenting as a couple, living together, progressing steadily toward greater life entanglement, and even getting legally married and having kids together. (Although asexual people may become parents via adoption, artificial insemination, or intercourse done strictly for procreation rather than sexual fulfillment — a practice that happens to be highly traditional, in some religious cultures.)

> *My life partner and I don't have sex; we both identify as somewhere on the asexual spectrum. We're monogamous and committed.*
> — *Katja, asexual and monogamous*

Invisible Identities

So far, asexuality and aromanticism aren't widely known. This can lead many asexual and aromantic people to feel isolated and invisible.

> *Thank you for listing asexual as a choice on this survey, not relegating it to the "other" section. This is the first place that I have seen this.*
> — *Annmarie, asexual and demiromantic*

Also, asexuality has sometimes been perceived as sexual dysfunction, similar to how homosexuality was historically pathologized by therapists, psychiatrists and physicians. While hypoactive sexual desire disorder is a recognized condition in the *Diagnostic and Statistical Manual of Mental Disorders (DSM-5)*, [68] that reference guide also explicitly recognizes asexuality as a sexual orientation and recommends that people who self-identify as asexual should not be diagnosed with this disorder.

Lack of visibility and assumptions of dysfunction contribute to social stigma about asexuality, and sometimes feelings of shame or vulnerability. As a result, many people are in the closet about being asexual or aromantic.

> *I know the isolation and feeling of being broken because sex was not something I was interested in. Sex is such a staple of western society that it is considered almost a disease not to want it.*
> — *Annmarie, asexual and demiromantic*

> *I wish society wasn't so obsessed with sex and the idea that a sexual relationship is more important than a nonsexual one. Because of this, my asexuality is a secret. Not even my closest friends know about this.*
> — *Gray, asexual*

The widespread lack of awareness about asexual or aromantic relationships also can make it challenging for asexual and aromantic people to establish deeper bonds with people they care for.

> *I'm living with a squish[69] and I also have another squish outside the household; one of each gender. No desire for anything beyond platonic relationships and occasional cuddles. Haven't explained this to them in clear terms, but everyone seems happy enough!*
> *I'm not really sure if they understand the strength of feeling I have for them. I don't want to come across as if I'm romantically interested in either of them. It's really difficult to discuss the concept of squishes with friends and family. They don't get it.*
> — *Cheryl, asexual and aromantic*

Yet for some individuals, embracing their asexual and/or aromantic identity is precisely what helps them access a wealth of mutually beneficial love and connection.

> *I am an asexual, aromantic woman. I am in a poly kinky relationship with a man; I'm his secondary partner. For four years, I've been living with a heterosexual female. Between the two of them, they make up my primary relationship.*
>
> *I would not be happy in a relationship that fits the norms. My current relationships give me the opportunity to have the relationships I want, without having to accept things that I am not interested in or dislike.*
>
> *If I tried to fit the relationships I have into norms, they would break. As is, it's a fantastic buffet where I can choose what works for me.*
>
> *— Indigo, asexual and aromantic*

Blended Relationships: Asexual and Sexual Partners Together

Asexual or aromantic people can end up in intimate relationships with partners who do feel sexual/romantic attraction (sometimes called *allosexual* or *alloromantic*, or simply *sexual* or *romantic*). As with other types of blended relationships, these may work out well, with negotiation.

Often, consensual nonmonogamy is helpful in resolving this difference.

> *We originally opened up our relationship so my partner could explore hir[70] polyamorous identity, but it turned out to be incredibly convenient since I'm an ace and not necessarily available for hir sexual needs for long periods of time.*
>
> *In fact, I'm frequently the one encouraging my partner to ask out the people ze's interested in.*
>
> *— Morwen, asexual in an open relationship*

Blended sexual/asexual relationships also can be monogamous.

> *My ex-boyfriend has suggested that we get married. When we were dating, we were very sexually incompatible. After we stopped dating, he discovered he was gay and I discovered I was asexual. However, we were — and are — still very close.*
>
> *After we came out to each other, he suggested a platonic marriage. He has personal reasons for wanting to be legally married. I have no objections to eventually having such an arrangement with him, although I'm unsure about doing that at this time.*
>
> *I would love to find another asexual person with whom I could be romantically and exclusively involved. Ideally, I would live with them. However, I am open to all types of relationships and partners, including*

an open relationship with a sexual person. The most important aspect for me is an intimate relationship with another person. The relationship can take any form, as long as it has intimacy.

— Nola, asexual

Of course, sometimes the asexual/sexual divide can create considerable tension in relationships, from either perspective.

I am an asexual woman, but my partner is a sexual man. We are committed to each other and have been together a very long time, but we do not have sex. In the past, I was in an open relationship where my partner engaged in sex outside of the relationship due to my asexuality.

Not having sex is always the biggest problem in my relationships. I'm willing to compromise — but sometimes my compromises aren't enough.

— Laverne, asexual

How do you prioritize asexual-but-intimate romantic relationships when you are not asexual yourself?

— Helen, in an open relationship

Story: A Journey to Asexual Awareness

Since asexuality and aromanticism are not well-known orientations, it can be a challenging and confusing process for people to discover that they might be asexual or aromantic. Marie described a very personal journey of discovery.

In high school, I was in a long distance intimate relationship with a fellow asexual. At the time, I considered it a typical romantic relationship — although, in retrospect, I don't think the presence of romantic attraction from either of us would have made any difference. Romantic or not, we loved each other and wanted to have a life together.

We were both asexual and we both wanted to live a celibate life. Had we been in the same location, we would've had a highly sensual and physically intimate but nonsexual relationship, since we're both big fans of sensual touch.

In a later relationship with another boy, we were never officially "a couple." However, it was definitely a romantic friendship during the first year we knew each other. He was a straight boy my age. I came out to him as asexual as soon as we met, so he knew I wasn't exactly a possibility for a stereotypical romantic-sexual girlfriend at any point.

However, we were powerfully drawn to each other immediately, and our relationship was intensely emotional.

He and I also were much more physically affectionate than typical friends, since we're both very tactile and highly value physical affection. We hugged a lot, we cuddled a few times, he would kiss my neck and give me massages.

During this first year of our friendship, he dated two other girls. His second romantic relationship devastated me. I was very sensitive to being subordinated by sexual partners of my sexual friends. I was sufficiently hurt that I immediately broke off our relationship without discussion. He was deeply hurt by my abandonment, even while he should have been in the initial honeymoon phase of his new romance. Two years later he and I rekindled our friendship. Thus far it's been an ordinary friendship, no longer a romantic one.

For me, the best part about these relationship experiences was that they contained so many elements of what I've always really wanted. I've always wanted passionate friendship — and I've had a specific, powerful attraction to nonsexual love which surpasses ordinary friendship in terms of emotional intensity and physical intimacy.

When I was a younger, many of my relationship difficulties came down to language. My friend and I had no framework easily and universally familiar to both of us that we could look at and say, "Okay, this is how we should conduct this relationship." Or, "This is what this means, this is how we feel," etc.

Language is tremendously important. I have it now, but only because I've been more heavily involved in the ace community in recent years. So I'm now educated and old enough to have come up with my own language, I didn't have it in the past. And I think that was one of the main reasons I couldn't get most people to understand where I was coming from — not the people I wanted to be intimate with, the ones who I was intimate with, or onlookers.

If my friend is a sexual person who wants to (or tries to) have a normative dating or sex life, their relationship with me can be a practical and emotional problem. This is yet another reason why I now only consider celibate asexuals or aromantics for intimate partners.

Outsiders just aren't going to get my asexuality. They're going to misinterpret what the relationship means — how I feel about my friend, how my friend feels about me, etc.

Asexual and aromantic visibility is a huge deal to me, not just because I'm ace, or for visibility's own sake. It's because I believe raising visibility for the ace and aro communities heavily corresponds with a rethinking of love and relationships.

I'd also like more visibility for cross-orientation sexual people. I really want to be a part of a movement that supports and promotes lifelong celibacy as a relationship/love choice, completely separate from religion and sexual moralism. Especially so that asexuals who genuinely desire celibacy can more easily be celibate for life or experience nonsexual love.

I would like nonsexual love, passionate friendship, nonsexual and/or nonromantic partnerships and tribes to become widespread realities.

Comparing Asexuality to the Relationship Escalator

Being asexual or aromantic means that one's intimate relationships will probably diverge from Relationship Escalator hallmark #4: *sexual and romantic connection.* The example Escalator relationship story of Chris & Dana *(see the preface)* featured several common indicators and impacts of sexual and romantic relationships:

Chris meets Dana, and they feel a strong spark of mutual attraction. They start talking and hanging out a bit, and then they go out on dates, just the two of them, quite romantic. They kiss, they feel excited. They start having sex.

...When out together, they hold hands or engage in other acceptable public displays of affection. As they fall in love, they obsessively think and fantasize about each other. Things get serious when they begin to say, "I love you."

...One night, Chris pops the question to Dana over a candlelit dinner, and Dana enthusiastically accepts.

Not every intimate relationship works this way. There are many ways to feel, and express, love and intimacy; sex and romance are not always required.

20

MORE NONSEXUAL RELATIONSHIP OPTIONS

People may have intimate relationships that do not include sex and/or romance even if they don't consider themselves asexual or aromantic.

Asexual and *aromantic* are personal identities or orientations, analogous to being gay or straight. In contrast to this, *nonsexual* or *nonromantic* are terms that describe relationships, not people. Relationships that are both nonsexual and nonromantic are commonly called *platonic*.

Just like sexual or romantic relationships, platonic relationships might involve profound emotional intimacy or love, strong commitment, substantial affection or sensuality, passion, emotional support and perhaps even life entanglement. They might even become life-partner relationships mirroring the pinnacle of the Escalator in many respects, even legal marriage. (Yes, some people really *do* marry their best friend.) Furthermore, important platonic relationships can include members of one's biological family, something almost universally taboo for sexual or romantic intimacy.

Intimate nonsexual relationships are incredibly common. They happen both on and off the Escalator, for different reasons.

In my survey, roughly 40% of participants mentioned that at least some of their important intimate relationships are (or have been) nonsexual or nonromantic — at least to some significant extent, or at some times. Also, one in five people specifically indicated that they are open to having nonsexual intimate relationships.

> *I do seek nonsexual intimacy with other people, but I find it sufficient to let my existing friendships deepen. I rely on my web of friends in an informal, ad hoc way.*

> *Someday I may want a more official commitment from these kinds of*
> *friends, but right now that's not important to me.*
>   *— Grace, single*

In mainstream culture, people commonly assume that relationships which include sex and romance have more staying power since they offer a path to the Escalator. However, nonsexual relationships often become very deeply committed and long-term. They can even prove more durable or less volatile than strongly romantic or sexual connections.

> *I'm in several relationships, including a 10-year committed (but not*
> *romantic, and only sometimes sexual) relationship with a woman.*
>   *— Cat, bisexual and polyamorous*

Friendship That's "Too Close"

Deep emotional intimacy and a strong sense of commitment often develop within very close platonic friendships, sometimes to an extent that doesn't comfortably coexist with Escalator relationships.

Under current social norms, friendship is assumed to be platonic. That's why this type of bond is usually acceptable, even for people who have an Escalator partner. Except, of course, if that friend might be sexually attractive or available. In that case, friendship (or at least, very close friendship) is often discouraged, since it's seen as a distraction from or threat to the Relationship Escalator.

Mainstream culture tends to rank friendships as a lower priority than Escalator partnerships. Therefore, friendships that involve significant shared time, logistical entwinement that is not purely for convenience, or other substantial commitments are, in a way, unconventional intimate relationships. That is, they might be perceived as "stealing" time, attention, energy and resources that "should" be reserved for one's current or potential Escalator relationship.

> *I'd like to be able to form close personal friendships with partnered*
> *people to whom I might be attracted, in a way that would be considered*
> *ill-advised in traditional relationships.*
> *Such friendships are rarely actually sexual, but they are closer than*
> *most monogamous people would trust or understand, in my experience.*
> *People often think such friendships would threaten a monogamous dyad.*
>   *— Helen, nonmonogamous*

Nevertheless, people sometimes form deep emotional attachments and logistical commitments, even nesting or life partnerships, with platonic friends.

> *My best friend is someone who I used to date over a decade ago. This person is my emergency contact, even when I have other significant (more primary-esque) partners.*
> — *Chloe, nonmonogamous*

> *I am currently in a totally nonsexual and nonentangled relationship with one of my housemates. I've never been so close with another person.*
> *This is the person I talk with late at night when something is on my mind and I need some help processing. This is the person who sees me early in the morning when I am just barely functioning but trying to embrace that space of vulnerability and creative illogic. This is the person who has watched me, during my celibate time, slowly recreate my relationship to sex, creativity and spirit.*
> *This is what I thought marriage was supposed to be, and what my own marriage never was.*
> — *Savanni, single*

Continuing Intimacy After the Sex Disappears

Not all nonsexual intimate relationships start out that way. Many partners start off with sex being an important part of their bond, but their relationship evolves to become comfortably nonsexual, either temporarily or permanently.

This is especially common in long-term nesting or life partner relationships, both on and off the Relationship Escalator. Sexual connection sometimes fades due to life or physical changes (common after a new child is born, or when a partner becomes ill or disabled), or a persistent loss of desire (for sex in general, or just with a specific partner). Despite these changes, partners often continue to share substantial love, companionship, support and even romance.

The Relationship Escalator has a venerable tradition of long-term monogamous relationships that eventually become nonsexual, sometimes called *companionate marriage*. These partners eventually cease having sex with each other, either mostly or entirely. To remain on the Escalator, they still must not share sex or romance with anyone else, even if they continue to have those desires (just not for each other). Sometimes this works out well.

> *We're an unconventional monogamous relationship. We have been together for 11 years. He is 41 and I am 71. At first, we were sexually involved. Over time, this aspect of our relationship has disappeared.*
>
> *We live together but sleep in separate rooms. We are very happy together and support each other in our work and in our relationships with our children. We expect to be together for the rest of our lives.*
>
> — Margaret, monogamous

> *It started 18 years ago when I moved in with and later married my best friend. Our relationship basically followed the Escalator, although I never meant for that to happen. I was depressed and sexually unsatisfied but did not want to lose everything else.*
>
> *Eventually, somehow, we came to a happier place where we love each other unconditionally and are mutually supportive. And we don't have sex with each other.*
>
> — Veronica, married

Even though it's quite common for sex to wane or vanish in long-term exclusive relationships, social norms tend to instill shame about this, unless a partner's lack of sexual desire or contact can be explained by physical concerns such as aging, recent childbirth, menopause, illness or disability.

> *Shortly after we moved in together, we officially stopped having sex or doing sexual activities with each other. It's now been over three years. Neither of us is very sure why we agreed to stop having sex, or why we continue to be more-or-less content to leave it this way.*
>
> *Being in a sexless relationship sometimes causes me internal shame and feelings of being sexually rejected, even though logically I know that this is a mutual agreement. I also see some benefits: no fear of STIs or pregnancy, no need to trust another partner's sexual safety practices.*
>
> *Neither of us has shared with anyone else that we don't have sex, and everyone probably assumes we do. I worry about being socially rejected if any of our friends were to know.*
>
> — Theresa, in a theoretically open relationship

As sexual connection fades, the structure of a relationship may change. For people who require monogamy, sexual incompatibility or cessation can lead to breaking up, divorcing, moving into separate households, etc., unless that would be prohibitively costly or risky. Alternately, if one or both partners still desires sex (just not with each other), this is often a point at which cheating occurs.

Another socially acceptable reason for transitioning to a companionate, nonsexual Escalator relationship is when breaking up over sexual incompatibility would cause too much disruption. For instance, Escalator partners might be co-parenting, or they might depend financially or logistically on maintaining that relationship structure.

But increasingly, former Escalator partners do disentangle from each other while transforming relationship. Usually, this involves a loss of sexual connection, but not always. Former partners can find ways to retain much of the companionship and at least some of the mutual support and affection they previously shared — just without the sex and romance.

> *I live with one of my exes in a stable, platonic domestic partnership.*
> *— Penny, poly and kinky*

> *Despite the fact that we are no longer married, and not sexual at all, I still feel very attached to her. I am glad to have her house key and am glad that she has called me in the past during an emergency etc. I still pay the phone bill for her parents.*
>
> *— John William, solo poly*

It's also becoming more common for partners to remain close, even if they must change the structure of their relationship or end their sexual contact to achieve this.

> *I've ended my romantic/sexual connection with my primary partner, but I am keen to keep up our nonsexual but fairly intimate friendship, even though we may each be dating other people.*
> *I have yet to see if this will work, but I want us to be open and honest about the fact that we like to hang out and are physically friendly. (We still hug, etc.)*
> *— Karen, single*

Some people even consciously plan for and negotiate such transitions.

> *I'm sexually involved with one of my best friends. We have agreed that if our relationships with others become more significant, we will stop and stay as "normal" friends.*
> *— Katarina, nonmonogamous*

> *Our relationship is long distance (which sucks) and open. It's also nonprimary, since we aren't sure about living together. We definitely are not interested in riding the Escalator toward marriage.*

> *We've committed to dropping the sexual part of our relationship if either of us needs to. Although we both value our sexual connection, we value the overall depth of our relationship more. We'd drop the sexual aspects of our relationship rather than drop the relationship entirely.*
> — *Alex, in an open relationship*

Kinky Relationships: Sex and Romance Not Required

Kink (bondage, flogging, power exchange, roleplay, fetish activities, etc.) can offer a powerful approach to physical and emotional intimacy and expression that need not be sexual or romantic in nature.

Of course, that depends on what "sex" means — and there is a wide range of views on this topic. Kink usually is highly sensual or erotic. Still, there's plenty of room in the kinkosphere for intimacy that does not depend upon sexual arousal, contact or orgasms. Kink might be strictly recreational, expressive, experimental or cathartic; or might be essential to achieve an intense sense of intimate connection.

By itself, kink usually does not constitute a step off the Relationship Escalator. Many people enjoy kinky play or eroticism within traditional relationships. Or they may view kink as a crucial aspect of their personal identity, separately from how they choose to structure their relationships.

It's fairly common for people in monogamous relationships to want to find people with whom they can share nonsexual kinky experiences.

> *I would like to find a partner to "scene" with. I am into bondage as a submissive. My husband is willing to occasionally play with me in that way, but he doesn't have much interest or experience with this.*
> *I would like to find a dedicated top. This would not need to be a sexual relationship, just someone I could scene with occasionally.*
> — *Rachel, married*

But in some relationships, nonsexual kink forms the core of the intimate bond. Such intimacy may or may not be deep. But when the intimacy of kink is the focus of the relationship, that can be a departure from the Relationship Escalator.

> *I enjoy playing in the BDSM scene. I have a nonsexual partner-in-crime, and for years we've been playing together with friends.*
> — *Elaine, nonmonogamous*

One of my partners is a man with whom I share a loving and intimate relationship, but we do not have penetrative sex. He spanks me, which we both enjoy.
— Sandee, polyamorous

Some kink-based relationships might be highly sexual but not at all romantic.

My long distance, power-exchange-based relationship is not intimate in the way most people think. We care about each other but not in a romantic way. He wants me to find someone to be romantically involved with someday.
— Kiana, nonmonogamous

Many people on the asexual spectrum enjoy kink and treasure it as a form of intimacy, expression, or physical release.
My partner is allowed to find a sexual/BDSM partner in his city since he has needs that I can't meet (such as lots of sex).
I'm allowed to have friends and nonsexual play partners for activities like rope bondage. I'm also allowed to have subs or slaves, especially if they make my life less stressful.
— Frankie, asexual and kinky

Even though a kinky relationship may include some sex or romance, the nonsexual or nonromantic aspects of that bond often are paramount. This is often apparent in consensual power exchange, where someone voluntarily agrees to surrender certain freedoms or decisions to others.

I'm a naturally submissive trans woman. I always find relationships in which I am the submissive, pet, little one, etc. I prefer 24/7 total power exchange relationships. My Dom, Master/Mistress, Owner or Daddy will make even my most basic choices for me, since these are difficult for me and trigger my anxiety
Many people jump to conclusions and judge me. They say things such as, "You aren't living a healthy lifestyle" or "You're not right in the head."
I try to spread the knowledge that I have healthy, loving relationships without fighting, hate, misunderstandings, lack of communication, and a lot of focus on partners being happy and in a good place.
I have a lot of friends who are not into this kind of lifestyle in the slightest. However, they appreciate learning about it. They accept it, and me, with open arms.

Typically I find that my power dynamic relationships are healthier. I care very much for my significant others. They, in turn, care very much for me. My safety and well-being are their main concern.

For instance, I was anorexic at the time when I entered the care of my first Master and Mistress. They took care to make sure that I ate healthy foods, in healthy amounts. They watched to make sure that I actually ate, that I didn't purge. They required a rule that I lick my plate clean to show my obedience and appreciation.

— *Amelia, kinky and nonmonogamous*

21

CHOOSING CELIBACY

Some individuals choose to be *celibate.* They might experience sexual desire and attraction, but they voluntarily refrain from having sexual contact with anyone. This can be a matter of personal preference, or a choice to support other goals.

In one sense, celibacy is very traditional. For millennia, priests, monks and nuns of various religions and spiritual disciplines have taken vows of celibacy. Also, in some cultures, women who have been widowed are expected to remain celibate during a period of formal mourning.

Many people occasionally consciously adopt celibacy as a temporary measure: to regain clarity and emotional balance after a relationship ends or a life crisis, to focus on a demanding effort such as medical school, as part of a spiritual practice or retreat, to focus on recovering health or sobriety, or to prepare for future relationships.

> As I began graduate school, I decided to try a year of celibacy, which became two years, which ended six months ago when I began to date and sleep with my co-parent of 14 years.
> — Hegen, polyamorous

> Due to the emotional turmoil of a breakup in which my civil-union partner left our relationship to move in with another partner, I made the decision to remain celibate and single for a year.
> I wanted to re-evaluate my own priorities and desires in romantic relationships, and also whether I still wanted to be involved in polyamory or nonmonogamy as a lifestyle choice. I decided that I did. One painful experience wasn't going to put me off a choice I knew made sense for me.
> — Bill, poly transmale

Generally, unless someone is entering a religious vocation, celibacy is expected to be just a phase, not a way of life. Furthermore, once someone's celibate phase is over, they're typically expected to eventually find an Escalator partner. Choosing celibacy indefinitely, with no religious justification, can be a very unconventional approach to handling intimate relationships.

> *I am bisexual but celibate by choice because of sexual trauma in my past. My girlfriend is simply asexual.*
> — *Joann, celibate by choice*

Celibacy is not necessarily at odds with Escalator norms. However, some people make the unconventional choice to stay celibate while maintaining nonsexual aspects of their intimate relationships.

> *My partner and I are on spiritual paths. Our primary commitment is to that, more than to our relationship. I recently had the intuition that I should be celibate for a while, so I'm doing that, and all my lovers are supportive and we still cuddle.*
> — *Ash, polyamorous*

Really Going It Alone: No Intimate Relationships Wanted

Some people simply prefer to avoid all significant intimate relationships: sexual, romantic, or perhaps even emotional intimacy.

> *I'm currently married, but if my marriage ends or my spouse dies, I don't want any more relationships. I'd rather be alone.*
> — *Molly, monogamous*

> *I am demisexual, and before my current open relationship, I was largely aromantic. I did not seek this relationship and have no intention to seek one in the future. Honestly, I just don't want a relationship. I don't, I never have. I tend to end up in them from time to time — but I don't seek them out and I don't feel like it's important to me to have one.*
> — *Sheva, in an open relationship*

The social stigma against adults who choose to avoid Escalator-style couplehood also affects people who avoid intimate relationships in general.

I prefer not to have any sexual or romantic relationships, not even casual ones. My friends are aware that I prefer not to date or sleep with others. However, this inevitably leads to a whole host of pretty personal questions that I don't enjoy being asked.

    — *Playelephant, solo*

Sometimes, women in late middle age or older choose celibacy even though they still enjoy physically sex — which many do, see Joan Price's excellent books about sexual fulfillment later in life.[71] This can be a strategy to maintain personal autonomy, which may have been trampled earlier in life by sexist social norms. Bug explained why she chose, and treasures, her celibacy:

I am not in a relationship, sexual or otherwise, and I have no desire to pursue an intimate relationship. I'm done. I am happiest living alone and have no need for a relationship other than a small network of friends. After my last divorce, I decided I'm done with trying to make a man happy. I am focusing on making me happy. I don't like to compromise. I want to live my life the way I want and not have to consider the feelings of a significant other.

I've been celibate since 1999. But well before that, if I did have a short-term relationship, I wouldn't allow a man to leave anything in my place, which often pissed them off. But this is how I feel: You have a place for your own for your stuff, so you don't need to leave it at my place. I consider such behavior territory marking, and I am not into that whole caveman mentality.

I'd like more information on women like myself who have chosen to eschew intimate romantic relationships. More women need to adopt the "take me as I am or hit the road" approach to relationships. Especially women of a certain age, like myself. I will be 60 in two months. I like sex, but I just don't want to have it anymore.

    — *Bug, celibate*

Sexual Avoidance

The choice of celibacy can be motivated by several reasons; some of which sound more positive than others. For instance, avoidance of sexual contact can be a reaction to past sexual trauma or abuse. While such experiences are always tragic, it's up to those individuals to decide whether they wish to try to overcome the resulting sexual avoidance. It's a valid personal choice to decline to undertake this considerable effort.

To some, sex doesn't seem worth the health risks. For instance, some individuals are especially vulnerable to infection, due to a highly compromised immune system.

But sometimes, sexual avoidance is more a response to the strong social stigma associated with, and widespread ignorance and misunderstandings about, sexually transmitted infections (STIs). When someone is diagnosed with an STI (especially HIV), this can trigger a dire fear of infecting others. Also, some people feel an extreme fear of contracting an STI through any sexual contact.

Almost always, there are options for people to share and enjoy sexual intimacy which minimize STI transmission risks, even if someone is known to have an STI. This can depend on how severe or treatable a specific infection is, as well as access to safer-sex supplies, nonjudgmental healthcare and sex education. Sometimes, learning more facts about STIs and safer sex helps people unravel this stigma and evaluate options realistically. Also, gaining familiarity, skill and enjoyment with a wide range of lower-risk sexual activities can decrease fear and avoidance of sex. For instance, manual stimulation can offer considerable mutual pleasure and intimacy, generally with a low risk of STI transmission.

Some people prefer to avoid sexual contact because they were raised in a strongly sex-negative environment that led to considerable shame, disgust or fear about sex. This is especially likely for people raised in strictly conservative religious families or communities — and it is as valid a reason as any for someone's choice to avoid sex.

Regardless of why people avoid sex, or whether others think their reasons sound or healthy: no one is ever obliged to have sex or to seek sexual contact. Consent matters. Every human being has a right to bodily autonomy. This includes the right to authentic, pleasurable sexual expression — as well as the right to not have sex, with anyone in particular or anyone at all, for any reason.

Things Sometimes Mistaken for Celibacy

It's common for people to strongly desire to have sex, but they lack the ability or opportunity to experience sexual contact with others. This circumstance may be quite temporary or a more permanent feature of life. But it is not quite the same thing as celibacy. Also, since it is not a choice, this circumstance might feel especially stressful and demoralizing.

Finding sexual partners can be challenging; most people experience difficulty with this during some parts of life. Indeed, one of the biggest perceived advantages of the Relationship Escalator is that it promises reliable, easy access to sex. Sometimes, it even delivers on this promise.

Some people face additional obstacles in having sex or finding partners. Lack of a conventionally attractive appearance, severe social awkwardness, lack of time, social isolation, and other issues are common and often considerable impediments. But also, illness or disability[71] can curtail someone's libido or physical ability to have sex.

Despite how sex-obsessed mainstream culture can be (especially in the U.S.), it's also strongly *sex-negative:* influenced by deep-rooted, ancient beliefs that sex is evil and dangerous, so therefore it must be tightly controlled. This is probably why, outside of ongoing intimate relationships, there are generally few socially acceptable, legal, safe and affordable options for people who are not in an intimate relationship to find willing or compatible sex partners. For instance, in the U.S., most sex work is illegal. Mobile apps such as Tinder and Grindr, and online services such as Craigslist, have made it somewhat easier for people to arrange casual sexual encounters. However, this can present safety risks, especially for women and transgender people.

Certain social circles can be more amenable to sensual and sexual contact as part of friendship, or as an activity at parties and festivals. Typically, active consent is paramount in such settings. Assumptions based on stereotypes (such as: that artists or college students are usually into casual sex) often go disastrously awry.

Note that the catchphrase *involuntary celibacy* has become problematic. In recent years, this term has been increasingly adopted by straight men who have not been successful in finding women who are willing to have sex with them. This spurs some men to become strongly resentful and angry. They may adopt sexist, entitled views that women owe them sex, but are vindictively or unjustly withholding it from them. Or that more confident and appealing "alpha males" are greedily consuming more than their fair share of female sexual availability.

This mindset can lead to toxic interactions and sometimes even dangerous behavior, from hate speech and harassment to stalking and assault. While related to frustrated sexual needs, this has nothing to do with actual celibacy. And, sadly, these attitudes and behaviors are all too traditional.

≈

Part 5 Questions to Consider and Discuss

- Aside from sex and romance, what do you think are some things that can make a relationship feel significantly intimate? How much do you value those types of intimacy in your relationships?

- How do you experience or express love, intimacy and commitment in your friendships?

- What are your questions about the role of sex and/or romance, or their absence, in intimate relationships?

- Which topics in Chapters 19-21 would you like to learn more about, and why?

Share your answers, or your own story, online*

OffEscalator.com/resources/book1questions

* By answering any of these questions or sharing other personal information via the Off the Escalator website, you agree that the Off the Escalator project may quote your responses in our books, web content and in other material. You can answer anonymously if you like.

PART 6

NOT ALWAYS AND FOREVER

22

BENDING WITHOUT BREAKING:
FLEXIBLE RELATIONSHIPS

How much change is acceptable within an intimate relationship before it feels like that relationship has ceased to exist?

Most traditional relationships are not completely rigid or static. The Relationship Escalator does allow some leeway — for partners to express more or less romantic connection, to spend more or less time together, to temporarily live apart due to external demands, to shift their rhythms of sexual contact, or even to eventually stop having sex at all.

Still, people tend to draw fairly clear lines demarcating when an Escalator relationship is intact, and when it's over.

Riding the Relationship Escalator is a one-way, continuous trip; permanence, continuity, and consistency are key Escalator hallmarks. Once two partners ride a fair way up the Escalator together (usually to the point where they claim and define their couplehood), they are not supposed to step back toward less entwinement, to pause for "too long" at a certain level of involvement, or to revise the structure or terms of their relationship. Rather, the only socially acceptable options are:

- **Keep riding the Escalator** until you reach the top. Then, stay there until someone dies.

- **Break up.** End the relationship. Traditionally, this has meant that former Escalator partners drop out of each other's lives altogether, or at least as much as possible — although that norm is changing. A definitive breakup clears the way to find a new Escalator partner and start riding again.

Consequently, a subtle step off the Escalator is to create or expand flexibility in the structure of an intimate relationship. For this to work, partners must agree that their relationship can change substantially, without necessarily deeming it "over."

> *People always change, needs and desires evolve. If relationships are to stay intact over time, adaptation must happen. Either the structure of the relationship, or the expectations of the people in the relationship, must adapt to suit changing needs and goals.*
>
> *Otherwise, the people in the relationship must continue to conform to an unchanging structure, which may involve ignoring or subverting their own changing needs and nature.*
>
> *This comes down to: which is more important? The people in the relationship, or the relationship as an entity?*
>
> *— Sierra, polyamorous and lesbian*

Sometimes partners cycle through various roles during the life of a long-term intimate relationship.

> *I've been legally married to my husband of 19 years. For most of our marriage, we were polyamorous with relationships of various intensities.*
>
> *Six years ago we entered into a poly family agreement with two other partners. When that ended abruptly after three years, our romantic attachment to each other ended as well.*
>
> *Since then, we have been living platonically, raising our daughter and sharing a household. He has a girlfriend and I am single, but we publicly maintain our family dynamic.*
>
> *— Otterdancing, in an open marriage*

> *I was once in an emotionally committed relationship with a man who had seven girlfriends. Eventually I realized we had some fundamental personality incompatibilities, so I chose to "downgrade" our relationship to something more akin to friends with benefits.*
>
> *He and I still love each other. We consider each other to be part of our greater poly family, and we support each other through good times and bad. We just don't expect as much time, energy or communication from each other as before.*
>
> *This has worked out very well for us. We no longer trigger those issues in each other on a regular basis, but we still share support and love when either of us needs it.*
>
> *— Ana, polyamorous*

Friend-Lover Fluidity

Several participants mentioned that their intimate relationships slip back and forth between being lovers (sharing a sexual, romantic or passionate connection) and a *platonic* connection that is nonsexual and nonromantic. But they may or may not shift to calling their relationship a friendship when its texture shifts this way.

Often such fluidity is a matter of simply adapting how partners in a relationship express love and care for each other, especially as circumstances change, including ripple effects from other intimate relationships.

> *My ex-boyfriend and I are somewhere in between being friends and boyfriend/girlfriend. We're not officially together, but we do love each other. While we were officially together, we lived together and had an open relationship. Neither of us is seeing anyone else at the moment.*
>
> *I don't know what would happen if either of us met someone else. But we are best friends and have always told each other and discussed everything. So I know I'd tell him, and he'd tell me.*
>
> *— Rylee, in a pause/play open relationship*

> *Our seven-year relationship started open and honest between us, with myself identifying as poly and him identifying as more of a serial monogamist. We have lived together in the past.*
>
> *There have been times when, because of a current partner's beliefs, we put the sexual part of the relationship aside — but continued to keep the deep friendship and emotional intimacy between us.*
>
> *We have never expected either of us to be anything but what we are, so there is a lot of fluidity to our relationship.*
>
> *— Lanikino, polyamorous*

People who don't differentiate much, or at all, between friends and lovers tend to have more flexible intimate relationships. This includes, but is not limited to, people who consider themselves relationship anarchists.

> *I am more interested in having friends than having lovers, and I'm only interested in lovers who are also friends. I'm working on exploring that hazy area between friends and partnership, and how that works for me and my friends.*
>
> *— Susanna, solo poly*

> *We both think that there will eventually come a time that, while our relationship will remain important to each other and at the same level of intensity, we may not live together. We're both fine with this. It would be neither a breakup nor a "demotion" of that relationship status.*
>
> *We simply both believe in personal freedom, growth, and expression — as well as the freedom for each of us to follow our own path. So if our paths end up taking us in different dwellings (or, as is likely in this case, different states), that's okay with us and our relationship.*
>
> *— Tylyn, queer and polyamorous*

Some individuals (including, but not limited to, people who consider themselves *demisexual* or *demiromantic*) require an existing strong friendship before they begin to feel a desire to explore sexual or romantic intimacy. This might make it somewhat easier to accept shifts in the other direction, as well.

> *I am pretty much only sexually attracted to people I respect, trust and like. Which means I pretty much can only make out with my current and future friends.*
>
> *This often means that my relationships are quite fluid, flowing along the friend/lover/partner/community/chosen family continuum.*
>
> *— Stefanie, nonmonogamous*

Flexible Merging

The Escalator hallmark of merging is supposed to move in one direction: toward ever-increasing entanglement of the infrastructure of life (especially sharing a home), and of identity (thinking and acting "as a couple"). But some relationships are more flexible about merging — especially in terms of living arrangements.

> *We used to live together, but we have not been living together since we decided to be open.*
>
> *I think we'd both like to live together again, but we are not in a rush. If we did, it would be with the intention of remaining open.*
>
> *— Valeria, nonmonogamous*

> *My primary partner and I have children together and consider ourselves "family." We live in two houses. Sometimes we stay at each other's houses, sometimes not.*
>
> *— Colleen, queer, partnered and open to options*

Flexibility around the concept of "home" can especially suit people who tend to move around.

> *I have two core partners. In one relationship, we sometimes share a household, finances, and a business together — along with 30 others in an income-sharing intentional community. They are largely not romantic or sexual partners to either of us.*
>
> *My partner M has lived in this community for five years. For the last three years, I've been spending half the year with M, and we have been sexually and romantically involved for most of this time.*
>
> *We don't have any expectations for our relationship, but I expect M to continue residing at the farm for the foreseeable future. Also, M expects me to continue spending time at the farm on a regular basis.*
>
> *My other partner is R, a translady with whom I've been romantically and sexually involved with intermittently for the last 12 years. For the last three years, I have been spending 4-12 weeks per year with R. She and I have a loving but zero-expectation relationship.*
>
> *— Rejoice, solo poly*

Intimate Tribes

One form of unconventional intimacy that many people in my survey voiced a desire for is the *tribe:* a persistent network of overlapping relationships, with some level of physical and/or emotional intimacy within that group. What makes a tribe different from any other network of overlapping intimate relationships is that tribes have some level of group awareness and cohesion, expressed through mutual care, respect, attention and support.

Think of a tribe as a strong circle of friends, where some relationships within that circle may include sex or romance. The sex or romance might be exclusive to some pairings, or there might be overlapping sexual/romantic relationships across the tribe. The movie *The Big Chill* portrayed a long-term tribe with a deep sense of mutual commitment, involving some elements of polyamory as well as strong nonromantic emotional intimacy.[73]

A tribe may include some members who live together, perhaps as life partners. However, more typically these networks are fairly informal and distributed across multiple households — or even multiple states, countries or continents.

> *There are many interdependencies in our poly community. This creates a close-knit group of people who feel more like family than friends. We help each other through heavy life issues.*
> — *Lux, poly and married*

> *I'm a married heterosexual woman living in the suburbs with my husband. We are part of a geographically distant tribe of chosen family. Most were originally friends on the early internet. Over the years, some of us have had, or continue to have, romantic and/or sexual partnerships within our family dynamic.*
> *The additional support that comes from multiple, interwoven, serious relationships is valuable. My tribe has gotten me through hard times where traditional family has failed. My tribe includes my two most important and longest-term relationships.*
> — *Wendy, polyamorous*

Sometimes, a tribe's shared identity can grow strong enough that its members consider each other family, and may make more formal or family-like commitments or investments as a group. More commonly, tribes are rather informal.

Polyamory, with its openness to deeper emotional ties and commitment, is especially likely to give rise to a sense of tribe or chosen family. This can include a sense of immediate as well as extended family.

> *One benefit is the extended poly family which I'm a member of. The arrangement of my relationship has allowed me the opportunity to bond with my partner's wife and her boyfriend. They feel like an extended family to me.*
> *My relationship with my partner may eventually change, but I cannot imagine that they would not be part of my life, wherever our relationship leads us.*
> — *Karen, polyamorous*

Tribes represent a step off the Relationship Escalator, even if some members are married, monogamous or otherwise on the Escalator. This is because a tribe is a committed intimate relationship that includes more than two people, even if not all of the intimacy being shared is sexual or romantic. Under social norms, one's strongest sense of intimacy, commitment, care and support is reserved for Escalator partners and their nuclear family.

The level of group awareness and cohesion in a tribe exists along a spectrum: from informal circles of friends where occasionally some of the friends have sex or fall in love with each other, to groups or communities who consciously value, consider and interact with each other as a family of choice.

> *We don't all live together, but our "hub" is the home that my husband and I share. Everyone spends some time in and out around here, and our girlfriend is probably moving in soon too. This will be different, but fun.*
> — *Niki M, polyamorous*

Typically, tribes form and evolve organically, rather than by design. Membership usually shifts over time: different people play more central roles, newcomers enter the fold, and others depart or step back. It's common for a tribe to exist for a while (usually several years) with a gradual dissipation of the group bond over time.

> *I've been polyamorous my entire adult life. This has always felt like being enmeshed in a community of people who share shifting romantic and sexual relationships, rather than being an isolated individual.*
> — *Steve, poly and married*

> *I share a room with a long-term primary partner. We live within the context of a collective communal household of 12 people with whom we also share finances, meals, responsibilities, and plans for the future.*
> *Within this community, different types of relationships occur. Some of the people who my primary partner and I live with are former sexual partners. Also, some of them are intimate friendships, some are more shallow, and some are wanting to be more intimate. They are all fluid and ever-changing.*
> *In addition, my primary partner and I have nonprimary partners outside of our household. I have a long-term nonprimary partner who I do not live with, but who is part of our mutual wider community.*
> — *Aster, polyamorous*

Like family, a tribe is often something that people can come back home to.

> *I have a poly family: my ex-girlfriend and ex-boyfriend, who live together. For many years I've had no sexual or romantic connection with them, but we still celebrate Christmas and other holidays together, along with their other significants. Also, I'm usually welcome to bring my significants to these celebrations.*
> — *Lynna, polyamorous*

> *I was in a tribe, to some extent, when living elsewhere — but then I had to move away for school. I still feel that I'm a huge part of the poly family where I used to live, and still visit when I can.*
>   — Anna, polyamorous

I was struck to see that more than half of my 1500 survey participants indicated a desire to having intimate relationships in a closely interwoven, tribal context. In fact, when I asked what their ideal relationships might look like, several people voiced excitement at learning a word, tribe, that describes their dream.

> *In a couple of years, I'll want kids. I'd like to have them with at least one more person. Or maybe I'd want the kids to be primarily mine, but share childcare responsibilities with several other people. Some kind of tribe might be amazing: living in a collective, sharing household and childcare responsibilities.*
>   — Annie, polyamorous

> *I didn't even realize that this was my ideal until I took this survey! It sounds like heaven.*
>   — Sylph, in an open relationship

Such a common and strong yearning for tribe, especially with some level of shared living arrangements, is rather poignant in a society where housing options and social norms rarely support such cohesion beyond a couple or nuclear family.

> *I really want a tribe, a group of folks who I share my life with. Some sexual, others not, some lifelong, others more casual. I'd like to share my home with several people. I'd like our relationships defined by what we want them to be, in combination with a commitment to our tribe.*
>   — Morgan, relationship anarchist

> *My ideal relationship structure would be founded by a core tribe of people cohabiting with varying degrees of involvement between the people of the tribe.*
> *The tribe does not have to be static. I would prefer it capable of allowing a flow of people in and out. Not all members of the tribe would need to live together.*
>   — Kevin, polyamorous

Story: Vision of a Relationship Anarchist Tribe

Chris, a relationship anarchist who lives with a partner, was especially eloquent about this vision:

> *As to my white-picket-fence vision, it's a home with several involved adults, co-parenting children who come from a variety of pairings. In a way, it is very tribal though not insular. The tribe is abstract, not real — the aggregation of all our close connections, but those individuals and connections are the important part, not the group identity.*
>
> *Maximal freedom, maximal responsibility, everyone contributing in their unique ways, but without coercion or compulsion. Children would be raised with that ethic: no coercion, just persuasion.*
>
> *I would want it to last a lifetime, but not out of obligation. I would hope it worked for people, that it supported and enriched their lives. And if it did not, then people would be free to leave — though if resources or agreements around children are in place, leaving would require some orderly exit and consultation.*

$\approx$

23

PAUSES AND LIMITS

There is a time for everything, but that time might not be very long. Also, absence can make the heart grow fonder. However, on the Relationship Escalator, "serious" relationships are not supposed to be on-again, off-again. Nor should they have a consciously, agreeably contained lifespan. An Escalator relationship is expected to become a permanent, dominant, unchanging feature of life.

However, relationships rarely work that way.

In the big picture, the vast majority of intimate relationships don't survive beyond a precious window of fleeting context. Most nascent intimate relationships fizzle quickly. Usually, people take this high fizzle rate for granted, so they tend to not count as "a relationship" any connection that ends fairly soon after it begins (within days or weeks). Thus, most short-term relationships don't count, when people are counting.

This benchmark for defining "real" relationships isn't wrong, but it doesn't leave room to celebrate the reality and value of love that doesn't proceed indefinitely along an unbroken trajectory.

For instance, partners may know and discuss that their intimate relationship has a clear time limit, whether for a summer or a night. Or perhaps they understand and accept their connection will last only as long as certain other circumstances permit, such as until one of them moves, or until graduate school ends, or until one of them hops on the Escalator with someone else. Even with such constraints, partners can find ways to recognize their connection as more than just a way to kill some spare time or release some spare energy.

This perspective represents a fundamental challenge to what a "real," or even "serious," relationship might be.

Some relationships that people consider to be deeply intimate and significant are deliberately, or at least agreeably, discontinuous or limited. By mutual consent, they may accommodate intermittence; or they may exist only for a certain time, or within a certain context.

From "whenever we're in the same town" romances, to vacation love affairs, to a one-night stand that touches the heart deeply, discontinuous or finite intimacy can be meaningful and rewarding.

In fact, up-front awareness of the limited scope of a relationship can amplify its intensity and significance. And sometimes, acknowledged limits are what allows a relationship to exist at all.

Pause/Play Relationships and Comets

It's common for strong platonic friendships to effectively pause and resume, with gaps in contact ranging from months to years at a time. Similarly, big gaps in contact can also be a characteristic of relationships that involve sex, romance or other forms of intimacy.

While such non-platonic relationships are often termed "on again/off again," the people in them generally do not consider their relationship dissolved during an intermission. Rather, it's more like hitting the pause button; when the partners reconnect and hit "play," their intimacy easily resumes.

> *I have a partner who I see multiple times a year at regional Burning Man events. Our physical connection evolved very slowly, due to relationship circumstances (other partners), and because we rarely see one another.*
>
> *I've enjoyed the speed of this development. It's low pressure and has developed an exciting sexual tension. We won't speak for weeks at a time, but pick up where we left off when we do.*
>
> *We enjoy each other's company, but we are also practical about how often we can see each other. There's desire, but not desperation. This has opened my eyes to the opportunity to develop other similar relationships without the fear or stress of "When will we see each other?"*
> — *Sheri, polyamorous and singleish*

A term that is gaining popularity to describe discontinuous, or less continuous, relationships is *comet.* An unattributed online post described it this way:[74]

A comet is someone who passes through your life repeatedly, who is intense and awesome. And when they are gone, you are still in contact with that person in some way — but they are not a continuous partner.

Example: Ana is excited to have her comet Fredrico visit because they have hot sex and a deep connection. This is despite him living in Granada, Spain while he focuses on his poetry, while Ana lives in Seattle with her primary partner.

I've found a hole in the poly lexicon. The term "play partner" doesn't fit non-casual partners. Play sounds trite. Some of these relationships can span years and even decades. Some are very deep, with a combination of intimacy, friendship, admiration, and shared history.

Poly circles use the term "pause/play," which also doesn't fit many of my comets since we don't really pause. I stay in touch with many of them daily or weekly.

Some comets come by every 18 months when our schedules line up; or to continue the metaphor, when the stars align. I have even heard some use the term partner-partner. As in, "they are a partner, but not, like, a partner-partner."

This is an example of that awkward lack of a term for someone who is somewhere between being fully in your life at all times and a casual play partner who you like but don't have an ongoing connection with.

Some people noted that intermissions can enhance the joy they find in these relationships, or allow them to relax more. Time apart can be a feature, not a bug.

I have had an ongoing pause/play relationship for some years. We live in the same state, but usually take a kind of break when one of us is going through something, such as being really busy.

When we feel able to get together again we are excited to see each other. Absence truly makes the heart grow fonder.
— Jennifer, polyamorous

I've often had pause/play relationships; for me, they're ideal. It's all good, for the most part. As long as we talk enough that I don't worry they're actually trying to pull a disappearing act for good, the time away often makes the time together feel more important and special — or at least less boring.
— Kenzie, solo poly

Permanently long distance relationships can be pause/play; partners don't always stay in regular or frequent contact between visits.

I've got a couple of intercontinental long distance relationships with which there's a good chance that we won't actually spend time together in real life more than a handful of times throughout our lifetimes.

The trick with finding fulfillment in these connections is simply that there's no attachment to any particular structured relationshippy future outcome — other than simply maintaining our emotional connection (online), and appreciating that for what it is. Also, it's nice to know that there are parts of the world where I can visit and essentially fall straight into the arms of a loved one there.

Personally, I find that discontinuity isn't a problem in long distance relationships, but it would be harder to deal with in local ones. I suppose it's just easier to fall into a pattern of seeing each other quite regularly when you're local, so then it feels lacking if it's not regular enough. But with distance, the discontinuity of spending time together in real life feels quite natural — and if anything, it can bring into focus just how lovely the more abstract emotional connection really is.

— Benjamin, relationship anarchist

It's not uncommon for relationships to begin with continuity and transition to pause/play. Periodically reuniting with old flames can be deliciously rewarding.

I have a good friend, a musician and filmmaker, whom I dated for a few months back in 2008. He then got a monogamous girlfriend, so I thought we were over romantically. He moved to New Orleans, while I lived in Florida.

When his band was touring near me, we visited, and he told me that he and his girlfriend were in an open relationship. So we were romantic that week. And this continued until 2014 when his band broke up.

Now, he's touring the country with a film he made. When he's in my area, we strike up our romance again. We text here and there, to keep up with each other, but not much else. Our here-and-there romance is very special to me.

— Devin, polyamorous

My first serious partner lives in Louisiana; I'm in Tennessee. We see each other once every few years, and talk 2-3 times a year. Whenever we're together, it's like we never split to pursue different dreams. We've been like this since 2011; we originally got together in '06.

I fit seamlessly into her triad when I'm there, and she usually slides perfectly into whatever relationship I'm in here.

— Silvester, polyamorous

Scene or Activity Partners

Sometimes people connect intimately, perhaps profoundly so, but only within the context of certain events or activities. They may be brought together by a recurring gathering (a conference or festival), or by a particular interest, kink or subculture.

Usually they acknowledge that their intimate relationship exists only within this context. There's no pretense, assumption or desire that it will expand into other parts of their lives.

> *I have had a relationship of sorts with a guy who has a foot fetish. Our relationship has been limited to public acts of foot worship.*
> *— Karen, polyamorous*

While such connections can certainly be one-time deals, sometimes they can be surprisingly enduring and meaningful.

> *I had a lover for a several years who was essentially only my lover whenever we happened to be at the same event, usually an annual kink convention that correlates with my birthday. Often, we had little to no contact in between these hookups.*
> *Still, something about being with this man felt like coming home. We connected on a level and with an intensity that has been unrivaled in any other relationship I have.*
> *I genuinely believe this was because we only saw each infrequently; we didn't have other "stuff" to focus on or worry about. When we came together, we were totally focused and in the moment for the time that we were together.*
> *— Bryanne, solo poly*

> *I have a few very meaningful pause/play relationships with loves who I only see at music festivals. One has been going on for a decade.*
> *— Lyndsay, polyamorous*

Short-Term Relationships

On the Escalator, serious relationships are intended to last a lifetime. Outside of a Las Vegas wedding chapel, you usually can't ride the Escalator very far in just a few hours, days, weeks or months.

However, significant intimacy can blossom and thrive even though the partners know they will share only a very limited time together.

Contrary to popular belief, short-term relationships are not intrinsically trivial, meaningless or pointless. They can profoundly affect people.

Short-term relationships can require some special skills.

> *Short-term relationships require more flexibility and compromise, I think. You can't expect people to act the way they would in an ongoing relationship. It's a chance to connect deeply in the moment and not have that loaded with a lot of expectations.*
>
> *It does take a special "be in the moment" ability, which some people may struggle with. I think of it like sweetness and savoring; a dessert you love that will be finished, and you want to roll that flavor around in your mouth after they leave. And since it's not long term, you don't have to be assessing the person for all the things you would if it were going to be long term. They can be totally who they are, and you can be, too.*
>
> *It's just a beautiful opportunity to accept someone and take them at face value. Love them and let them go. It's rather romantic, actually.*
> *— Ruth, poly and married*

> *It's a super vulnerable feeling sometimes to trust the present and not worry about the future.*
> *— Colleen, queer, partnered and open to options*

Some relationships are short-term not because of a hard deadline (like a planned move to another city or country, or the end of graduate school), but because partners know their lives are on different paths, crossing only temporarily.

> *I dated one man for many months until he met his current girlfriend and became monogamous. I have had a few other short "stepping stone" relationships where I will date a person who is in transition or between monogamous relationships.*
>
> *I enjoy being a part of that transition and being around when they are going through a big change in life — such as about to move far away.*
> *— Darla, in an open relationship*

Knowing that a relationship won't last terribly long can amplify its intensity.

> *Knowing that a relationship is a time-limited can allow me to be more intense, since early intensity of feelings in a relationship can be (and perhaps usually is) taken as a sign of the relationship being "serious" in the Escalator sense. That level of intensity isn't sustainable.*

> *However, that isn't relevant when a relationship definitely can't last very long, and when we are aware of this from the start.*
> *— Sy, solo poly*

> *Something about knowing a connection is time-boxed seems to free me, and my partners, to really go all in; to experience true intimacy as well as freedom.*
> *In contrast, my relationships that are not time-boxed (but which still allow for an amount of flexibility and freedom that works for me) tend to lack intimacy.*
> *— Kelly, solo poly*

In contrast, *flings* are short-term romances that are mostly about enjoyment and excitement. That doesn't necessarily make them trivial. Brief flings can enrich lives, broaden horizons, and awaken people to joy and possibility.

Jaclyn, for example, treasures her flings.

> *Oh, Dario was this guy I met at a Porcupine Tree concert who was only in the US for a few days. That was a sweet little intense thing. I was 21 at the time and he was 18 and just so damn cute. He started talking to my friend and me, and we hung out during the show. We exchanged numbers and he told me he was going back to Mexico in two days but would love to see me once more.*
>
> *So the next day we met at the Jersey City waterfront and basically spent hours just talking and looking out at the river and city. He was super sweet and very romantic.*
>
> *We shared a bit of our stories with each other, talked about music, held hands and kissed a bit... and he said all of this cute stuff. We went our separate ways knowing we would likely never see each other again. We emailed a couple of times but it didn't last. That was probably for the best, since the memory sort of kept its magic that way.*
>
> *And it did all feel very magical, like something out of a movie. It was like we got this little frozen moment in time together, you know? Its finiteness made it special.*
>
> *Then, this was this Turkish guy I met at a bar meetup. Again, we connected on music, sharing love for the same band. He was here for work for a few more days. We ended up spending a bunch of time together in a short period, spent hours talking, had some really awesome sex, and got to know each other quite well. It was a very romantic and intimate time, although brief.*

> *Obviously, we both knew it was temporary — but he was coming back here since his company is based in my city. So we kept in touch and saw each other again. However, it ended up not being quite as special the second time around (long story).*

Comparing Fluid/Discontinuous Relationships to the Escalator

Traditional intimate relationships are supposed to continue, without gaps or role shifts, until at least one partner dies. However, some relationships diverge from Escalator hallmark #5: *continuity and consistency.*

The example Escalator relationship story of Chris & Dana *(see the preface)*, had no gaps. From the time they began dating, these partners remained an important part of each other's life on a daily basis, even when doing so meant making sacrifices:

> *...When Chris gets accepted into a prestigious graduate program in another state, Dana makes a career sacrifice so they can move and stay together.*

Also, in that story, Chris & Dana firmly identified as partners and spouses. They never shifted to referring to each other as friends.

Often, Escalator partners are indeed good friends, in addition to being intimate and life partners. Many people who ride the Escalator happily note that they "married their best friend." Still, it's most common for established Escalator partners to refer to each other as partners or spouses, rather than friends. This is because, on the Escalator, being "just friends" would be perceived as a demotion of the relationship.

24

WHY BREAKING UP IS HARD TO DO

The vast majority of intimate relationships, traditional and otherwise, end short of someone's death. Since this is so common, then why is it often quite difficult to end an intimate relationship, or to step back from certain types of intimacy that once were shared within it?

Also, why are stark, hostile, painful breakups (featuring inconsideration, blaming, unaccountability and other bad behavior) so common that they might, like cheating, be considered part of the underside of the Relationship Escalator?

Some of the most unfortunate aspects of the Relationship Escalator kick in when relationships wane or end. There is almost no gray area here: Escalator relationships are supposed to be either intact or finished. They are not supposed to linger in intermediate phases, or transition to another form (such as friendship, whether platonic or sexual), without the original Escalator relationship being deemed "over" at some point. This starkness often breeds negativity.

> *In my experience, people in relationships either grow more intimate,*
> *trusting, and move steadily toward a satisfying relationship — or else*
> *they stagnate into a dull, tense, unsatisfying routine.*
> *— Kimberly, in a noncohabiting, monogamous relationship*

Regardless of structure, any kind of relationship can end badly. However, the process of questioning Escalator norms and exploring unconventional relationships can, incidentally, illuminate options for exiting or downshifting intimate relationships on peaceful, positive terms.

Simply knowing that there are options to more happily or peacefully conclude relationships can, by itself, feel like a substantial departure from the Escalator.

> *I value being able to redefine relationships and end them humanely,*
> *instead of being limited to the disaster-centered Escalator exit script.*
> — *Chaos, polyamorous*

Some people feel that nonmonogamy provides a buffer that can mitigate the emotional pain and disruption of a breakup.

> *Not putting all your apples in one basket mutes the impact of a*
> *breakup. It makes it less hard and total to lose someone. It's still utterly*
> *hard, but not as life altering.*
> — *Morgan, relationship anarchist*

But when a consensually nonmonogamous relationship breaks up, it can hurt just as much as anyone's, they sometimes receive less compassion or sympathy.

> *There can be a lack of understanding and support from friends when*
> *my relationships end. "You still have a husband, so you can't really be*
> *that heartbroken."*
> — *Ninny, in an open marriage*

The Denial of Relationship Mortality

To better understand how partners can conclude or downshift their relationship on positive, peaceful terms, it helps to clarify social norms about breakups. Most Escalator relationships live in denial of their own mortality. The goal of the Escalator is to merge into life-entwined couplehood and stay there until one partner dies.

As with physical death, there's a pretty strong taboo against acknowledging, especially early in a relationship, that the most likely outcome is that relationship will end. Silence and ignorance tend to not bring out the best in people.

> *I'd like to see people become aware that often monogamous*
> *relationships progress up the Escalator because the people involved are*
> *afraid that they'll end. Once people begin to observe that fear and deal*
> *with what is underneath it, it may no longer be such a compelling*
> *mindset to be monogamous and headed toward a wedding and babies.*
> — *Flame, married and polyamorous*

People who are in, or seeking, an Escalator relationship often feel blindsided or bitterly disappointed when these "forever" hopes get dashed. Also usually, people don't like to improvise while they feel emotionally vulnerable.

This can be exacerbated by social presumptions. An Escalator relationship is supposed to form the foundation of how people organize their life and future, and even how they perceive their own identity and self-worth. When someone loses or leaves an Escalator relationship, it can feel like their whole world is falling apart.

Mainstream culture generally equates the ending of an intimate relationship with failure, which is why the phrase "failed marriage" is so commonplace. This is just one of many social assumptions that can make it daunting to leave or substantially change an Escalator relationship or to emotionally recover from a breakup.

> *It's sad if a relationship is no longer working, or if two people no longer enjoy spending time together. But it's far worse if they don't tell each other.*
> *Staying together simply because it's the default is an awful thought. This usually guarantees that cheating and deception will follow.*
> *— Bob, polyamorous*

The stigma of singlehood (the flip side of couple privilege) is another social norm that exacerbates the pain, stress and fear of exiting an intimate relationship. In a society that strongly venerates and privileges couplehood, facing the stigma of being an unpartnered adult can feel like a personal blow, as well as a loss of identity.

And then, there's the general fear of loneliness.

> *I've watched so many people stay in stagnant, soul-numbing relationships because they don't want to be alone.*
> *I am fine being alone. I only want a relationship if it adds value to my life, and if I add value to my partner's life as well. This does not mean I bail at the first sign of trouble. However, I don't stay in a relationship that has ultimately stagnated.*
> *— Agnes, nonmonogamous*

Also, it's widely assumed that a lifelong Escalator relationship must be everyone's goal. So, if someone falls or jumps off the Escalator, typically they're expected to seek a new Escalator partner eventually, if not immediately.

If someone hopes to attract an Escalator partner, it might appear suspicious or threatening, or at least unhealthy, if they maintain strong, positive connections with former partners, even when sex and/or romance are no longer part of that picture.

Positive afterships often are viewed as a sign that perhaps someone "hasn't really moved on," or that they might even be hoping to "rekindle an old flame." That might seem to limit the chance for a new Escalator relationship to begin, and to eventually take over as the unquestioned top priority. Demonstrating a "clean break" reduces impediments to hopping back on the Escalator.

> *At the moment I present myself as recently single and avoid being openly affectionate with my ex-partner, especially near any women he is considering dating.*
>
> *I also do this when we're around friends, to avoid gossip or upset any dates or potential dates before they have been informed.*
> — *Karen, transitioning partnership to friendship*

> *I have a some very good friends who are also exes. I also have more intimate relationships with several of my friends and exes than society would deem appropriate.*
>
> *These relationships caused me a lot of angst when I was single and worried about having to explain them to future partners. I'm lucky that I found a poly boy to date. Now my intimate friendships don't have to be pruned back to socially acceptable levels of friendship.*
> — *Miriam, polyamorous*

In my survey, some people noted that the skills they developed through exploring unconventional relationships help them to conclude relationships in more positive ways, or even to execute a transition instead of a breakup.

> *When my partner and I finally did choose to break up, we realized that it was a logical decision and that we could still totally love and care about each other. We didn't need to become enemies and we didn't need to hate each other.*
>
> *This felt like a tremendous shift from the "normal" breakup narrative. I think it was made possible from our communication skills that had been built up from being polyamorous.*
> — *Michelle, polyamorous*

> *It may be a little counterintuitive, but it's great to know that if anything starts breaking, I'll be told first and there'll be an attempt to keep it working.*
> — *Ania, nonmonogamous*

Harshness, Animosity and Heartbreak

The Relationship Escalator has what might be called an emotional "gravitational field." Once life/identity merging with an intimate partner has begun, it can feel logistically daunting and emotionally painful, to extricate oneself and re-establish an independent path. Achieving sufficient "escape velocity" to leave, or to regroup after that partner leaves, can require substantial energy. Negative emotional energy can be an especially powerful motivator.

The patterns for how relationships wane, stagnate or end are, in some ways, very similar both on and off the Escalator. For instance, inertia occurs in unconventional relationships, too.

> *Being poly makes it harder to break up with people. There's less opportunity cost to the relationship. So unless something's really making me unhappy, it can be tempting to go along for the sake of my partner's happiness, even if I'm not interested anymore.*
> — *Ten, polyamorous*

Breakups that start off peacefully often grow contentious during the process of life disentanglement. Dividing property, moving out, separating finances (or negotiating ongoing financial support), navigating changed social and family ties, and reworking parenting arrangements commonly breed tension and conflict.

Few people truly relish the possibility of a fight, or of major life disruption. This reticence can foster inertia, as captured in this *Urban Dictionary* entry:

> **Relationshit.** *An intimate relationship that has gone sour, but both parties are too scared and/or lazy to call it quits.* [75]

Escalator social norms have fostered the vivid language typically used to discuss how intimate relationships end. These words tend to imply harshness, which can fuel energetic emotional reactions. Often, people need to psych themselves up to leave a relationship, or to justify this choice to others.

For instance, the "break" in *breakup* implies a clear ending, not a transition. It also implies that something is "broken" (as in, damaged or severed beyond repair).

And then there's *heartbreak:* the painful, complex, churning emotions commonly experienced after the loss of an intimate relationship, or when treasured aspects of a relationship (such as sexual connection) disappear. This may have the intensity of a dire physical injury, sometimes with physical and psychological effects. Heartbreak also may require considerable time for healing. People rarely die of a broken heart, but often they are quite damaged by it, at least for a while.

The experience of heartbreak can be very real. However, framing this experience as the socially loaded bundle called "heartbreak," rather than dealing with the component emotions which comprise it, tends to mire people in rumination of the past. Assuming that great relationships last forever often leads people to focus on things that cannot be changed: *"Why did that relationship fail? How might it have been saved? Is there any way to rescue it from the rubble?"*

Backward-looking rumination tends to delay healing. Finding ways to focus on current life and feelings, including grief, often promotes emotional recovery.

The common language of relationships can complicate dissolution and moving forward. For instance, when onetime partners end their relationship, they suddenly become exes. To *"ex"* someone is a verb that implies crossing someone out, negating their existence or importance. Thus, *ex*-partners generally are *ex*-pected to *ex*-it each other's lives to the greatest *ex*-tent possible, barring ongoing obligations such as co-parenting or financial support, or inevitable social or family contact. Such severance tends to disrupt almost every part of life. It often is disorienting and distressing for former partners and the people who know them.

In my survey, several participants noted relief that letting go of Escalator norms made them freer to conclude or de-escalate intimate relationships in happier or more peaceful (or at least, less destructive) ways.

> *It seems that, once you step out of the crazy idea that a breakup is some kind of tragedy, the road to happiness is open to all involved.*
> — Keir, single

In addition to evocative language, it's common for people to leverage animosity to provide momentum to leave a partner, or to cope with being left. Despising, fearing, resenting, blaming or feeling hopelessly annoyed, frustrated or bored by one's partner can psychologically fuel the initiation of a breakup. Reaching rock bottom can provide justification: down is often the way out.

Animosity is so common in breakups that it yields some odd social conventions. For instance, it's common for friends to "choose sides," retaining connections with one former partner while ostracizing and perhaps vilifying the other. This can make future social interactions less awkward, but at the cost of considerable social capital.

The assumption of post-intimacy division of social ties is why, when people hear that former partners are maintaining an active, genuine friendship, they often remark, *"Oh, it's so nice that you and your ex are still on good terms!"* This is always well intended, but it begs the question: why should *not* hating or ostracizing a former partner be at all remarkable?

> *Some people are genuinely happy for their exes. It's allowed.*
> — *Veronica, nonmonogamous, in a monogamous relationship*

Aftermath: Pain and Renewal

When a relationship ends, traditional or otherwise, it can really hurt. However, since unconventional relationships tend to be automatically devalued, people often don't receive much support after these breakups.

> *Being in an open relationship has forced me to learn how to let go of love, with or without support. When any relationship fails, it hurts. Still, I believe there's a perception that if you still have another a relationship (especially if it's your oldest or main relationship), you aren't allowed time and space to grieve.*
>
> *Once, a man I'd loved and been dating for a year suddenly broke up with me and immediately cut off all communication, so he could pursue a monogamous relationship. The lack of support I experienced was really difficult. I couldn't turn to friends for support after this breakup without the inevitable response, "Well, you've still got your primary partner, so how is this so bad?" Meanwhile, I couldn't talk to my primary partner about this. It made him feel like he wasn't good enough.*
>
> *I felt like someone had died. However, since I still had living people around me, I wasn't allowed to grieve because the living took my sadness personally. If this had been a traditional relationship, I would have had space to process it fully — and I would have gotten over it a lot faster. I still have nightmares about it.*
> — *Sabrina, polyamorous*

There can be a special brand of resentment or bitterness when someone ends an unconventional relationship in order to ride the Escalator. This circumstance can lead the partner left behind to feel outraged by social norms. Sometimes it causes people to judge themselves harshly; to effectively blame themselves for not being conventional enough to hold on to love.

> *I had a long-term friends-with-benefits relationship that ended when he found someone to ride the Relationship Escalator with. After that, I had a black period. I basically thought, "The person he's picked over me*

is very similar to me, but she is more conventionally feminine and pretty, less queer and more into conventional relationships. Why would anyone ever pick someone like me when there are people like her around?"

I felt cast aside in favor of the better model of woman — and that I was supposed to bow gracefully out of the way to make room for his meet-the-parents, 2.4-kids-destined, picture-perfect relationship that would get all the social support it needs.

Breakups are bad enough without feeling like the whole world is on the other side.

— Melinda, nonmonogamous

Sainthood is no more common off the Escalator than on it.

Unconventional relationships can end badly, too. This is especially common when people are new to unconventional relationships, or where veto power is a factor.

Exploring unconventional relationships for the first time, at any point in life, is like learning to date as a teenager. It can make people more prone to unwittingly treating other human beings as experiments or crash test dummies.

During initial forays off the Escalator, people generally lack relevant skills and experience. This can spark especially vivid emotions and reactions. It's also common for people to continue to unconsciously harbor opinions and expectations rooted in Escalator norms, even if they consciously disagree with these norms. All of this can hinder one's ability to navigate new waters smoothly. Experience can make this process easier, but that takes time, and people can be rather impatient when they feel a desire or need for intimate connection.

Yet, even with considerable off-the-Escalator experience, partners may still treat each other spectacularly poorly as their unconventional relationship ends.

I was in a 14-year open relationship that ended badly last year. My partner unilaterally turned a visiting houseguest into his new primary partner, and me into his nonsexual housemate. There was no good communication about this.

— Tunia, polyamorous

Story: A Misunderstood Breakup

Escalator social norms can undermine people's ability to express the truth of their own relationships: how and why they work, and how and why they end. The pressure to rewrite the authentic story of the end of a relationship, so that it conforms to social norms, can lead to feelings of dissonance and discouragement.

This can make it much harder to get appropriate support as a relationship ends. It can also hinder former partners from maintaining a positive connection. Bill, a poly transmale, shared this story:

> *My civil-union partner broke up with me. He wanted to pursue a deeper relationship with another partner. But because not many people knew about his other relationship, when our relationship ended I didn't get the kind of sympathy or understanding that would have been helpful.*
>
> *People were all, "Oh my God, I can't believe he's such a cheating cunt!" And: "She's such a homewrecker/husband stealing bitch!" None of that was true, yet I still needed to adjust my own narrative and reactions to conform to societal expectations.*
>
> *I wanted to say, "My relationship with my civil partner broke down because he chose to prioritize another relationship over ours. It sucks, and I'm sad, but shit happens." But I could feel myself having to play the part of a wronged man.*
>
> *When I turned to people for sympathy and support, they expected me to be bitter and angry about some societally perceived (but nonexistent) breach of trust. That's kind of what I became, without even realizing it.*
>
> *I think a lot of that came down to the fact he and I were in a state-sanctioned relationship. I think if we hadn't had to deal with the societal expectation of what the end of a state-sanctioned relationship should look like, we'd probably have been able to remain better friends at the end of it.*

25

HAPPIER, FUZZIER SORT-OF-ENDINGS

There are, as Paul Simon sang, *50 ways to leave your lover*, at least.[76] Fortunately, this process need not entail trauma or abandonment, or even a complete exit. Just as there are many options for having intimate relationships, there also are many ways to conclude them or to shift gears.

There are many graceful, peaceful, constructive options for letting go of some or all intimate aspects of a relationship. This can yield considerable long-term benefits — not just to partners, but also to their families, friends and communities. These options apply to traditional and unconventional relationships. However, if an intimate relationship is already off the Escalator in some significant way, that vantage point can make it easier to see these options.

This theme emerged very strongly in my survey. Sometimes positive afterships emerge from how people manage their own emotions, and sometimes it's a matter of how they acknowledge or approach the process of concluding relationships.

> When I attempt monogamy, I invariably end up falling hard, then being hurt for months or years when he loses interest and moves on. It's easier for me to accept the gradual end of a relationship if we've always been open with each other about who else we're interested in.
> — *Deb, polyamorous*

> I've found it quite easy to handle significant changes in relationships when Escalator-ness is not on the table, but almost impossible when the Escalator is assumed.
> — *Karen, transitioning a partnership to friendship*

For some people, the flexibility of stepping off the Escalator is what enables them to maintain intimate relationships, contradicting the common belief that consensual nonmonogamy is a way to avoid commitment.

> *My friends tend to not understand why I don't just break up with someone if we hit a rough patch because I have "other options."*
> — *Ashleigh, polyamorous*

Knowing that loving relationships need not come to a complete halt can be a relief.

> *I enjoy having the freedom for my relationships to change, grow, wax, wane, shift, adapt, etc. — without anyone fearing, "Oh noes, breakup!"*
> — *Avory, solo poly*

> *We were great while we were together, and now we're great as friends. There's no point in pretending to be something we're not.*
> — *Keir, single*

Transitioning vs. Ending Relationships

People in unconventional relationships often speak of transitions, or ebbs and flows, about as often as they mention breakups or endings.

> *In unconventional relationships, "breakups" aren't usually breakups. Usually, they are evolutions of relationships into other forms.*
> — *Andrew, nonmonogamous*

> *When an Escalator relationship breaks up, it's often seen as the end of everything. For me, it is a transition to a nonprimary loving relationship. Many people don't have a frame of reference for what that means and what type of process that can involve.*
> — *Melody, solo poly*

This tendency to think in terms of transitions may be understandable. Off the Escalator, the point when an intimate relationship begins or ends can be blurry. Thus, my survey did not ask about the longevity of intimate relationships. It's also why any statistics about the longevity of unconventional relationships warrant scrutiny.

> *I've had several poly relationships that had no clear beginning nor end and thus are not clearly definable as "past" relationships.*
> — *Andy, polyamorous*

However, some people prefer to have clarity about the status of an unconventional relationship. They might acknowledge the end of a chapter, even if the story of their relationship is continuing in a new direction.

> *I've recently ended an eight-year, two-person relationship. We're trying to transition to nonsexual intimate friendship.*
> *I'd prefer to treat this as a form of polyamory, so everyone is on the same page and can accept this friendship-relationship as well as other relationships, rather than think that one will trump the other eventually. I wouldn't want either of us to look intimidating or like a threat or impediment to the other's new relationships.*
> *— Karen, polyamorous*

Intimate relationships often overlap during transitions. This is widely considered normal and good in consensual nonmonogamy, and it doesn't necessarily mean that any of the relationships involved is waning.

Meanwhile, in *serial monogamy*[77] (the way monogamy is typically practiced these days), it's not always the case that one relationship clearly ends before the next one begins. In fact, cheating is a common strategy to transition between monogamous relationships. This is another way that cheating is a complement to, not a departure from, the Relationship Escalator.

Often, someone in a traditional relationship will surreptitiously commence a new relationship, continuing their existing (and ostensibly monogamous) relationship until they're ready to leave, or until this behavior is discovered. At that point, the person who has been cheating may directly shift into a new acknowledged Escalator relationship with their formerly clandestine partner.

This kind of overlap allows people to ready a new Escalator relationship. It allows the person who had been cheating to avoid the socially inconvenient and stigmatized phase of temporary singlehood, while also enjoying the comfort of emotional and sexual intimacy. However, the partner who was left behind often faces difficulties on all these fronts, in addition to possibly feeling blindsided and betrayed by someone they may have loved and trusted.

Off the Relationship Escalator, and especially in relationships that are considered poly or open, there tends to be transparency when one relationship wanes as others grow. This can help make these shifts less surprising or traumatic, if not completely seamless or comfortable.

> *My last relationship was with a polyamorous woman. I identified as asexual at the time, so we had no sexual contact.*

> *Near the end of that relationship, I started sleeping with my current boyfriend. She was fine with that and happy that I'd found someone I was comfortable with sexually. But when I started to fall in love with him, the contrast between those relationships seemed immense.*
>
> *I had to come to terms with the fact that I didn't love my girlfriend as anything more than a friend — something I'd known for months, but hadn't really accepted up until that point. So, we broke up.*
> *— Genevieve, poly*

People often hope that if their intimate relationship ends or downshifts, that they could remain close to their former lover. Stepping off the Escalator can support this.

> *Something I've loved about my polyamorous adventure is that I'm on good terms with all of my former partners. Before I discovered ethical nonmonogamy. I almost never talked to any of my ex-girlfriends. Even without any direct animosity, it was just sorta understood that we'd moved on to other loves and didn't require further contact.*
>
> *But in my nonmonogamous relationship, my previous partners and I mostly acknowledged our incompatibility (or whatever) and inhabited less invested roles in each other's lives. We still talk, hang out and regard each other as positive people. But we aren't romantically involved.*
>
> *Last week I went to dinner with my BIG ex — my game changer. We hadn't seen each other since our breakup over a year ago. Still, we were able to feel the same familiarity in our dynamic, while acknowledging why it can no longer be constant. It was pretty amazing to be able to speak about our breakup and the life changes we've both since seen, without pointing fingers or fighting for reconciliation.*
>
> *There's a huge difference in viewing someone as part of your past, vs. seeing them as having an alternate role in your present and future. I understand that this isn't possible in every poly breakup, but I've been lucky in this journey.*
> *— Kevin, married poly relationship anarchist*

De-Escalation

Any intimate relationship might *escalate* (become more intense, entwined or committed), even if it's not riding the traditional Relationship Escalator. However, the all-or-nothing nature of the traditional Relationship Escalator leaves scant room for graceful de-escalation. There is just no good way down.

Several participants have found the Relationship Escalator's automatic, presumed escalation to be quite stressful.

> *Things were great with my boyfriend before we stepped up higher on the Escalator and started using words like "boyfriend," "girlfriend," and "love." Also before we started sharing certain domestic responsibilities.*
>
> *I plan to change those things when I get home because that isn't where I want this relationship to go. I want to live alone and do my thing, but of course, I also want to have love in my life. It needs to work for me instead of making me feel pulled in weird directions.*
> — *Kacie, in a don't ask don't tell relationship*

De-escalation, or *downshifting,* happens when partners step back from some or all of their forms of intimacy or merging. This could involve any of several decisions or actions, including:

- Reducing or ceasing their sexual connection.
- Shifting how they express care and affection toward each other, toward being less romantic.
- Changing what they call their relationship, between themselves or to other. For instance, substituting the label "friends" for "partners" or "lovers."
- Spending less time together, and/or communicating less frequently.
- Separating a shared home or finances.
- Letting go of plans for a shared future.

> *I once had a friends-with-benefits situation with an ex. It was more what I've termed "dating light." This was a way for us to step back from the Escalator while still enjoying each other emotionally and sexually.*
> — *Miriam, poly*

De-escalation can be a temporary or permanent shift. It may happen organically or deliberately. Partners may discuss these changes before they happen, or acknowledge them to each other after they have taken place. Or sometimes they simply accept or assume changes without discussing them.

> *My partner is significant to me, but we live in different states (only seeing each other a few times per year) and we are not monogamous. We were monogamous until I saw that I'm not wired to be monogamous.*

> *Two years ago, I told him that I felt like we needed some space from each other. We sort of transitioned to nonmonogamy. However, we have never really had a conversation about this, mostly because I am afraid of how he will react to what I really want.*
>
> *Since then, we have been intimate when we see each other, and we talk on the phone occasionally. But I mostly do my own thing here. I see other people, and we don't talk about it.*
> *— Mary, nonmonogamous*

De-escalation can mean changing how partners share intimacy, not just creating distance. For instance, friendship is an important type of relationship that can involve deep emotional intimacy and support, and it may or may not include sex.

> *I once had a primary (and master/pet) relationship with my former partner. Right now we're very emotionally close friends who have sex.*
> *— Jack, poly and kinky*

Under current social norms, it's mostly taboo to acknowledge or discuss the possibility that one's intimate relationship might not ride all the way to the top of the Escalator, or stay there. Such conversations can be construed as hinting that someone already wants to end the relationship. Or, as with talk of death, discussing how partners might eventually de-escalate may foster a superstitious sense of "jinxing" a relationship. This is one reason why, in mainstream culture, negotiating prenuptial agreements often becomes a contentious matter.

Meanwhile, off the Escalator, such negotiations are fairly common. Partners may even plan ahead, or at least consider and discuss early on, how they would prefer to manage de-escalation or detachment.

> *We have no kind of plan to continue our relationship in the future, but we have agreed to tell each other if we're ending it.*
> *— Caroline, in a sexual friendship*

> *Our marriage vows weren't 'til death do us part. We enjoy each other and are deeply committed to each other's well-being.*
>
> *But sometimes a breakup or divorce is for the best. We're also open to living apart or disentangling finances once our intensive child-rearing phase is past.*
> *— Rhiannon Laurie, married and polyamorous*

Pre-negotiating how to disengage from an intimate relationship can be one way for partners to retain their individual autonomy within a relationship, including the ability to pursue independent goals or adventures.

> *I am currently married to a man who I consider my life partner, and I live with him. We are polyamorous. Within a year or two, we plan on living in separate households, while remaining married life partners. I intend to go to Japan to teach English while he will stay in the U.S. and finish his bachelor's degree.*
> *— Jesse, married and polyamorous*

Some people wish to retain the option of riding the Escalator, even if they're currently exploring unconventional relationships. This possibility is also something that partners can discuss and make agreements about.

> *My partner and I have dated separately during our time together. On his end, since he doesn't identify as polyamorous, that means when he dates another girl, he leaves our sexual relationship behind. But he doesn't leave me behind.*
> *We love each other; we just know that the sexual part of our relationship won't last forever. That's okay, because we've made a more realistic promise: To be good for each other as long as it lasts, by letting each other be who they are and do what they need to do to be happy.*
> *— Murasaki, polyamorous*

Some relationships repeatedly de- and re-escalate. Sometimes this is comfortable; in other cases, not so much.

> *Our Escalator has gone up and down. Last fall I needed a break from the intimate side of our relationship, but we stayed friends. Eventually, we rebuilt and renegotiated our relationship. It's now better than before.*
> *— Leigh, nonmonogamous*

> *De-escalating has been difficult for us. In the past (and currently, to some extent), we have separated and reconciled over and over again. This has been enormously painful, and totally unnecessary.*
> *We keep returning to one another because of our connection. Yet we keep letting the Escalator get in the way of us having a healthy, fully functioning relationship. It's madness.*
> *— Tisha, open to nonmonogamy*

De-escalation is not widely understood or appreciated. Consequently, it tends to elicit dismayed or pitying reactions from other, as if de-escalation is an inevitable signal that a relationship is failing. Such invalidation can breed self-doubt, and make it harder for people to make authentic, if unconventional, relationship choices.

> *When I moved out of my husband's house, into my own apartment, we lost a lot of friends. They assumed our relationship was over or broken. They didn't/don't understand that we just want to live our own lives; that we will remain married, but this is no longer a primary relationship.*
> — *Lori, in an open, noncohabiting marriage*

Disengagement Styles

As people gain relationship experience, on or off the Escalator, they tend to develop patterns for how they exit intimate relationships. Styles of disengagement vary widely. An individual's habitual approach may evolve over time.

Discussing the end of a relationship isn't everyone's style. Some people prefer a "rip the Band-Aid off" approach: suddenly leaving a relationship that no longer suits or serves them. They may choose to announce this departure or to simply leave without a word. Others prefer to gradually, quietly disengage from relationships, especially emotionally and sexually — perhaps only acknowledging their withdrawal when a partner says something about it, or perhaps denying it until it has grown blatantly obvious.

Some people are more proactive about disengagement. When they realize that they wish to leave a relationship, they initiate a clear conversation where all partners' feelings and issues are acknowledged. In this process, partners often celebrate the value that their relationship yielded while it lasted, and acknowledge the roles they played in how it waned.

A popular approach, especially in traditional relationships, is to strive to fix persistent problems, perhaps with the help of a relationship therapist. Often partners disengage only if such measures do not succeed. This path to eventual dissolution can support healing and moving forward. It also can be emotionally, mentally and financially exhausting.

Some partners attempt to heal or revitalize their relationship by changing its structure or terms. This is a popular motivation for stepping off the Relationship Escalator. Sometimes this yields a viable new path for moving forward together, but sometimes it merely prolongs an inevitable dissolution. Particularly in polyamory, the *"Relationship broken? Add more people!"* approach is notoriously problematic.

My marriage ended with divorce after we transitioned into an open marriage. It turned out to be more of a transition to breaking up.

Most likely it would have ended anyway, just a little earlier if we hadn't decided to try the open thing to make things work. Still, that choice probably drew the unfortunate breakup period out longer than would have happened otherwise.

— Nika, in a long distance open relationship

Some people prefer to exit relationships through retroactive demotion or erasure: reframing a relationship to minimize its importance or nature, or even its existence. It can feel easier to leave something that must not have really mattered much. But on the receiving end, this type of disengagement might feel like an insult, gaslighting[78] or a betrayal. One way to execute this strategy is to avoid clear conversations about a relationship as it develops.

We don't say everything that we could
So that we can say later
"Oh, you misunderstood..."
— Ani DiFranco, "Anticipate"[79]

Usually, the end of an intimate relationship isn't equally or mutually desired by all partners. In this common circumstance, discrepancies in disengagement style can substantially amplify the pain of ending a relationship. Behaviors intended to be kind might feel cruel, and efforts to repair or restore the relationship might appear desperate or controlling.

It helps for individuals to have an awareness of how they tend to disengage from intimate relationships. Here, patterns of actual past behavior can be more telling than one's beliefs or intentions. It also helps, in any kind of intimate relationship, to be able and willing to discuss disengagement styles, ideally before disengagement happens. This lets partners consider how they might someday disengage with consideration and kindness if that becomes necessary.

Planning, communication, and negotiation don't necessarily make it easy to let go of an intimate relationship.

Some people feel little pain or stress when concluding intimacy. But for many people, this particular kind of change is especially uncomfortable and stressful — even when it's what everyone involved wants, or when it's obviously the best choice. Also, it's common for people to start letting go of an intimate relationship well before they consciously grasp what they are feeling and doing, and why. The process of realizing what they are doing can be distressing.

Differences in disengagement styles can lead to painful misunderstandings and breakups. Complaints that partners have grown clingy or aloof over time may signal such a difference.

There's a tendency in some alternative relationship circles to denigrate people's feelings of being emotionally attached to a partner or relationship — as if emotional attachment is somehow less evolved.[80] In other words, it's sometimes assumed that easy, painless detachment denotes greater emotional intelligence or more advanced relationship skills. However, emotional attachment can be a feature, not a bug.

For instance, emotional attachment can support empathy — as well as motivation to work through difficulties, offer support in hard times, or commit to shared projects or goals. These things can become especially important off the Escalator, where emotional attachment can be what primarily sustains relationships which have little or no external reinforcement, such as legal marriage, a shared household or logistical or financial entanglement.

> *A recent ex of mine thought I wouldn't get too attached to him since I was also involved with others. When he suddenly dumped me, he was surprised, and pretty cold to me, when I told him I was hurt by this.*
> *— Jennifer, nonmonogamous*

Disentangling one's emotions from a lengthy or intense relationship can be a long process. Even when concluding the relationship is definitely the right thing to do (or where there is acceptance that the relationship is ending, and why), it can still take a while for the heart to catch up with the head.

However, such challenging experiences can help forge skills that yield smoother transitions in other relationships.

> *I dated a guy for a year as mainstream, conventional, monogamous boyfriend-girlfriend. We were starting to fall in love, but then we broke up because he was uneasy about commitment and riding the Escalator.*
>
> *We remained affectionate and extremely attracted to each other. Eventually, we started having sex again as friends with benefits. Taking our relationship in this direction felt awesome to me! I gained a sense of balance and ease in this arrangement that felt fresh and very welcome.*
>
> *Over three years, our relationship went through various phases of more and less involvement and commitment. Eventually, it came to an end, due to our different wishes about commitment and escalation.*

This ending was quite painful for both of us, I think. As of today, we are very rarely in contact. It's not too pleasant to recognize this, but the fact is, I had become very emotionally invested. And when I ultimately couldn't get what I wanted from him, I also could not quickly "divest." It's years later now and I'm still doing that divestment.

Today I have three lovers, each in different cities, and each in a new or transitional phase. ("Transitional" meaning that we went from friends to friends-with-benefits fairly recently.)

I care about all of my lovers, and now it's not difficult for me to adjust the terms of our relationships in response to conflicts or life changes. For example, I am about to move across the country, away from one lover (an established "casual" connection with a lot of affection) and towards another (a new one who I only met recently).

— Anna, nonmonogamous

Story: Finding a New and Better Level for a Relationship

Fortunately, even after the most painful, stressful breakups, sometimes former partners find their way back to a close, supportive, friendly or loving connection. This can take work, but often it just takes time. John William shared his journey through a breakup to a happier ever after.

X and I were married for seven years after knowing each other in graduate school for about a year. People thought we were a great couple. In many ways we were, but we had a libido mismatch, oops! Now, X identifies as asexual (or at least gray-a). I made the classic mistake of hoping: "Maybe polyamory will fix my broken marriage!" Hahaha... In some ways it did — it helped it to end sooner!

While our separation was a horrible emotional mess, now that we've gone through the crucible we still respect each other. We now meet up about once a week to play old-time music together.

Part 6 Questions to Consider and Discuss

- How have your own intimate relationships shifted between being lovers, partners and friends? Did you negotiate this?

- How do you feel about extended gaps in intimate relationships? Does that feel like an ending, or a pause? Why?

- Did you ever have an intimate relationship that felt significant, even though you both acknowledged that it could only last for a limited time? What was that like?

- How have you tended to disengage from intimate relationships? What do you feel, say and do as you make your exit?

- What does it mean to end an intimate relationship well? What skills help support this outcome?

- What more would you like to know about any of the topics from Chapters 22-25? (Relationship fluidity or discontinuity, breakups, intimate tribes, etc.)

Share your answers, or your own story, online*

OffEscalator.com/resources/book1questions

* By answering any of these questions or sharing other personal information via the Off the Escalator website, you agree that the Off the Escalator project may quote your responses in our books, web content and in other material. You can answer anonymously if you like.

CONCLUSION:

MAKING FREE, CONSCIOUS RELATIONSHIP CHOICES

Once you know that several viable options exist for unconventional intimate relationships, how might you put that knowledge to use? How might it influence the way you approach relationships — intimate or not, traditional or otherwise?

I had a conversation about this with Addie, who has had considerable experience with both conventional and unconventional intimate relationships. At various times she has been partnered with women and men, monogamously and otherwise, nesting and living apart. She's enjoyed both deeper and lighter intimate connections, from recreational sex to marriage.

One of Addie's most important insights came from letting go of what might seem to be a minor hallmark of the Relationship Escalator: continuity and consistency. This is the belief that good relationships should last a lifetime, in a fairly unchanging form.

> There are many strains to the Escalator, many pieces of scaffolding holding it up. For a large part of my life, some of it did feel like it was just a given, how to do relationships right.
>
> Probably my deepest assumption was that successful relationships last forever, which is why many people describe past relationships as having failed. I truly believed that, and it gave me an enormous amount of grief when my relationships changed course. Even when we handled it very well, ending still equaled failure.
>
> In the last five years especially, I've had an epiphany: ending is not failure! As I've been rethinking my current and past relationships, I've realized that I actually would not want to still be in my past relationships

that ended. Furthermore, I regret very few of my past relationships. Most of them were incredibly rewarding, joyful and powerful. They still hold much value for me, whether they lasted a few months or a few years.

In hindsight, one benefit of experiencing unconventional relationships has been giving up the tradition of labeling as failures relationships that end. Or assuming that a relationship which may not last forever is not worth my time.

Questioning and reconsidering this Escalator belief led to another insight which has helped Addie in her more recent relationships.

There have been times when I have wanted something outside of my current relationship structure. When this happened, I thought, "There is definitely something wrong with me."

I've had many experiences in the last 20 years where my feelings changed, or my partner's feelings changed. That was when things would inevitably get really hard. I believe there is a stigma against changing feelings. People generally don't get much support or practice to sit down and talk honestly about this.

When someone's feelings change, or they might want to handle some important aspects of a relationship differently, it's tempting to just assume they "have intimacy problems." Anyone who develops doubts, or whose feelings no longer align with the original plan for the relationship, can easily be labeled "broken" by others, and by themselves, too.

Through accepting how feelings and relationships change, Addie fostered skills to check in regularly with her partners. These conversations leave room to consider a broader range of options than the Escalator typically allows.

I now believe it's crucial to periodically have a conversation just to take the pulse of how everybody in the relationship feels. How does it feel to be monogamous or polyamorous? How does it feel to be having sex, or not? How does it feel to live together or apart? How do we feel now about having children, or about how we are parenting? Do we want to be married or not? Do we want to be public or private about our relationship? This stuff does not stay static.

Having these conversations, practicing this skill, has helped me accept that it's completely normal to feel different things at different times, or to want things that are unconventional. And you can't really have these conversations without understanding that you really do have options.

Currently, Addie would prefer a nesting monogamous relationship. On the surface, this might appear quite traditional. But how she arrived at this preference has been profoundly influenced by what she knows about unconventional relationships.

> *Right now I am feeling like I want a partner who I can live with. I love the kind of teamwork involved in living together. I have done that for many years and have really enjoyed it.*
>
> *However, I have a lot of caveats for living together. It's not just that we sleep in the same place, but that we are really compatible in terms of how we operate, how we spend money, when we sleep. It's difficult to try to force living together with somebody who operates quite differently.*
>
> *I am also pretty open to a monogamous relationship. I don't feel like I am polyamorous by nature. In the time that I've spent partnered with someone with whom I share a good sex life, I've felt a certain charge to the monogamy that I have enjoyed. So I am absolutely game for that again if it comes up.*
>
> *Right now, I'm dating a few people, including someone who I've been seeing long-term, for about three years. We are not monogamous at the moment. But in the past, this person and I have been monogamous with each other, and we enjoyed that focus. We have also lived together and enjoyed that collaboration. Still, what we're doing right now isn't based entirely on the promise of that more traditional structure. There is something about just doing the friendship and the romance, by itself, that feels right, for now.*
>
> *We discuss this roughly every week or two. We continually revisit how our relationship is working, and how it might work.*

Aside from her personal experience with diverse relationship styles, Addie also benefited greatly from getting to know other people who were practicing various types of unconventional relationships — from exploring sexuality beyond monogamy, to group households, and more.

> *It has been really nice to know people in unconventional relationships who are willing to talk about what's working and not working for them.*
>
> *In the moments when I have been in a relationship and thought that I might want something that is not expected, not traditional, not the norm, having this context has helped me negotiate with my partners. It's helped me figure out what might make me happy and what might make my partners happy. It's also helped me see which things I might want simply because they are traditional.*

> *The fundamental liberating factor is that I have a choice. It is okay to choose a relationship based on tradition, or based on what someone else wants, or based on what I desire in my heart.*

As I readied this book for publication in early 2017 (as Donald Trump assumed the U.S. presidency amidst a profoundly divisive social, cultural and political climate), I realized that unconventional relationships might not seem like the most important topic. However, Addie reminded me that awareness, acceptance and appreciation of all kinds of diversity hold deep value, not only for individuals and their relationships, but for society and the world.

> *This may sound dreamy and optimistic, given the state of the world, but I think one of the core things that makes us suffer is the assumption that if someone does something different from what you're doing, then that means they're criticizing you. That if five people have different beliefs about religion, or politics, or marriage and love, then four of them must be wrong.*
>
> *It sounds crazy, right? But unfortunately, that does seem to be at the heart of a lot of the conflict right now. I look forward to a day when people will consider that nobody needs to be wrong.*
>
> *I hope anyone who is learning about unconventional relationships, for any reason, understands that you don't have to judge anyone's relationship as right or wrong. You don't have to agree with what they're doing, and you don't have to change what you're doing.*
>
> *Most people who have unconventional relationships are not claiming that traditional relationships lack value. I think they're just advocating choice. They're advocating close examination of relationship traditions to see which ones resonate. They're brave enough consider a particular tradition and say, "You know what? I'm gonna pass on that one."*

Thanks for reading this book!

Please rate and review this book on Amazon.

Bit.ly/StepOffEscalator

What did you think of this book?
OffEscalator.com/Resource/Book1feedback

See **OffEscalator.com** for more books, and for more ways to support this independent project. Subscribe to our email updates, or send private feedback. Your participation makes this project possible!

NOTES

Most of these sources are available online, and are worth checking out. For links, see: **Bit.ly/OffEscNotes1**

More resources, see the *Off the Escalator* Resource Guide·
OffEscalator.com/Resources

1. Google Trends tracked the first online mentions of the phrase "Relationship Escalator" in 2012.

2. An interview with Jackie Stone, creator of the polyamory-themed web series *Compersion*, was featured on episode 498 of the podcast *Polyamory Weekly*, Dec. 21, 2016.

3. *Compersion*, a fictional web series about being black and polyamorous, launched in 2016.

4. *The Adventures of Ozzie and Harriet* (1952-1966) was a classic American TV sitcom featuring a highly traditional nuclear family.

5. "Fewer than half of U.S. kids today live in a 'traditional' family," Pew Research, Dec. 22, 2014.

6. "The Monogamy Hangover," by relationship coach Mel Cassidy, Aug. 31, 2016.

7. "Marry Me," song by Dolly Parton, on the album *Little Sparrow*, Sugar Hill Records, 2001.

8. "Many cheat for a thrill, more stay true for love," Jane Weaver, MSNBC.com, April 16, 2007. Also, in 2016, *Statistics Brain* published a compilation of cheating statistics from various sources.

9. "At least with cheating there is an attempt at monogamy: Cheating and monogamism among undergraduate heterosexual men." Research by Eric Anderson, University of Bath, England. Published in the *Journal of Social and Personal Relationships*, Vol 27, Issue 7, 2010.

10. Example of sex/relationship advice celebrity Dan Savage's axiom on cheating, "Sometimes you do what you need to do to stay married and stay sane," can be heard on the *Savage Lovecast* podcast, Magnum Edition, episode 517, 1 hour 10 minutes in, Sept. 20, 2016.

11. *The Wisdom of a Broken Heart: How to Turn the Pain of a Breakup into Healing, Insight, and New Love,* 2010 book by Susan Piver.

12. "The High Price of Being Single in America," by Lisa Arnold and Christina Campbell, published in *The Atlantic,* Jan. 14, 2013. This article documents how "over a lifetime, unmarried women can pay as much as a million dollars more than their married counterparts for healthcare, taxes and more."

13. The term *singlism* was coined by social psychologist Bella M. DePaulo, who researched this phenomenon extensively and has published books about it. See: *Singled Out: How Singles Are Stereotyped, Stigmatized, and Ignored, and Still Live Happily Ever After* (2007), and *Singlism: What It Is, Why It Matters, and How to Stop It* (2011).

14. Scientific evidence contradicting the conventional wisdom that monogamy is more "natural" for either sex is presented in the 2010 book *Sex at Dawn: How We Mate, Why We Stray, and What It Means for Modern Relationships,* by Christopher Ryan and Cacilda Jetha. See also: *Race, Monogamy, and Other Lies They Told You: Busting Myths about Human Nature,* 2012 book by Agustín Fuentes. Several data sources are cited in the article "Data should smash the biological myth of promiscuous males and sexually coy females," by biologist Zuleyma Tang-Martinez, published in *The Conversation,* Jan. 20, 2017.

15. "Monogamy's Law: Compulsory Monogamy and Polyamorous Existence," by Elizabeth F. Emens, Columbia Law School. Published in the New York University Review of Law & Social Change, Vol. 29, p. 277, 2004.

16. "Compulsory Monogamy and Sexual Minorities," by essayist, activist and educator Pepper Mint. Presented at the International Academic Polyamory Conference, 2013.

17. "How to Define Emotional Infidelity: Different Types of Cheating," by Seth Myers, Psy. D., published in *Psychology Today,* June 22, 2011.

18. President Bill Clinton uttered the now-infamous phrase "I did not have sexual relations with [Monica Lewinsky]" during a press conference. Historical retrospective, *U.S. News & World Report,* 2013.

19. "Prevalence of Experiences with Consensual Nonmonogamous Relationships: Findings From Two National Samples of Single Americans," by M.L. Haupert, et al, published in the *Journal of Sex & Marital Therapy,* April 20, 2016.

20. "1 In 5 People Date Non-Monogamously, Says Wide-Ranging Survey — Finally," by Mariella Mosthof, published in *Bustle,* Aug. 26, 2016.

21. In my survey, some participants used the term *open* to describe their own relationships. I've preserved this when quoting them directly. However, elsewhere in this book, I use the more precise term *consensual nonmonogamy.* This is because, in my survey, it became clear that some people's

definition of "open relationship" allows for cheating, which usually does not involve all-around informed consent from everyone in the network.

22. "The Fewer the Merrier? Assessing Stigma Surrounding Consensually Non-monogamous Romantic Relationships." Terri D. Conley, Amy C. Moors, Jes L. Matsick, and Ali Ziegler, University of Michigan. *Analyses of Social Issues and Public Policy*, Volume 13, Issue 1, pgs. 1–30, December 2013.

23. "Fear of the Polyamorous Possibility," by Elizabeth A. Sheff, Ph.D., published in *Psychology Today*, Nov. 4, 2013.

24. *More Than Two*, 2014 guidebook to ethics in polyamory, by Franklin Veaux and Eve Rickert.

25. "Relationship Bill of Rights," by *More Than Two* authors Franklin Veaux and Eve Rickert, 2014.

26. *Opening Up*, a 2008 book by Tristan Taormino. See chapter 5, "Partnered Nonmonogamy."

27. Kasidie is a membership-based website that describes itself as "the adult community for sexually adventurous people." Members use this site to connect with each other for swinging, swinger parties, erotic events and more, with a focus on having fun.

28. *The Lifestyle: A Look at the Erotic Rites of Swingers,* book by Terry Gould, 2010.

29. "Are Swingers Freaky and Deviant?" by Edward Fernandes, Ph.D. *Psychology Today*, Oct. 9, 2013.

30. Scarlet Ranch is an adults-only Lifestyle club near Denver, Colorado.

31. Desire Riviera Maya Resort is an adults-only, clothing-optional Lifestyle resort in Cancun, Mexico.

32. "Women, Swinging, Sex, and Seduction," by Edward Fernandes, Ph.D., published in *Psychology Today*, Nov. 13, 2013.

33. "Meet the Monogamish," column by Dan Savage, *The Stranger*, Jan. 4, 2012.

34. "What is Polyamory?" History of the term, and of various poly styles and movements. Published on the website of Loving More, a U.S. nonprofit group supporting polyamory and relationship choice.

35. The *Polyamory in the News* blog, by Alan M., tracks mainstream and niche media coverage of polyamory.

36. *Polyamory Weekly,* podcast hosted by Cunning Minx with various co-hosts.

37. *More Than Two,* 2014 guidebook to ethics in polyamory, by Franklin Veaux and Eve Rickert.

38. *The Polyamorists Next Door: Inside Multiple-Partner Relationships and Families,* 2013 book by Elisabeth Sheff, Ph.D.

39. In the culture of polyamory, *unicorn hunter* tends to be a derisive term. A common critique of unicorn hunting is that this practice, while typically well-intentioned, tends to be unfair, unrealistic and sexist. In a 2012 educational

essay, "So, Someone Called You a Unicorn Hunter," David Noble offered advice for how couples can approach polyamory in a less ethically fraught manner.

40. *Safecalling* is a buddy-system strategy to protect the physical safety of sex workers, people who do online dating or sexual hookups, and people who commonly face dating violence (such as trans people). Explained in "Safe Dating, the Silent Alarm, and Signs of Predation," a 2008 post in the *Trans Group Blog.*

41. Batman and Robin (also known as the Dynamic Duo) are a crime-fighting superhero and his young protégé, both male. Part of the DC Comics universe, these characters were introduced in 1949.

42. *Thelma and Louise,* 1991 adventure film about the close friendship between a waitress and a housewife who go on the run after one of them shoots a rapist.

43. *Star Trek,* U.S. TV series that aired 1966-69. The three male protagonists (Captain Kirk, First/Science Officer Spock and Dr. McCoy) shared a close and often contentious platonic personal bond that fueled the drama in many episodes.

44. *Cagney & Lacey,* U.S. TV drama that aired 1983-88, about two female police detectives who cooperate closely in their work and personal lives.

45. *Butch Cassidy and the Sundance Kid,* 1969 U.S. film about two male Western bank robbers/con artists on the run from the law. A third partner in this relationship is Etta Place, a female schoolteacher who is both lover and partner-in-crime to both male protagonists — a rare instance of polyamory in mainstream entertainment.

46. *Sex and the City,* U.S. TV series 1998-2004 about the close friendship between four women in New York City.

47. "Apartners Live Happily Ever After, in Places of Their Own," by Bella Di Paulo, Ph.D. Published in *Psychology Today,* April 5, 2016. Also, as this book went to press in early 2017, director Sharon Hyman was creating a documentary film, *Apartners: Living Happily Ever After, Apart.*

48. "The live-apartners: How one million couples live in separate homes," by Steve Doughty, published in *The Daily Mail,* Sept. 30, 2010.

49. "Market Values in Cohousing," by Jim Leach, Founder/President of Wonderland Hill Development Co. (Boulder, CO), and Chairman of CoHousing Partners. June 20, 2012.

50. *Singled Out: How Singles Are Stereotyped, Stigmatized, and Ignored, and Still Live Happily Ever After,* 2007 book by Bella DePaulo, Ph.D.

51. *Romance in America,* 2006 study by the Pew Research Center.

52. "Single by Choice," by Janelle Nanos, published in *Boston Magazine,* January 2012.

53. "Polygamy and Wife Abuse: A Qualitative Study of Muslim Women in America," 2001 paper by Dena Hassouneh-Phillips, Ph.D., School of Nursing, Oregon Health Sciences University. *Health Care for Women International,* 22:735–748.

54. There is a popular belief that religiously-motivated *patriarchal polygamy* (where one man has multiple wives, all of whom are sexually exclusive with him alone) is inevitably abusive toward women and children. This is often true, but not always. Some women, as well as men, find this approach to intimacy and family to be

fulfilling and supportive, as well as in alignment with their personal values and spiritual practice. The HBO TV drama *Big Love* (2006-2011) portrayed the ups, downs and nuances of such relationships. Also, plural marriage is illegal in most western nations, so stigma and risk place extra stress on polygamous families.

55. *More Than Two: A Practical Guide to Ethical Polyamory,* 2014 book by Franklin Veaux and Eve Rickert. See Ch. 10. "Rules and Agreements."

56. "You Say Morals, I Say Ethics: What's the Difference?" by Paul Walker and Terry Novat, University of Newcastle. Published in *The Conversation,* Sept. 17, 2014.

57. *More Than Two: A Practical Guide to Ethical Polyamory,* 2014 book by Franklin Veaux and Eve Rickert. See Ch. 3, "Ethical Polyamory," under the subhead "On the Subject of Rights."

58. The term *sneakyarchy* was coined by Keiren Stephenson in an online discussion, Jan. 14, 2016. (Attributed here with permission.)

59. *Bill & Ted's Excellent Adventure,* 1989 cult classic comedy movie.

60. The saying, "Don't be a dick," became known as *Wheaton's Law* after actor and author Will Wheaton used this theme for his keynote speech at a major video gaming expo. Wheaton recounted this story in a 2013 interview on the online news show *The Young Turks.*

61. According to Wikipedia (Jan. 16, 2017), a *Hobson's choice* is, "A free choice in which only one option is offered. Because a person may refuse to accept what is offered, the two options are taking it or taking nothing. In other words, one may 'take it or leave it.' The phrase is said to have originated with Thomas Hobson (1544–1631), a livery stable owner in Cambridge, England, who offered customers the choice of either taking the horse in his stall nearest the door or taking none at all."

62. "Love Is Not a Pie," part of the 1993 collection of short stories by Amy Bloom, *Come to Me.*

63. "Difference Between Equity and Equality," unattributed explanation published in *DifferenceBetween.net,* date unknown.

64. *More Than Two: A Practical Guide to Ethical Polyamory,* 2014 book by Franklin Veaux and Eve Rickert. See Ch. 13, "Empowered Relationships."

65. Loving More, a leading U.S. group supporting polyamory and relationship choice.

66. "The Short Instructional Manifesto for Relationship Anarchy," 2006, by Andie Norgren, who coined the term *relationship anarchy.*

67. *Romantic-coded behaviors* are things that people do which are commonly perceived as expressing romantic feelings or intent. An extensive list of examples was included in 2016 blog post about Aromantic Spectrum Awareness Week.

68. "Asexuality in the DSM-5," posted in the *Asexuality Archive,* Oct. 20, 2015. Includes images of relevant DSM-5 passages.

69. *Squish* is sometimes used in the asexual community to refer to a platonic crush: a strong desire for emotional (usually nonromantic) intimacy, sometimes coupled with a strong desire to spend time or communicate with one's squish.

70. *Hir* and *ze* are two gender-neutral pronouns, which some people use to overcome gender bias in language or to refer to someone with a gender identity that is neither male nor female. See the Wikipedia guide to gender-neutral pronouns.

71. Joan Price has authored books and other information about sex for people age 50 and older.

72. *The Sessions,* 2012 film that offers a nuanced portrayal of a severely disabled person (who is also a devout Roman Catholic) who learns to enjoy sexual intimacy with help from a professional sex surrogate.

73. *The Big Chill,* 1983 film about a group of baby-boomer college friends who reunite after 15 years when one of their group suddenly commits suicide.

74. "Introducing a new term to the poly lexicon: Comet." Posted to the Reddit Polyamory forum in 2016, as an unattributed repost of an essay that originally appeared on Fetlife, a social network for kinksters.

75. "Relationshit" was defined in the *Urban Dictionary,* March 1, 2005.

76. "50 Ways to Leave Your Lover," song by Paul Simon from the 1975 album, *Still Crazy After All These Years.*

77. *Serial monogamy* is the practice of only having one sexual/romantic relationship at a time; where after one monogamous relationship ends, another may begin. Historically, monogamy was often construed as limiting oneself to having only one sexual/romantic partner during one's entire life. But these days, serial monogamy is commonly accepted as the social norm. See: "Americans Prefer Serial Monogamy to Open Relationships," opinion piece by sociologist Andrew J. Cherlin, published in the *New York Times,* May 21, 2013.

78. *Gaslighting* is a technique to manipulate, or to deflect confrontation or personal responsibility, by invalidating someone's memory or perceptions. Further explanation: "A Message to Women From a Man: You Are Not 'Crazy,'" essay by Yashar Ali, published in *The Huffington Post,* Aug. 23, 2013.

79. "Anticipate," from the 1993 album *Like I Said* by Ani DiFranco.

80. In the context of intimate relationships, *emotional attachment* refers to when someone values existing intimacy, and they also strongly desire for that bond to continue, usually in its current form. Thus, they may experience emotional pain or difficulty if that relationship ends or significantly shifts form, or if it becomes less mutually valued. See "What Is Attachment," by Kendra Cherry, published on *VeryWell,* Apr. 5, 2016. (Note that this is different from *attachment theory,* a popular theory of how early upbringing affects how people approach intimacy and bonding. Attachment theory is problematic in the context of unconventional relationships, since it is heavily grounded in Escalator assumptions.)

81. Gender spectrum resources: "Gender Revolution," a special issue of *National Geographic* magazine, January 2017. See also "Explainer: What Is Genderqueer?" by Jessica Kean and Rillark Bolton, published in *The Conversation,* Oct. 25, 2015.

GLOSSARY & PRIMER

The words most people use to describe traditional relationships often don't suit unconventional relationships well. Thus, many people who have stepped off the Relationship Escalator have created new words, and repurposed existing ones, to make it easier to discuss their relationships.

This glossary doesn't merely define some key terms used in this book that might be less familiar to some readers. It also explains how some terms are related and differentiated, and what their implications can be. Thus, it's not just a glossary; it's also a primer.

Asexual. The sexual orientation of people who experience little or no sexual attraction or desire for sexual contact.

Along similar lines, *aromantic* is an emotional orientation: having little or no experience of, or desire for, the intense surge of feelings traditionally associated with romance or falling in love. As with any human orientation, asexuality and aromanticism exist along a spectrum.

Casual Sex. *(Also: Hookup, Booty Call, No-Strings-Attached or NSA)*. A physically intimate encounter that is solely about erotic enjoyment or sexual release. Emotional connection plays little or no role, and there are no relationship expectations or intentions. Such encounters may be recurring or one-time-only.

In many social circles, casual sex is acceptable behavior for people who are *conventionally single* (not currently in an emotionally invested or otherwise committed relationship), but only as long as hookups don't happen "too often" (a highly subjective benchmark), only if singles intend to ride the Escalator someday. *(See: Mainstream Culture/Society)*

Many forms of consensual nonmonogamy allow for casual sex. In some relationships, this might be the only allowable departure from monogamy. For instance, this is often the case in *monogamish* relationships and in *swinging*.

Cheating. In an intimate relationship, this is when a partner violates a relationship rule or other commitment made to their partner(s). Thus, cheating can be considered not-fully-consensual nonmonogamy, since at least one person involved does not have the opportunity to consent to a significant change in the terms of their existing relationship. *(See: Consent)*

Cheating is highly subjective and context-dependent. Under current social norms, cheating typically is construed as agreeing to monogamy but then having sex with someone else. *(See: Norms)* However, some people in monogamous relationships extend this concept to also preclude kissing, cuddling, flirting, or sharing emotional intimacy with others. When partners make assumptions about what monogamy means to them, disagreements about whether someone cheated are common.

Cheating can happen in any kind of relationship. For instance, in hierarchical consensual nonmonogamy that includes rules, someone might be accused of cheating if they do something with a secondary partner that previously they'd agreed to reserve for their primary relationship. *(See Primary/Secondary Hierarchy)*

In mainstream culture, cheating is strongly vilified. It is also quite commonplace: studies often find that half or more of all people have cheated in their monogamous relationships. Also, far more people say they would cheat if they were confident it would never be discovered. Thus, cheating is not unconventional; there are well-established social conventions guiding how it usually works. *(See: Mainstream Culture/Society)*

Typically cheating is handled secretively. But sometimes people do not hide the fact that they're cheating — or at least, they don't try very hard to hide it. People can, and often do, break rules as a means to end, or change the terms of, an existing relationship. This approach can be effective, but it's usually a more destructive approach than communication and negotiation.

Only the partners in an intimate relationship get to define what "cheating" means for them, if it means anything to them at all. Thus, while it's common for people to refer to consensual nonmonogamy as "cheating with permission," this doesn't actually mean that consensually nonmonogamous people are behaving unethically. It only means they're being judged, perhaps out of ignorance, for making an unconventional choice.

Cisgender. This is when a person's internal sense and outward expression of their own gender is either male or female in the conventional sense — and this also matches their innate biology. Cisgender people may be of any sexual orientation or prefer/practice any relationship style.

Gender is a spectrum, not an either/or choice.[81] Cisgender men and women represent only part of that range. Some less common but equally valid gender identities are *transgender* (where gender does not correspond to biological sex), *nonbinary* (a custom blend of gender traits and expression), *agender* (being without gender) and more.

Closeted vs. Out. Someone who is *in the closet* acts to conceal the aspects of their relationship style, sexuality, or gender that fall outside the social mainstream. For instance, people in consensually nonmonogamous relationships often strive to maintain the appearance of *social monogamy* by being discreet about their additional intimate connections or relationships. *(See: Mainstream culture/society)*

Usually, closeting is done to minimize stigma, discrimination or danger to oneself or loved ones. *(See: Privilege/stigma)* It can also be intended to gain or keep the privilege and advantages associated with *passing* as socially normal *(See: Norms)*

Being closeted about consensual nonmonogamy can be ethically fraught. It can involve requiring at least some of one's partners to be complicit in concealing their own relationships, perhaps against their wishes or interests.

In contrast, being *out* means not concealing the ways in which one's orientation, identity or relationships diverge from social norms. This can involve active disclosure, but it can also simply mean not hiding or denying. *Outness* entails its own risks and benefits. People who also belong to generally marginalized populations (by race, class, disability, etc.) tend to face disproportionate risk from being out about their unconventional sexual orientation, gender or relationship style.

Being closeted, or out, is a spectrum; sometimes people are closeted only in certain contexts, or about certain aspects of their identity or relationship styles. The decision to be closeted or out is profoundly personal. It has many ethical, logistical, safety, relational and emotional implications. Unfortunately, being out not always a matter of choice; people can be outed against their wishes, accidentally or otherwise. Book 3 in the *Off the Escalator series* will focus on these topics.

Some people choose not to share any information about their intimate relationships, whether those relationships conform to social norms or not, based on strong preference for privacy. This sort of discretion can resemble closeting, but it isn't quite the same thing, especially if applies uniformly toward all of a person's intimate relationships.

Compersion. A term primarily used in discussions of polyamory, compersion means feeling happy because one's partner is finding joy in another intimate relationship. Compersion is sometimes called "the opposite of jealousy." More accurately, it's the opposite of *schadenfreude*: delight at the misfortune of others. *(See: Polyamory)*

Consensual Nonmonogamy. When two intimate partners explicitly agree that their relationship does not require mutual sexual and romantic exclusivity.

In practice, this usually means, at a minimum, that people actively disclose their nonmonogamy to all of their intimate partners. This gives everyone involved the opportunity to consent (or not) to being in a nonmonogamous relationship. Opinions and practices about disclosing nonmonogamy vary widely.

Consensual nonmonogamy differs significantly from *cheating,* which is not-fully-consensual nonmonogamy. That's because, when someone violates an agreement to exclusivity, at least one involved party has not consented to that situation. *(See Cheating)* Consensual nonmonogamy also differs from tradition-al *casual dating,* where individuals do not necessarily disclose that they might be sexually or romantically involved with more than one person.

Open relationship is a common colloquial way to refer to nonmonogamy, However, in the context of this book, that term proved problematic. In my research, I learned that people who say "open relationship" often equate it with a very specific approach to nonmonogamy. However, rarely do they agree on the details. A few individuals even contended that open relationships can include cheating.

Another popular term is *ethical nonmonogamy.* However, what constitutes "ethical" depends on the ethics of the individual using that term. *(See Ch. 16)* To avoid confusion, and to clarify all-around consent, this book use the term *consensual nonmonogamy*.

All relationship styles warrant active consent by everyone involved. However, since monogamy is so strongly supported by social norms, often monogamy is assumed rather than overtly negotiated.

Consent. This is established when people communicate about and agree to participate in some activity or situation — without misleading through false or incomplete information, and without coercion, duress or impairment.

Consent is most reliably established through verbal communication. In addition, visual cues, tone of voice, vagueness or body language also can be crucial. For instance, a person who does not wish to have sex may fear saying "No" directly, but instead give many other cues that they are not consenting to sexual contact.

Many people, including the author of this book, consider consent to be a foundational value; a cornerstone of both personal ethics and shared morality. For that reason, the *Off the Escalator* project addresses only fully consensual relationship options involving adults who are capable of giving consent.

Disclosure is a key consideration for consent. Usually, this means proactively volunteering relevant information and context. However, some people believe that disclosure is necessary only in response to direct, specific requests. Also, at least one popular type of unconventional relationship relies on partners agreeing to not disclose certain kinds of relationship information. *(See: Don't Ask Don't Tell)* Thus, practices such as cheating and *sneakyarchy* compromise consent. *(See: Cheating, Primary/Secondary Hierarchy)*

Privacy is another related consideration. People have the right to consent to whether their personal information (health, relationship details, personal history, etc.) may be shared with others. This gets notoriously thorny around discussions of sexual health in consensual nonmonogamy, as well as in conventional dating around and casual sex.

Social norms can create a subtle duress for intimate relationships, leading partners to rely on assumptions rather than active consent. For instance, it can feel quite risky or taboo to discuss the possibility that a relationship might be anything other than monogamous. This often leads partners to assume monogamy and how it will be practiced, or to dodge discussions about it, rather than to discuss, negotiate and arrive at conscious agreement and consent. This approach notoriously can yield unpleasant misunderstandings and surprises.

In the context of intimacy, full consent is an ongoing process, not a one-time decision. Partners remain free to ask questions, negotiate and renegotiate. Where choices are presented as irrevocable, unquestionable or take-it-or-leave-it, consent becomes questionable, especially for relationships that have become established or emotionally invested.

Don't Ask Don't Tell. A style of consensual nonmonogamy where intimate partners agree to be nonmonogamous, and they also agree to refrain from telling each other some or all information about their other intimate relationships or encounters. Often this is intended to prevent jealousy, but it can have other goals. This approach is consensual but not fully informed, by mutual agreement. *(See: Consensual Nonmonogamy)*

Escalator, Relationship. Explained in detail in Ch. 1. *(See: Norms, Mainstream Culture/Society)*

Ethics, Values, Morals. Explained and differentiated in Ch. 16.

Kink. Any unconventional sexual or erotic predilection or practice. This can include bondage, domination/submission, and sadism/masochism (collectively, *BDSM*); role playing, fetishes and much, much more. More conventional sexual/erotic tastes are sometimes called *vanilla, but* that term can seem derogatory.

Mainstream Culture/Society. The predominant way that people interact. It's what's considered "normal" behavior, priorities and preferences across the general population. The social mainstream encompasses aspects of life, behavior and relationships that tend to be widely known and understood, and thus do not generally require explanation, justification or clarification. The Relationship Escalator is a very mainstream approach to intimate relationships. *(See: Norms)*

The mainstream is a fuzzy, controversial concept since it's subjective and shifts over time. It also varies by geography, one's social circles or upbringing, and other factors. In the context of this book, it refers primarily to Western cultures, especially North America. Some people consider this term derogatory, others prize it. But in this book, *mainstream* is a descriptive term, not a value judgment.

Furthermore, what's commonly deemed mainstream is often shaped to accommodate the preferences or norms of privileged groups. Unfortunately, this tends to outweigh the norms and perspectives of marginalized groups. So what might be normal in, say, an immigrant neighborhood might be very non-mainstream outside that context.

Metamours. People who each have a more-than-casual intimate relationship with the same person. For instance, if Dana has intimate relationships with both Chris and Lee, then Chris and Lee are metamours to each other. *(See: Polyamory)*

Metamour interaction is a matter of preference and agreement. Sometimes metamours get to know each other, perhaps quite well. In some cases, metamours also become lovers, friends or partners to each other. But this is not always a requirement. Sometimes metamours are aware of each other's existence, but they have little or no direct interaction. Some people prefer to know little or nothing about their metamours. *(See Don't Ask Don't Tell)*

Metamour relationships exist even where they are not acknowledged since all relationships in a network can affect and influence each other. Traditionally, metamours are presumed to be rivals or enemies, because they're not supposed to exist on the Relationship Escalator — even though they often do, especially via cheating. *(See Cheating, Mainstream Culture/Society)*

Monogamish. A style of consensual nonmonogamy where a two-person relationship is mostly sexually and romantically exclusive. However, the partners agree to allow occasional, fairly casual sexual encounters with others. Such encounters may need to involve both partners (threesomes or moresomes), or they may occur independently, depending on the agreement. Most people in monogamish relationships are closeted about this; typically they prefer to maintain the appearance of social monogamy. *(See: Closeted)*

Monogamy. The most significant hallmark of the Relationship Escalator, typically this is when two people sharing sex and romance exclusively with each other. There is considerable diversity in how monogamy actually gets practiced.

Many people in monogamous relationships do not behave monogamously. Notably, cheating is common, perhaps even prevalent, in monogamy. *(See: Cheating)*

Social monogamy is the practice of maintaining the appearance of monogamy. This can include private agreements about discreet nonmonogamy. People sometimes choose to do this while secretly or discreetly practicing consensual nonmonogamy. *(See: Closet, Consensual Nonmonogamy)* Typically, this is done to preserve privilege or avoid stigma. *(See: Privilege/Stigma, Social)*

Nesting. Sharing a home, and otherwise combining the infrastructure of life, with one or more partners. This goes beyond expense-sharing arrangements, such as housemates. It's more about mutual investment.

Under social norms, it's most common for nesting partners to also be sexual or romantic partners. However, this is not always true, on or off the Escalator. For instance, siblings or platonic friends are sometimes nesting partners.

Network. In consensual nonmonogamy, this is a set of relationships where there is some overlap because some partners are in more than one concurrent intimate relationship. Sometimes called a *web* or *polycule*.

Some nonmonogamous relationship networks are highly structured, with well-defined roles. *(See: Primary/Secondary)*. Some may even be sexually or romantically exclusive, just including more than two partners. *(See: Polyfidelity)*. More commonly, relationship networks are freeform and fluid.

New Relationship Energy (NRE). The strong surge of emotion, energy, excitement, giddiness and often obsession that can accompany the start of a new intimate relationship. Sometimes called the *pink fluffy stupids*.

Normal. Behavior, relationships, or sense of personal identity or orientation that mostly aligns with whatever is currently most prevalent in society.

Being "normal" is commonly construed as intrinsically positive and beneficial, or at least of neutral value. It can support a deep sense of emotional security and social safety by allowing people to fit in.

In contrast, digressing significantly from one or more social norms is commonly viewed negatively. *Abnormal, weird* or *special* can carry the taint of an inferior, flawed, suspicious or dangerous state, vulnerable to stigma and ostracism. These perceptions vary by culture, subculture and issue.

Normal is a very loaded word. Many people equate it with being dull, conformist, or uncreative, and dislike being called normal. Yet in matters of sex and relationships, people often want to know what normal is, in part to gauge whether their desires or choices might be unhealthy or stigmatized.

Norms, Social. The basic grammar of human society; the common customs of behavior and engagement. Norms vary by culture, subculture and context to define what's appropriate, expected and, quite literally, what is *normal*. Norms are emergent, not designed, so they evolve over time. Consequently they tend to be messy and inconsistent.

The *Relationship Escalator* is the set of norms in Western society that define how intimate relationships are normally supposed to work: two-person sexual and romantic exclusivity, cohabitation and more. Intimate relationships that diverge from any of these conventions in some significant way are *unconventional*, maybe just a little bit off the Escalator, or maybe quite a lot.

Norms exist primarily to simplify the process of connecting and dealing with people. Knowing basically what to expect from others, and how to read cues and participate in interactions, can reduce friction and misunderstandings and help people feel calmer and safer.

However, some norms are a poor fit for certain individuals or relationships. They can even feel oppressive or harmful. Such discomfort leads many people to explore unconventional intimate relationships. This can be quite rewarding, even though it rarely feels as natural or simple as following social norms.

Diverging from social norms, especially for intimate relationships, presents some challenges. First, it can be hard to find guidance or models for handling unusual interactions and situations, both from the perspective of the people who are doing something differently, and to people who interact with them. Flying blind can feel unsettling for everyone, at least at first.

Second, there's "the devil you know." It's human nature to assume that more popular or established choices are probably better, or at least safer. New or unfamiliar ways of doing things are typically assumed to be weird, bad or riskier, until they become established *(normalized)*.

Third, deviations from social norms tend to be stigmatized, especially regarding sex, gender and relationships. For instance, people commonly worry that if they do relationships differently (or simply might want to), then this might mean there's something wrong with them or their relationships. Or they might fear prejudice, harm or alienation, or sacrificing opportunity or social status, if their steps off the Escalator get noticed. *(See: Privilege/Stigma)*

Pansexual. The sexual orientation where one might feel sexual attraction to individuals from any part of the gender spectrum. Increasingly, this term is supplanting *bisexual*, which some people now view as reinforcing the traditional male/female gender binary. *(See: Cisgender)*

Being pansexual or bisexual does not determine whether one is monogamous or not. Also, a pan/bisexual individual might have any gender identity.

Pan/bisexual people are often misunderstood and sometimes face unique tensions and marginalization when interacting with either straight or gay/lesbian communities. They might be perceived as straight or gay depending on the sex/gender of their current partner *(bi-erasure)*. They might face difficulty or risk due to stigma against homosexuality, or be resented for having the option to gain privilege by "passing as straight."

Play. Shared sexual, erotic or kink experiences where the pleasure and emotional content might exist outside of the context of an ongoing relationship. For instance, gatherings where guests might have casual sexual interactions are often called play parties. *(See: Hookup)*

Partners who do share an ongoing intimate relationship, even a monogamous one, might also deem some of their shared intimate activities to be play. But more commonly, this term refers to indulging in such activities for their own sake.

Polyfidelity. A relationship network which includes more than two partners, who all mutually agree to share sex (and possibly romance or other emotional bonding) only within that closed group. These partners may or may not all be intimately involved with each other. *(See: Network)*

Usually, a new partner can join an existing *polyfidelitous* network only with the agreement of all existing partners.

Polyamory. A style of consensual nonmonogamy that allows for more than one intimate relationship at a time to become more than casual. Hence, the word *polyamory* was coined to mean "multiple loves." There are many ways to practice polyamory; this book explores several in depth.

Slightly more than half of the people who responded to my survey practice polyamory or consider themselves polyamorous by innate inclination. Also, many people are open to participating in *poly* relationships, even if they don't personally identify as poly.

Primary/Secondary Hierarchy. This is how intimate relationships often are ranked, and sometimes labeled, in some types of consensual nonmonogamy.

In a hierarchy, the *primary* relationship tends to take precedence and gets to set the rules for all relationships in the network. *Secondary* partners typically are expected to defer to the primary relationship in at least some circumstances or choices. *(See: Networks)* In some cases, primary partners reserve the right to call an end to each other's secondary relationships. *(See: Veto)*

Some people say *primary/secondary* merely to indicate which of their relationships are more established or life-entwined, with no intent to limit certain relationships.

Hierarchy is also a powerful social norm, indeed, it's a hallmark of the Relationship Escalator. Typically, one's Escalator relationship gets prioritized over almost any other adult relationship, such as friendships. *(See: Mainstream Culture/Society)*

In polyamory, historically hierarchy has been commonplace, perhaps because it's a way to make polyamory resemble monogamy, by bolstering social couple privilege. *(See: Privilege/Stigma)* However, these days many poly relationships are more *egalitarian,* and strive to avoid default ranking.

Hierarchy is an aspect of relationships that warrants consent from all parties involved. However, some people in poly/open relationships neglect to disclose their hierarchy up front to new or potential partners. Or they may end up resorting to hierarchy despite their intentions or claims; mainstream social norms are hard to unlearn. This can lead to *sneakyarchy* (unacknowledged or undisclosed hierarchy), which typically is an unpleasant surprise, especially for partners who did not have the opportunity to consent to be secondary. *(See: Consent)*

Hierarchy tends to be a defining feature of styles of consensual nonmonogamy that usually focus on recreation or escapism. *(See: Don't Ask Don't Tell, Monogamish, Swinging)* In such cases, it's common for recurring nonprimary partners to be called *play partners,* rather than to acknowledge those connections as secondary relationships.

Privilege/Stigma, Social. *Privilege* is when people automatically gain access to certain benefits or support, or face fewer challenges in life or relationships, because they happen to belong to a group that is favored by social norms.

Most people who are *privileged* believe that they are simply *normal,* since norms generally reflect and support privilege. *(See: Norms, social)* One of the most pervasive, subtle and powerful benefits of privilege is being *out* by default, with rare negative consequences or questions. *(See: Closeted/Out)*

Privilege is not a choice; it is conferred by social norms, whether an individual wants it or not. Someone may choose not to exercise their privilege, but it's almost impossible to avoid being treated as privileged by others.

People who lack privilege often face social *stigma:* a default negative bias that can manifest as prejudice, suspicion, marginalization, underestimation, discounting, reduced opportunity (including actual barriers) or increased risk. Both privilege and stigma may be conscious or unconscious, overt or subtle, externalized or internalized. It's usually difficult to point at a particular decision, opinion or policy and announce definitively, "There! That's it!" Still, their accumulated effects profoundly shape people's lives, a fact recognized by considerable academic and scientific research.

Historically privilege was recognized only for traits that people are born with, such as race *(white privilege),* ethnic or religious heritage *(Anglo or Christian privilege),* sex and gender *(cisgender male privilege),* sexual orientation *(straight privilege)* and more.

Also, privilege can be accorded to characteristics that might change throughout life, or that might be deliberately chosen or worked for. Thus, privilege and stigma are commonly associated with wealth, class, educational attainment, physical appearance or relationship status/style. In particular, forming a socially visible, ongoing, life-entwined and ostensibly monogamous intimate partnership tends to confer *couple privilege.*

Privilege and stigma are highly controversial. Their role is often denied, rationalized or dismissed, especially when tied to non-inborn traits. Privileged people often don't feel privileged, since their lives are never trouble-free. Or they may assume that they've earned all the advantages they enjoy, or that stigma is the appropriate result of choices that society deems inferior or abnormal.

People who lack social privilege sometimes enjoy narrow advantages in certain contexts, but this does not erase social privilege. For instance, Ladies' Night at a nightclub does not erase male privilege; nor does a white person being received coolly in a black neighborhood erase white privilege.

Complicating this picture, people often are simultaneously privileged in some ways but stigmatized in others. Thus, a straight, cisgender, monogamous married couple would still face social stigma if they were also poor, Muslim, black and not college-educated.

Queer. A way to describe people who are not, or not fully, heterosexual or cisgender. Increasingly, this term also includes people who are asexual or aromantic. *(See: Cisgender, Asexual)*

Genderqueer refers specifically to people whose gender identity does not align with the traditional male/female binary in some significant way. This may or may not correlate with an unconventional sexual orientation.

Queerness also encompasses people who are *intersex:* their innate biology falls somewhere in the gray area between male and female.

Being consensually nonmonogamous or kinky typically do not fall under the queer umbrella, unless these people otherwise diverge from the mainstream of gender identity, sexual orientation or sexual biology. *(See: Consensual Nonmonogamy, Kink)*

Solo. More a way of life than a specific relationship style, someone who is *solo* does not merge their life or identity with intimate partners, Escalator style. Most solo people do not live with any intimate partners, and they tend to identify strongly as an individual, even while in significant relationships.

Solos don't necessarily live alone. Many live with housemates or family, or are nomadic. Solo people might prefer either monogamy or nonmonogamy, or to only have very casual/uncommitted relationships. A few prefer to abstain from intimate relationships altogether.

Many people choose solohood due to their strong desire to maintain and emphasize personal autonomy. Others may be solo by circumstance, not preference or choice.

Being solo is different from being single. Under current social norms, *single* means the state of not having any significant sexual or romantic relationships. However, it's normally assumed that most singles do hope to eventually "settle down" in a life-entwined relationship, if possible.

Thus, off the Relationship Escalator, someone might be both solo and also in one or more significant intimate relationships. Meanwhile, under Escalator norms, a person may be either single or partnered, but never both at the same time.

Solo Polyamory. Being polyamorous without having, and perhaps not wanting, to share a household or otherwise become life-entwined with any intimate partners. *(See: Nesting, Polyamory)*

The rise of this term highlights the growing awareness of the diversity of approaches to polyamory. Historically, the culture of polyamory has mostly presumed that poly people should have, or want, at least one nesting or otherwise life-entwined relationship.

Solo poly people face unique issues and concerns. Notably, they lack couple privilege. *(See: Privilege/Stigma)* This makes most solo poly folk averse to participating in relationship hierarchy, since the deference typically expected of secondary partners can hinder one's ability to self-advocate. *(See: Primary/Secondary Hierarchy)* This can, in turn, conflict with one's sense of autonomy and agency, which solos tend to prize highly. *(See: Solo)*

Swinging. A type of consensual nonmonogamy where people engage in recreational sex, usually within a well-established subculture called *The Lifestyle*. Swingers often connect through Lifestyle parties, clubs, resorts and websites; although informal swinging sometimes occurs between friends.

Swinging tends to be fairly couple-centric; most swingers are in established opposite-sex couples. Swingers may be single. In general, swinger culture tends to be very accessible and welcoming to single bisexual women, but not to single men of any sexual orientation.

Typically, swinging focuses on recreational sex, while downplaying or discouraging emotional connection or deeper relationships beyond an established couple. Thus, some swingers consider themselves monogamous in an emotional sense, even though they are not sexually monogamous. But the lines between swinging and polyamory are blurring; these approaches are not necessarily mutually exclusive. *(See: Polyamory)*

Historically, Lifestyle culture has not been especially welcoming toward genderqueer and transgender people. *(See: Queer)* And while female bisexuality tends to be celebrated in swinging, same-sex encounters between men are far less common and sometimes discouraged. However, these biases are waning in some swinger communities.

Triad, Quad. Types of polyamorous relationship networks where three or four partners all consider themselves to be in a single collective relationship. Partners need not all be sexually or romantically involved with each other. *(See: Networks, Polyamory)*

The awareness of this meta-relationship mostly is prioritized above the various two-person connections *(dyads)* it encompasses. Sometimes called *family-style polyamory*, on rare occasions such arrangements include even more partners.

Triads usually form when a new partner "joins" an existing relationship (even though this actually means that all of the people involved have created a new, expanded network). *Quads* usually form when two pre-existing couples begin to share intimacy. But there are many exceptions, and three- and four-person group relationships may originate in many ways.

Triads and quads are commonly sought in polyamory, however they are notoriously challenging to deliberately create.

V. The simplest and most common structure of a nonmonogamous relationship. *(See: Consensual Nonmonogamy, Network)* In a V, one person has two concurrent but independent intimate relationships. For instance, Dana might have a relationship with Chris, and also a relationship with Lee. This makes Chris the *hinge* of that network, and Lee and Dana would be *metamours* to each other. *(See: Metamour)*

Unlike quad or triad relationships, which emphasize the meta-relationship that partners share, usually people in a V tend to view and manage their overlapping relationships independently of each other. *(See Triad/Quad)*

Veto. In hierarchical nonmonogamy, this is when primary partners have a rule that gives them the power to end, suspend or significantly curtail each other's secondary relationships or other intimate connections. Usually, this is justified as being necessary to protect the primary relationship. *(See: Primary/Secondary)*

Sometimes a veto may need to occur before a new relationship begins, or very soon thereafter. Or it might be possible at any point, even if a secondary relationship has endured for years. It may be allowed only under certain conditions, or for any reason or no reason. Negotiation with the partner being vetoed may not be required.

Veto power is common, and usually uncontroversial, in more recreational approaches to consensual nonmonogamy. But in polyamory, veto power is highly controversial and risky. Exercising a veto on an emotionally invested relationship can harm or end the primary relationship it was intended to protect. *(See: Polyamory)*

Veto power also can be an unpleasant surprise. Sometimes people attempt to exercise a veto when they become distressed, even if no prior rule about veto or hierarchy existed. Similarly, a primary partner might exercise an *indirect veto* by creating so much stress and pressure that their partner's secondary relationship(s) become untenable.

FUTURE "OFF THE ESCALATOR" BOOKS

Thanks for reading the first book in the *Off the Escalator* series. I do have far more to show for the four years I've been working on this project (so far) than just this one book. The next two books are mostly done, as well.

10 Common Questions about Unconventional Relationships has been written and is awaiting final editing and production. I expect to publish it later in 2017. That book will address what survey participants had to say about the following common questions about unconventional relationships:

1. **Parenting.** What about the children?
2. **Commitment.** Who can you count on?
3. **Difficult emotions.** Don't you get jealous?
4. **Oh, the drama...** How can you stand it?
5. **Sex.** You're getting laid all the time, right?
6. **Slut!** *(Yeah, I know that's not a question. Rather, it's an insinuation that consensually nonmonogamous people often encounter.)*
7. **Sexual health.** Aren't you scared you'll catch a disease?
8. **Working things out.** Isn't this just too hard?
9. **Dating.** How do you find people to date?
10. **Communication and negotiation.** Don't you get tired of talking?

Book 3, *Off the Escalator, In the Closet,* will be published early 2018. This volume will explore how people navigate being out vs. closeted about their unconventional intimate relationships, as well as how we might all help make the world a friendlier place for all consensual intimate relationships styles. Many survey participants spoke passionately about these topics. Stigma and the closet were by far the biggest and most frequently mentioned challenges of unconventional relationships.

Beyond these titles, I intend to publish smaller books reflecting popular demand about specific topics. I have a wealth of information and perspectives, from my survey and elsewhere.

On that note...

How You Can Participate

Participation is cornerstone of this project. I was amazed, humbled and honored by the strength of the response to my original survey. I love to hear what people have to say about their unconventional relationships and their views on how social norms shape the way people love each other.

I found my initial survey so enriching, and so many people said that they enjoyed participating, that I will continue to offer ways that people can share their stories and insight on unconventional relationships.

Most of this will happen via this project website: **OffEscalator.com.** There you can read and comment on the project blog, subscribe to e-mail updates, and engage in other ways. For starters, I'm posting online versions of the discussion questions that conclude each of the six parts of this book.

(See **OffEscalator.com/Resources/Book1Questions**)

I also plan to post an updated version of my full survey, to gather even more views and experiences. And I will post special-purpose surveys, to support smaller books on more focused niches. All surveys on my site may be answered anonymously.

Off the Escalator has been a 100% bootstrapped process so far. As I move forward, I may seek crowdfunding support for certain projects. Stay tuned for these and other opportunities to support this project.

Stay in Touch

- Off the Escalator website: **OffEscalator.com**
- Subscribe to e-mail updates: **OffEscalator.com/Updates**
- Contact form: **OffEscalator.com/Contact**
- Facebook page: **Facebook.com/OffEscalator**
- Twitter: **@OffTheEscalator**

ACKNOWLEDGEMENTS

This book wouldn't have been possible without the candor and, often, the bravery of the 1500 people who participated in my online survey, many of whom feel they must conceal their unconventional intimate relationships. Stigma can be brutal. I'm glad I could help give these people a voice, they really need to be heard. Over the last four years, when I've struggled with this project, I've kept returning to their survey responses, to hear their passion, frustration and hard-won insight. I've learned more through this process than I ever could have imagined.

Profound gratitude to my dear friend Emily Wilson. She contributed her grace, attention to detail and uncanny ability to call bullshit, especially while hot tubbing in the snow. My former spouse Tom Vilot has shared this journey with me for nearly 30 years and inexplicably still likes me. He also helped me figure out how to wrangle survey data from my poorly chosen initial collection tools.

Michael Kirk fueled this project with a steady supply of good music and highly inappropriate jokes. (I miss you!) Catherine Dold offered much practical advice to help me feel less intimidated by self-publishing.

Several people volunteered to read various sections of this book as it took shape. Their sharp eyes and frank assessments yielded a far better result.

Many friends have urged me to keep going, and offered support: Susan Mernit, Angela Bowman, Scott and Eva Hill, Jeff Gamet, Randy and Kit Cassingham, Catherine Taylor, Beth Kanter, Cunning Minx, J.L. Forrest, Chris Bruggers, David Baron, the entire Hopkins clan, Kathy Giaccio, and far more than I can list here

As with my survey participants, several of my friends and supporters feel the need to stay in the closet about their own unconventional relationships. If this book helps ease their burden and make the world a safer place for them and the people they love, then that would be the best possible outcome.

My friends at the weekly Boulder Polyamory Meetup (especially organizer Jessie Glasscock) taught me the value of community, especially when swimming against the tide. My co-moderators and the nearly 7000 members (so far!) of the Facebook Solo Polyamory group taught me that I need to shut up and listen more; I hope this project shows how I've been working on that.

Lee Rainie of Pew Research assured me I wasn't crazy for doing this. Also, my media mentor Dan Pacheco offered considerable insight and expertise on the nuances of ebook publishing.

My benevolent feline overlords Wasabi and Taz graciously oversaw this entire effort, and mostly approved. But Taz did puke on an early draft. Everyone's a critic...

My cabin neighbors Jan and Morris Schneider graciously loaned me their porch for a considerable chunk of my writing time. I also became a fixture at The Cup Espresso Cafe in downtown Boulder; I highly recommend their blue couch and keemun tea.

At the tail end of this project, Anne Feustel pitched in with heroic proofreading efforts and much-needed good humor. Clarice Streets and Gina McLaughlin were my angels in the late stages of print design.

Way before started this project, or became a journalist, my dad Jack showed me how creativity, serendipity, helpfulness and interdependence are essential to self-employment success. I've applied these principles to my life and relationships, as well as my career. I'm grateful that my mom, Joanne, never expected me to be normal; she has always been in my corner, even when we disagree. My parents have ridden the Escalator together for nearly six decades. So yes, I know that it can work, too.

My five siblings, many nieces and nephews (plus their kids) and members of my large extended family have also offered me considerable support and encouragement — despite the huge pain that I was as a kid, and undoubtedly still am. I know several people who were rejected by their family of origin simply for being who they are and loving who they will. Never take the love and support of family for granted.

With love to my Aunt Harriet, an inspiration in my life who probably would have appreciated this book very much. She had a talent for diverging from conventions. Consider this my "hat trick" for 2017!

— *Amy Gahran, Boulder, Colorado, February 2017*

ABOUT THE AUTHOR

Journalist Amy Gahran lives in Boulder, Colorado — although she hails from southern New Jersey, and so occasionally still says "wutter."

Her journalism has appeared in CNN.com, Entrepreneur.com and many other venues, mostly covering energy, the environment, mobile technology and business. She worked closely for many years with the Society of Environmental Journalists. For the John S. And James L. Knight Foundation, she covered emerging local news media. And for the Poynter Institute, she covered the intersection of journalism and technology.

Amy has also engaged in unconventional relationships since 2001. In 2012, she launched the blog *SoloPoly.net* using the pen name *Aggie Sez*, which has since stuck as a nickname. She published that blog until 2015. During its run, this blog vastly increased awareness of people who explore polyamory without having or wanting a life-entwined relationship.

One of her early blog posts, "Riding the Relationship Escalator, or Not?" (Nov. 29, 2012) attracted broad attention. This sparked the *Off the Escalator* project, which was initially intended to be based on a couple dozen in-depth interviews, with a six-month timeline to publication. But as it turned out, 1500 people had intriguing, involved and diverse stories to tell...

Amy speaks at conferences and events on unconventional relationships and other topics.

Made in the USA
Middletown, DE
15 July 2022